Praise for
No Matter What

"In one sense or another, all of Catherine Keller's books are about everything. The end of all things; the beginning of all things; the excess and entanglement of God, world, and everything that composes them. But even for those familiar with Keller's everything, *No Matter What* somehow gives us *more*: the climate, the quantum, surging nationalisms, Black life, Ukrainian persistence, and the interdetermining breath that makes another way still possible."

—**Mary-Jane Rubenstein**,
author of *Astrotopia: The Dangerous Religion of the Corporate Space Race*

"A riveting collection by the leading theologian in the USA today, magisterial in scope, iridescent in style, Keller ranges over matters that matter, theological, ecological, and political, a tour de force on everything from process thought, postmodern theory, and feminism to climate change and the war in Ukraine. Everything we expect from Catherine Keller. This is exactly what theology should look like today."

—**John D. Caputo**,
Thomas J. Watson Professor Emeritus of Religion, Syracuse University,
and author of *What to Believe? Twelve Brief Lessons in Radical Theology*

"There are few theologians who have such luminous insights and spirited sensibilities to capture the hidden possibilities of a vital Christianity for our unraveling world. With steadiness and tenacity Keller weaves a fresh language for future ecotheologians to develop further. Her contributions in these essays reside in the realm of penetrating originality and unparalleled brilliance."

—**Mary Evelyn Tucker**,
Yale Forum on Religion and Ecology

"When Catherine Keller writes about the earth, love, power, politics, and more, it matters! Admittedly, it's tempting to believe doomsday scenarios will prevail. But Keller's process alternative—expressed in enticing prose—offers hope, meaning, and the Lure of Love. Read this book; it matters!"

—**Thomas Jay Oord**,
author of *The Death of Omnipotence and Birth of Amipotence*

"Catherine Keller is a theologian who does not write about the prospects of Christianity or theology. She writes luminous, theopoetic, brilliantly astute essays and books about entanglement, eco-apocalypse, racial capitalism, divine weakness, and creative becoming. *No Matter What* is vintage Keller at her liveliest."

—**Gary Dorrien**,
author of *In a Post-Hegelian Spirit:
Philosophical Theology as Idealistic Discontent*

"Catherine Keller is the most profound and creative theologian of our time. Taking seriously the many threats that loom large in politics, climate, and warring claims on God, like a divine magpie she draws out of disparate sources bright truths and teases ancient, sacred wisdoms toward a more just planetary vision of justice. This marvelous constellation of essays brings together key elements of her thought and is an essential guidebook for theologically minded seekers of the good."

—**Laurel C. Schneider**,
Vanderbilt University

"God-language has been used to despoil the earth; could it help support planetary thriving? In this timely volume Catherine Keller tells the story of the deep entanglement of theological and ecological crises, tracing how dominating divine spirit and the eco-crisis were interwoven from the beginning. Gradually the reader begins to discern the emergence of a more immanent spirit, now liberated from dualistic and colonizing chains and reconnected with the earth—the pathway toward a genuine planetary theology."

—**Philip Clayton**,
compiler of *The New Possible: Visions of our World beyond Crisis*

"Catherine Keller has done it again. In this latest installment of her groundbreaking and spiritually uplifting work, Keller carries us beyond nationalist, secular, and Christian exclusionists toward an eco-earthy, "amorous agonism." Always infused with hope that catastrophe will be avoided, and thoughtful strategies to carry that task out. An exciting and indispensable book today."

—**William E. Connolly**,
author of *Stormy Weather: Pagan Cosmologies, Christian Times, Climate Wreckage*

"Vintage Keller—brimming with vibrant justice-seeking theopoetic creativity, a testimony to and even a manifesto for theology's ongoing vitality. If you find yourself despairing that theology has died along with the God it proclaims, pick up and read. This is urgent and electric public theology—ecological, feminist, interreligious, political, and dialogical. This is theology done for a variety of communities, not just for whom the word "God" matters but also for communities for whom a living earth matters and multiracial and pluralistic democracy matters. Keller is at it again; her readers, old and new, will be delighted."

—**John J. Thatamanil**, Professor of Theology and World Religions at Union Theological Seminary, and author of *Circling the Elephant: A Comparative Theology of Religious Diversity*

NO MATTER WHAT

No Matter What

Crisis and the Spirit of Planetary Possibility

CATHERINE KELLER

Fordham University Press
NEW YORK   2025

Copyright © 2025 Fordham University Press

All rights reserved. No part of this publication may be reproduced, stored in a retrieval system, or transmitted in any form or by any means—electronic, mechanical, photocopy, recording, or any other—except for brief quotations in printed reviews, without the prior permission of the publisher.

Fordham University Press has no responsibility for the persistence or accuracy of URLs for external or third-party Internet websites referred to in this publication and does not guarantee that any content on such websites is, or will remain, accurate or appropriate.

Fordham University Press also publishes its books in a variety of electronic formats. Some content that appears in print may not be available in electronic books.

Visit us online at www.fordhampress.com.

Library of Congress Cataloging-in-Publication Data available online at https://catalog.loc.gov.

Printed in the United States of America

27 26 25   5 4 3 2 1

First edition

Contents

Introduction ... 1

PART I: Dis/Closures of Democracy and Earth ... 9

1 Creeps of the Apocalypse: Climate, Capital, Democracy ... 11
2 The "We" of Catastrophe, the Throb of Cosmogony:
 Eco-Thinking with Sylvia Wynter ... 25
3 Political Theologies at War:
 A Virtual Talk with Students in Ukraine ... 35
4 Apocalypse After All? Climate, Politics,
 and Faith in the Possible ... 50

PART II: Power and Its Alternatives ... 63

5 Nationalism and a New Religion:
 Foxangelicals and the Agonism of an Alternative ... 65
6 Power, Theodicy, and the Amipotent God ... 77
7 Weakness, Folly, Insistence, Glory:
 The Phenomenal God of John D. Caputo ... 87
8 Poiesis of the Earth: "A Black and Living Thing" ... 100

PART III: Love-tangles of Theology — 107

9   Amorous Entanglements:
  The Matter of Intercarnation — 109

10 "Birds with Wings Outspread":
  Islam, Christianity, and the Earth — 122

11 Animality, Animacy, *Anima Mundi*:
  Toward an Age of Enlivenment — 133

12 Dear Young Theologian — 145

Acknowledgments — 153

Notes — 155

Index — 179

No Matter What

Introduction: No Matter What

CRISIS AND THE SPIRIT OF
PLANETARY POSSIBILITY

No matter what. Listening, say, to Bach's Goldberg Variations, isn't that what you hear? Something that matters, *no matter* what sorrow, joy, or exhaustion you have brought to the moment? No matter what hope or despair, what skepticism or confidence? Still, an ambiguous phrase. It suggests that there is "no matter" that will make a difference—regardless of what obstructs or intrudes. And at the same time: that the matter at hand *matters*—regardless. No matter what other matters obtain, something is materializing in the music, something unconditional relative to the complex inter-mattering of score, players, instruments, soundwaves, ears, hearts, brains. . . . Without that matter, those conditions, what? But nothing?

"No matter what," in the context of a somehow theological inquiry, carries an echo of Paul Tillich's "ultimate concern," its "ground of being" reverberating. But that existential abyss manifests not just at a mystical depth but in dense materializations, in the mattering multiplicities of collective crisis and planetary life. In matters political, ecological, economic, religious—the ground beneath us, of us, trembles with the effects of power. There is no escaping the planetary scales of power and of crisis in this century: forces systemic and inflicted; but also and, yes, no matter what, powers that answer back. "Our" response-ability—that of a "we" endlessly differentiated in the categories, traps, and denials, in the exploitations, abuses and breakups of our collectivity—keeps mattering. So maybe the Bach moments matter all the more: not to escape or transcend the crises that loom but to tune our (my, your) ability to respond. No matter what crisis. For our responses matter even when minor. They materialize.

The essays in this volume are not preoccupied with the so-called new materialism, but certainly share its concern to rescue our matter, indeed materiality itself, both from the old (modern) reductions and from the far older transcendings of earth's matter. Most of these essays mind theological renditions of materiality, degrading or affirmative; and some of them indulge in theological constructions of their own. Of course, theology itself—the discipline, the tradition, the discourse—is at increasing risk of not mattering. Along with its largely Christian institutions, not to mention the *theos* they purport to represent, theology has long been in crisis. And its crisis unfolds alongside, in no simple ways correlated with or separable from, the crises of the material Earth. So then the theology voiced in this volume does not—and *minds* that it does not—transcend the causes, let alone the effects, of the secular materializations of ecosocial emergency.

If theology is to matter—is to find fresh incarnations amid the problems and possibilities of a lively planet—it will maintain an ecological attitude toward its own history, the histories of theology itself. It will neither surrender them to their very present and toxic remainders nor waste their ancient resources of social justice and love. Rather it will selectively recycle those sources, as the multiple liberal/progressive theologies at home for over half a century in mainline institutions persistently seek to do, indeed, to do in evolving solidarities with the materiality of vulnerable bodies, human and otherwise. This was, for example, passionately explicit in the theological voices of second wave feminist reclamation of the body—of our bodies from sexist objectification, and of the body of the Earth from ecological depredation. So we need not now dump in the "out of fashion" barrel the intensive twentieth-century work on the maternity, the *mater*, of matter, earth goddesses shrieking against their male abusers.[1] That *mater* now resurfaces as Gaia, who as in this millennium Isabelle Stengers and Bruno Latour insist must be distinguished from any unitary organism, let alone personifiable mama. None of this volume's essays delve into the *mater* per se. But in recycling ancient animacies, neither do they filter out her densely mattering traces, Those belong now to the compost of emergent theo-, eco- and ecotheo-talk. Ecological theology, a discourse responsive to multiple and multiplying sites of emergency, grows in complex conjunction with challenges to the political, economic, racial, and sexual paradigms.

Not all the essays in this volume attend to the Earth as such. Certain all too human political issues have demanded their own theological response. Each of the essays does witness to current crisis—*current* as in the shifting and choppy flows of power, and as in the temporality, its present tense hoping to broaden with its readership, of a book. Although the familiarity of proffered examples may fade, the exemplified crises of climate, capital, and democracy remain still "now" (fortunately for the currency of publication, unfortunately for the world) in play.

Let me, however, underscore how the titular *crisis* names something other than *catastrophe*. In terms of devastation, crisis may be just as extreme—it may result from or issue in catastrophe—but it does not signify mere overturning or sheer destruction. Crisis stems from the Greek *krinein*, "to decide." There is something in a crisis that calls for decision; there are choices that can and must be made, choices that precede and may elude the sheer "too late" implied by catastrophe. Such decisions may multiply to the scale of the crisis and alter its currents. So a crisis as moment of decision carries not critical distance but a critical imperative. De*cision* carries the etymology of "cut," as in the "cis" of "scissor." It rather emphatically cuts through the paralysis, passivity, or indifference that catastrophe might produce. A crisis met with indecision might explode into catastrophe. But crisis as decisive moment does not itself dictate the needed actions, let alone the possible outcomes. These are still being decided. No matter what. So these essays do not prescribe practices. Rather they hope to strengthen (decisively) possibilities of right action.

Indeed the concept of possibility comes here charged with planetary potential—but only if it pulses, spiritedly, toward counter-catastrophic actualization. And that pulsation has *deep* theological reverberation: In Genesis 1:2, darkness covers the deep, while the spirit vibrates bird-like, pulses, *meherephet*, over the waters.[2] Over the currents of energy yet to be materialized in "the creation," over the waves, themselves pulsing, of sheer potentiality. Ever yet? So in a literal sense—well, a sense true to the Hebrew letters—that *ruach* (breath/wind/spirit) signifies the "spirit of planetary possibility," in a vision in which the earth is the only named planet.[3] And in which all materiality emerged from the currents of the deep, not supernaturally from nothing, but rather, as complexity theory puts it, "at the edge of chaos."[4] *Ruach* suggests no omnipotent creator, but the spirit of possibility—of manifold possibilities materializing amid the boundless currents of creative process.

But don't I really mean "God" when I write "spirit"? Isn't this theology? Well, yes it is, and no, I don't equate spirit with God. Ruach is not the same as Elohim. As common usage attests, all manner of spirits exist—moods, energies, personalities, good and ill, strong and weak, human and otherwise. Spirit is traditionally, even biblically, and also not in the current text, a synonym for God . But what "God" signifies is traditionally and also in this text certainly "spirit." Spirit is not God, but God is spirit. Spirit expresses an immense planetary ecumenism—of any religious or Indigenous paths and of variously secular sensibilities. In manifold spiritualities and routine secularities (the orchestra, or the pitcher, or the student, offers a spirited performance), the metaphor of spirit sustains a free-form ecumenism. And we readily apply it to the wilderness, to any creatures felt as live, as enlivened, enlivening. These aren't all the *same* or single spirit, nor do they add up to one. But they all signify an animacy that lives only in vast force fields of interactivity, of "intra-activity" (in physicist Karen Barad's quantum sense). And even the doctrinal focus named pneumatology may take heed of the breadth of this *pneuma/ruach*/breath—as Jürgen Moltmann demonstrated definitively in *The Spirit of Life*: "God's Spirit is life's vibrating, vitalizing field of energy: we are in God, and God is in us."[5]

"The spirit of planetary possibility" surely signifies such a field of animating energies in the life of its particularly earthbound materializations. And no doubt such an *anima mundi*, spirit of the world, may sometimes meaningfully be called God—when and if such naming fosters rather than represses the vitality. When it energizes the wild and the cultured ecumene of the earth. The *ecu*, from *oikos*, home, does not then mean domestication (by one religion, one race, one language, one gender, one nation . . . even one species) but inhabitation. Home signifies space where we belong, not real estate that belongs to (some of) us. To expand our sense of belonging as individuals, localities, communities, and diverse painfully entangled collectives to the scale of the planet now seems imperative to our planetary future. And—as alternative to sheer catastrophe—that scaling up might, must, force the downscaling of the current globality of neoliberal capitalism. The *oikos* of the planetary *ecu*mene comes embedded in the *oikos* of *eco*logy and therefore now in the politics of *eco*nomy.

In other words, theologically charged words, the critical imperative of the current crisis carries now the double-edged sword of the Apocalypse: threat of untimely End and Revelation of creative alternative. As in some sense it has for two millennia. That New Creation—promised and promising—lands on the ground of the old one. But it lands its spirited re-genesis only as a disturbingly current and radically conditional possibility.

The spirit of this eerie but ever earthly possibility does not return us to some cozy geocentrism or advance to a utopic Gaiacentrism. Being at home in the earth opens our perspective into the universe, into the sparkling immensity that teaches our species the rarity of our species of planet, with all of its lively species, *Homo sapiens* shining in its uniqueness only as one of and among them. Our singularity might read then not as *exception* but as *inception*.[6] If we can resist Musky temptations to colonize other planets—at least until we heal ours—we might become true cosmopolitans, citizens of the cosmos.⁷ Citizenship does not mean ownership. We might, guided by "Indigenous teachers, Saturnalian musicians, Black counterutopians, scientific heretics, and the leaders of the three largest Christian denominations, cry out that we've simply got to stop trying to own the whole universe."⁸ We might work the univers/ality of our matter into a new earthworthiness of our politics. We might find ourselves minding what matters.

No Matter What branches into three parts. The first, *Dis/Closures of Democracy and Earth*, begins and ends in *apokalypsis*—in its original sense of revelation rather than closure. It opens with "Creeps of the Apocalypse: Climate, Capital, Democracy" (Chapter 1). Those three creeping temporalities of contemporary crisis are converging—"now"—more swiftly than an earthworthy future might bear. In the interest of a polyrhythmic present tense in which salvation appears as the salvaging of earthly possibility, chances, many of them fragile or last chances, do keep flashing up. No longer serving the political economy of the exception, might we intensify a polyrhythmic solidarity of the inception?

We? Who? "The 'We' of Catastrophe, the Throb of Cosmogony: Eco-Thinking with Sylvia Wynter" (Chapter 2) meditates on Wynter's reclamation of a new "we" from the grips of catastrophe. She exposes the crisis exploding out of a medieval and modern history of the pale "over-representation of Man," in His assertion of order against the chaos of the Other. As this order speeds toward "unparalleled catastrophe for our species," Wynter conjures a humanity capable of a great "Turn/Overturn." I tug her cosmogonic "code made flesh" into its resonance with a process eco-cosmology of interdependent becoming—in order to amplify her summons (no guarantee) of an "unprecedented Second Emergence." ⁹

Of course, there can be no such Emergence if "we" are at war. The third essay reflects on the military conflict that has been going on in the Ukraine for a decade. Invited to a virtual conference by Ukrainian students wanting to continue their education despite the horrific interruption, I wrote "Political Theologies at War: A Virtual Talk with Students in Ukraine" (Chapter 3). It analyzes the exceptionalism driving Vladimir Putin's aggression. His persistence comes theologically well supported not just by Patriarch Kirill's theocratic version of Russian orthodoxy, but by the earlier writings of Ivan Ilyin, for whom "fascism is a redemptive excess."¹⁰ Whitehead's insistence that "God is not to be treated as an exception to all metaphysical principles" but as "their chief exemplification" may suggest a fruitful alternative to any political theology of autocratic rule.¹¹

The last essay in Part One returns to the trope of the apocalypse (in case we ever left it). "Apocalypse After All? Climate, Politics, and Faith in the

Possible" (Chapter 4) reflects on modes of nihilism and denialism that play off against each other, allowing little breathing room for the third way of a responsible realism. Such a realism lacks certitude even as it takes no refuge in its unknowing. In the dark of the improbable, and against the ongoing depredations of a so white and right exceptionalism, a mindful intersectionalism presses on.

Part Two reflects on power and its alternatives—alternatives not to power itself but to its dominant forms. "Nationalism and a New Religion: Foxangelicals and the Agonism of an Alternative" (Chapter 5) considers the political theology of the sovereign exception as manifest in the faith of Fox news evangelicals and in its political secularizations.[12] If the repudiation of this Christian nationalism demands not a reactive antagonism defined by enmity but the (Christian) alternative of an amorous agonism, will the latter appear weak, even delusional? And yet does it not carry the potential of a planetary ecosocial solidarity?

Chapter 6, "Power, Theodicy, and the Amipotent God," hears anew the agonizing outburst from the cross. Its devastating cry of God-forsakenness incites a meditation on the old question of theodicy: How can an omnipotent God permit, or even cause, undeserved suffering, and still be thought "good"? Amid the world-threatening crises of this century, false theological hopes and self-defeating attributions of blame obstruct needed action. Thomas Jay Oord's "amipotence" names the process theological alternative: a conceptualization of divine power as characterized not by top-down control but by seeds of potentiality.[13] Does the loss of classical omnipotence, however, abandon theists after all to a mere ghost of what is meant by "God"?

Chapter 7, "Weakness, Folly, Insistence, Glory: The Phenomenal God of John D. Caputo," considers his *Specters of God* as an apophatic alternative to the gory glories.[14] This essay engages with a theopoetics turning cosmopoetic. It imagines not a God to fix the world but perhaps—even in the face of whatever deaths at whatever scale, even ultimately the heat death of the universe—to keep a future, possibly including "our" future, open. Enlivening in its spectral hope, a poststructuralist sense of the im/possible may prove key to a theopoetic new creation.

Chapter 8 brings this Part to a close with a too brief meditation on the poetry of Lucille Clifton (1936–2010), particularly on the titular poem of this essay, "Poiesis of the Earth: 'A Black and Living Thing.'" Exposing the "white ways" of death—"he kills his cities / and his trees," her prophetic poetry discloses another way.[15] Calling upon the blackness of skin, of bear, of hawk, of universe, Clifton invokes "perhaps / a final chance."[16] Because a last chance may be a real chance, we cannot in good faith slam the door on hope. Precisely in its darkness.

That possible last chance exposes us to each other, in our delusions and projections, our denialisms and our nihilisms. In the fragile desires, disappointments, desperations of what we call love. Intimate or infinite. So Part Three finds itself caught in the love-tangles of theology. Love, so globally privatized, so pathetically depowered, so routinely depressed.[17] And all along embodied as the core matter of Christian theology. Chapter 9—"Amorous Entanglements: The Matter of Intercarnation"—therefore reconsiders the possibility of a messianic mattering. Its matter would find liberation not from the Incarnation but from the exceptionalism that dogmatically entrapped that ancient event of embodiment. The "agential intra-action" of Karen Barad's material bodies then joins forces with Mel Chen's and Sharon Betcher's queered and ecological embodiments of disability. Might such emergent bodies of intercarnation also enact a panentheism of radically relational creativity? Amid whatever ruins we face?

"'Birds with Wings Outspread': Islam, Christianity, and the Earth" (Chapter 10) then twists into a comparative ecotheology. With Jürgen Moltmann it asks: Might the great *world* religions become *earth* religions? And actually matter again? Drawing on the example of an ecologically minded Islam and its Qur'anic exegesis, this chapter considers how interreligious and intercreaturely solidarity can join in in an unprecedented cooperation, in an Earthbound solidarity resistant to predatory capitalism.

"Animality, Animacy, *Anima Mundi*: Toward an Age of Enlivenment" (Chapter 11) presses, against the numbness of every reductionism, the question of materiality's own liveliness. Rolling from contemplation of the animal—ourselves and all the others—toward the animacy of matter itself, it invites Jane Bennett's vital matter, Bruno Latour's Gaia, and Merlin Sheldrake's entangling fungal life to draw us into the force field of Earth's vibrancy. There the long-discarded trope of the *anima mundi*, for which the world is the animal body, performs an irresistible appearance.

And then a final slip of a chapter turns on the fragile life of theology itself, in its odd convergence with the fragility of the earth habitat (Chapter 12). Might the death of God be ceremonially accompanying the demise of our civilization and all that it lovelessly takes with it? This "Dear Young Theologian" considers, most inconclusively, a livelier possibility.

Avoiding the doomsday processional—that seems to be what all these essays want. Is that what matters, no matter what else? Or is there something that matters even if the "white ways of death" and the bogus apocalypse—with no new creation on the horizon—prevail? To answer that latter question may remain for this anthology impossible. For to say "no" is to wipe out the cosmic context and the dark depth of any spiritual, let alone theological, imagination. But to say "yes," something other than the Earth matters unconditionally, plays right into varieties of transcendent indifference. And so will help The End along. Instead let's just begin.

No matter what.

Part I: Dis/Closures of Democracy and Earth

The future. Is there one?

Such a question might be read metaphysically. "Is" there any such thing as that which by definition does not yet exist? For if the future signifies something that "is" already, then it is nothing but an extension of the past—closed in advance. But if possibilities "exist," so do multiple futures. Yet the existence of the future comes into question for a more *existential* reason: Our species has so exhausted and contaminated the planet that we may have closed ourselves into a few remaining decades. That hardly suggests a future, at least on any historical scale answering to that of our past, not even of our two hundred millennia as "modern" humans. The planetary systems in and as which we exist may not much longer bear our exploitation. We seem to be shutting down the future. At least the future of this species that envisions futures.

Of course, that species misplaces its own concreteness. Ecosocial justice advocates expose its—our—vastly divergent levels of responsibility, monstrous asymmetries syncing with those of "our" democracy. And anyway, why take responsibility, why pretend we can make a needed difference, if the future itself is closing down? Such rhetorical questions now haunt all discourse aimed at planetary transformation. For futurity now merges with planetarity. Local movements for justice—movements economic, racial, sexual, environmental, social, democratic—can now only be extracted from our planetary collectivity by an abstraction violent at once metaphysically and physically. For if local struggles get abstracted from their materiality—from the shared matter of the earth—they can be kept closed to (rather than close to) each other.

Perhaps only through an overstretched ecology of issues do the challenges of our present moment open—against those *closures*—into the future tense. Then the *tense* binary of denialism and nihilism opens into some indeterminate realism. Perhaps democracy can shake freer, and then more free, of both the spreading threats of autocracy and the globally spread table of capitalism. Perhaps in recognizing that doors are slamming on our planetary future, *we* may respond more insistently to specific struggles for social liberation and material sustainability. And vice versa: Those local struggles stretch into their earthly magnitude. Their planetary mattering.

The essays in this Part recognize the improbability but not the impossibility of such dis/closure. They circulate through that *apokalypsis*, that un/veiling, that may or may not signify any final closure. Sometimes they surface a political theology at play in the fraught temporality of the ancient apocalypse itself, as it reverberates through not just religious radicalities but secular social orders and earthly possibilities. Amid those conflicting futures the present will keep exposing its uncertainty. That uncertainty will not cover over the determinate consequences of present actions, any more than the future that "is" will free us from the imperatives of a hope for what is not.

1 / Creeps of the Apocalypse

CLIMATE, CAPITAL, DEMOCRACY

I am not name-calling.[1] The titular creeps are not personalities but temporalities. They suggest how slowly the material evidence of global warming registers publicly, even now rarely blazing into the news cycle. Yet the time of anthropogenic climate change, read as *a* time, an age among ages, a geological epoch—anthropocene, capitalocene, pyrocene, plantationocene or otherwise obscene—seems to move not at a creep but a gallop (okay, I admit it, horse of the Apocalypse). So a tragic paradox has come into play. The climate crisis is now moving too fast for any full-fix reversal, and at least for a wide and not only denialist public, too slowly to grasp. The temporality of climate change pulses in an eerie convergence of the imperceptibly slow closure of the epochal window and the accelerating accumulation of planetary effects.

Add to the problem of its speed-creep this perplexity: There is no responsible way of grasping climate crisis without entangling its science, already dangerously complex for popular consumption, in the divergent temporalities of politics and economics. But the time of politics throbs at the rate of daily news and periodic elections. As US democracy lurches spasmodically toward new electoral deadlines, it casts white Christian supremacist shadows of creeping authoritarianism. That political creep does not signify any predetermined outcome but rather what William Connolly calls "aspirational fascism."[2] He does not predict its victory but calls for great struggles to prevent such.

And of course the fragility of democracy constitutes a now multinational phenomenon. In this menace our political moment mirrors, indeed intensifies, the high-pressure threat of global warming. Not surprisingly a rhetoric of apocalypse—not necessarily as "the end of time" but as a catastrophic disruption of human history—now edges even sober secular fears for both the democratic and the ecological future. So in the intersections of politics and climate, divergent speed-creeps form a complicated planetary temporality, overdetermined and yet indeterminate. Repair appears improbable. But still possible.

What, however, of the third temporal creep, that of economics? In its dominant form the current economy funds both the ecological and the political threats yet presents as itself unthreatened. Far from the disruptive discontinuities of ecopolitical time, it claims an opposite sort of temporality: that of the smooth continuum of assured progress. The current global capitalism depends on one US party's war against corporate regulations joined with white evangelical climate denialism. At the same time it promises that "Capitalism Is the Key to Fixing Climate Change."[3] This ever more greenwashed capitalism claws its way from a determining past into its guaranteed future by way of a resiliently continuous present. Indeed, in theologian Kathryn Tanner's analysis of "the new spirit of capitalism," it is this temporality, with its self-reproducing continuum, that defines the economic dynamism of the current neoliberalism.[4]

So the *ecological* repair that is still possible demands improbably immense and fast *political* change in order to slow—quickly—the *economic* drivers of the crisis. Does this triple time not appear to be materializing as a speed-creeping apocalypse? I am here imagining that those three asymmetrical temporalities might be helpfully read in their systemic entanglement—from a mindfully multitemporal perspective. Such a polyrhythmic point of view emerges in this case as the thought experiment of a theology not just multidisciplinary in perspective but *trans*disciplinary, aiming through and beyond disciplinarity itself toward practice. Indeed toward practice *in time*—quickly enough to make the difference. Such theology takes place not outside of time in a heavenly retreat center, nor in some end-of-time headquarters. If in this case practice in time demands a bit of theological attention to the ancient future temporality of John's *Apocalypse*, it also attends to the present precarity of theology itself. We seem to have to do with a fourth temporality. And this horse knows that its own *trans* could swing all too apocalyptically into the creeping death of *theos* and therewith of theology.[5]

Alternatively, that theo-precarity might release the uncertainty, the opening, of a more plural and volatile possibility. In its contracted multitemporality, the tense present appears to crack open a planetary indeterminacy, a space (creepily) framed by apocalyptic *over*determination. Speaking theologically: *apokalypsis* read responsibly, even correctly, does not close. It "unveils." It dis/closes.⁶ The present meditation, therefore, folds the temporalities of climate, beset by capital and betrayed by democracy, into the transdisciplinary opening of a polyrhythmic present. And because such disclosure is steeped in an ultimate concern, one that accepts certain theological tropes, the present tense may just keep opening—however tensely—into possibility. No matter what catastrophe approaches.

Economic Endgame

"A kind of unbreakable continuity exists between past, present and future—they in fact collapse into one another, fuse with one another—in ways that make any radical break with the present order seem impossible." Thus Kathryn Tanner characterizes the current capitalist temporality. The financialized transactions of the regnant economy operate at split-second virtual speeds—and yet move as though in an unchangeable frame. "This is a constantly changing economic order or regime, requiring constant change from the participants in it, but one offering no escape from it; the future simply promises more of the same." So, in fact "the present monopolizes attention in ways that chain one to it."⁷

We might call it the propertied present. It is founded on a classical substance metaphysics, where the subject—as first of all man of substance, sovereign over his properties—presents at the creep-speed of an essentialized self-identity through time. Reproduced in endless innovations, risks, and resiliencies, the smooth time of capital can capitalize every difference by remaining commodifiable as the *same*. Endlessly. And so even in view of the meltings, the floodings, the burnings: It has no end in sight.

Thus, Trump's second secretary of state, Mike Pompeo, announced that the ever more swiftly melting sea ice presents "new opportunities for trade." "The Arctic," he continued, "is at the forefront of opportunity and abundance. It houses 13 percent of the world's undiscovered oil, 30 percent of its undiscovered gas, an abundance of uranium, rare earth minerals, gold, diamonds, and millions of square miles of untapped resources, fisheries galore."⁸ This winning optimism thus monetizes melting glaciers.

Faced with planetary volatilities of climate, politics, virus, war, and a recent capital-driven economic meltdown, the current form of financialized capitalism projects the image of a propertied present continuously progressing. Therefore, its growth can only be conceived as infinite. The very notion of any limit to the market's growth, let alone some ecological or democratic constraint, remains economic heresy.

Theology, in several minor keys, has labored to expose both the secularized infinite as the all-propertied idol of capitalist orthodoxy and the creeping Christian collusions with the political and economic status quo. Over half a century ago there arose in the global South the great movement of the Roman Catholic liberation theologies on behalf of the poor, and eventually also, with Leonardo Boff and Ivone Gebara, of the Earth; in the North, Jürgen Moltmann, John Cobb, and Joerg Rieger have guided their diverse Protestantisms against the jointly ecological and human destructiveness of the capitalist absolute.

Rieger nails the problem: "We now understand that where the goal of production is the generation of profits—the categorical imperative of the Capitalocene—production must drive consumption, evolving in a vicious cycle that results in ecological destruction and climate change."[9] So global warming and the global means of production cycle dangerously around the planet. In *Of Divine Economy: Refinancing Redemption*, Marion Grau reconstructs the economy theologically, for the sake of an ironic *commercere* as "common investment," seeking to undo the self-centered and domesticated divinity of late capitalism.[10] Exposing its increasingly dominant financialized form in *Christianity and the New Spirit of Capitalism, theologian* Kathryn Tanner reads with and against Max Weber to show how this spirit feeds on a dominant form of puritan Calvinism.[11] She pursues her critique not as sociologist but as a theologian, in fidelity to her "own, quite specific Christian commitments."[12] These diverse theological critics all discern the spirit of an alternative *oikonomia*, a divine economy vibrating with the ancient possibility of an actually, radically, *common* good—even amid the buyouts and sellouts on behalf of the goodies of the competing economic absolute.

In the meantime, the enthroned capital continues to accept worship, religious and secular, whereby it is granted its due: faith in its creeping infinity of growth. Funding the household, the *oikonomia*, of its economic elites, its propertied present despoils in this time the space, the *oikologia*, of its species. So the present economy assembles at its speed-creep the new figuration of an "uninhabitable planet."[13] Because the *eco*logy of a hospitable earth can no longer coexist with the present form of the *eco*nomy, the self-contradiction within the *oikos* cashes the temporality of capitalist gradualism into the accelerating volatility of the planetary habitat. Capitalist time conquers earth's space. It is not that time itself dominates space. Rather the infinitude of the propertied present tense of a few jeopardizes the habitable space of a majority. And the finitude of space in (this) time manifests ever more desperately—at least as concerns the habitat hospitable to the majority of humans and nonhumans.

As Bruno Latour notes, the economic elites already recognize this. They no longer pretend that wealth will trickle down to all. They have "understood that, if they wanted to survive in comfort, *they had to stop pretending, even in their dreams, to share the earth with the rest of the world.*"¹⁴ They have realized there isn't enough space, enough planet, enough stuff, for us all; there will be less and less, for more and more people. They have begun to prepare their own climate change households in lovely locations up north, thus offsetting any looming guilt as to their grandchildren's futures even as they make their high-speed profits at the future's expense. In "How Big Business Is Hedging against the Apocalypse," Jesse Barron lays out how that hedging is not happening in ways that environmentalists will like. Without even the excuse of ignorance, major companies like ExxonMobil continue to profit from climate destruction.[15]

Does the future thus capitalized rule out the high-speed temporality needed for a political turnaround? Toward—what shall we call it? Ecosocial justice, slowing of climate change, revolution in economico-political practice? The salvation of a whole bunch of species, including even ours? The salvaging of the yet habitable planet? Some earthwide assemblage of and for a *common habitability*? And yet. Any such turnaround would require, as each recent IPCC report makes grimly clear, international cooperation for an economic withdrawal from fossil fuels requiring political transformation larger in scale and faster in speed than anything known in history.[16]

How probable is that? Inasmuch as chances can be calculated and the future predicted, the Game Over chorale will keep swelling in volume. Under these eerie Earth circumstances, the new normalization of a perfectly secular vocabulary of ecological apocalypse—of glaciers melting, coastlines flooding, fires around the globe raging—can only spread. I used to disdain most public uses of "apocalypse" as extremism. But then at a certain point the public eco-apocalyptic rhetoric reached beyond any putative hysteria in such headlined studies as the "Insect Armageddon" (based in Germany) and then "Insect Apocalypse" (in two Americas). The insects form the basis of our food-chain. Their die-out portends our own.[17]

If only due to the ancient imaginary of planetary catastrophe, theology creeps, not quite visibly, into a new public speech—a speech of the unspeakable. *Apokalypsis* blurs into *apophasis*: An apophatic Anthropocene that no mystification can save from the unspeakably destructive impact of its *anthropos*.

The relation between the volatile ecological and the relentless capitalist speed-creep has locked into the internal contradiction of the Anthropocene itself. The power of a small portion of the anthropos over the Earth increasingly turns Earth against the Anthropos at large. Planetary systems unfortunately cannot aim the effects of man-made change at the "exceptional" wealthy white guy. And that economic exceptionalism invests in political support of, for instance, the white US (and Christian and heteromale and successful) exceptionalism. As political theology has demonstrated already at its Schmittian root, it is by manipulating emergency that the exception makes itself the rule.[18] So power can smoothly take advantage of the very emergencies—of climate, of class—that it has caused. Sovereignty democratically elected may then turn autocratic, indeed fascist, by way of its nationalist manipulation of the white supremacist public.

As to that whiteness, another important, underacknowledged, correlation between politics and economy unfolds. It happens between race and class, and it happens *ecologically,* in what J. Kameron Carter all too accurately names the "plantationocene." Carter summons for a time of climate change what W. E. B. Du Bois had called *"the propertization of the world."*[19] Already a century ago Du Bois captured its political theology, indeed the ecologico-economico-political theology, with prophetic sarcasm: "Whiteness is the ownership of the earth forever and ever. Amen!"[20] In the present moment a polyrhythmic theology must heed Carter's articulation of the needed turnaround: to a "'non-class culture' that heralds nothing less than the apocalypse of the (plantation as) World." No straight "end of the world," this *apocalypsis*—but the doom of a civilization that has rendered the earth its plantation. Carter's stunning "Black Malpractice" can be read as a new manifestation of a long history of revolutions. That counterhistory, as the Marxist philosopher Ernst Bloch demonstrated seventy years ago in *The Principle of Hope*, translates the apocalyptic radicality of the biblical legacy into political motivation—into a collective refusal of the organization of culture by class.[21] To face that civilizational economy, as it antedates and produces whiteness and blackness right along with capitalism, the "principle of hope" now depends on a persistent confrontation of the entanglement of race and class.

White world without end: Is that the face of the propertied present and its infinite growth? No matter how many ethnic diversities and skin tones it is able to commodify, advertise, and monetize? The racial register of the propertied present that came into its own through the Euroamerican slave trade brands the half millennium old beginning of the plantationocene as Modernity itself. As Tanner observes, such a present partakes theologically of the early modern temporality that "in a traditional Protestant ethic also finds an insidious analogue in the new spirit of capitalism."[22] Hardly limited to the Puritan experiment but ecumenical in its Christian capture of the Americas, this half-millennium-old modernity barely pauses in its self-replication as we pass into postmodernity. It speed-creeps along as though endless, self-continuously racing, raced, through various ends of the modern: differences, dispossessions, and disasters. All cashed out and reinvested in its propertied present, its *proper* infinity.

Porn Queen of the Apocalypse

Now, however, we note a recent, still undertheorized, shift in the relation of economics to politics. We must not miss the deep tension between, on the one hand, global capitalism in the neoliberal format of the past half century, the form that we on the academic left presume and criticize, and on the other, the white nationalist—*anti-globalist*—politics with which that capitalism converges in recent US history.

Here an apocalyptic anachronism creeps up on me. One of the most garish parodies presented in the Book of Revelation stages what can be read as an ancient form of the tension of politics and economics: The Beast of empire riding "the Whore (*porne'*) of Babylon"—the original porn queen? The beast symbolizes the Roman *polis*. The "Great Whore" must be decoded as the embodiment of another dimension of empire: global trade.[23] The text cashes out in detail the lament of the urban and marine merchants at her fall, and at the loss of *twenty-six* luxury products of the ancient world: "cargo of gold, silver, jewels and pearls . . . purple dye . . . wine, olive oil. . ." with "slaves—human lives" providing the climax of the list (Rev 18:11–13).[24] There could hardly be a clearer symbolization of a global economy.

The porn-apocalyptic image, like the text as a whole and like most of its world, colonizer or colonized, partakes of a systemic misogyny. So when toward the end of the last millennium I wrote *Apocalypse Now and Then: A Feminist Guide to the End of the World*, the vilification of the female figure as slut distracted me from its economic radicality. (I befriended her, called her Babs, blamed John for blaming economic imperialism on her.) But in *Facing Apocalypse* I recognized that the author's aim is not to strengthen male supremacy as such (he hardly needs to). In the flashing image of the imperial prostitute (with her sovereign status one can hardly call her a "sex worker") the Great Babylon vision cultivates horror at the limitless commodification—unto the life of one's most intimate flesh—imposed by the sovereign globalization of trade. And as today, that commodification imposes itself not by extrinsic force but by the seductive formation of desire. In part because of its indubitably creepy sexism, the prophetic force of Revelation's exposé of the precapitalist form of imperial global economy as idolatrous has been underappreciated by even the Christian left. But when the Beast turns on his royal Porne and devours her, is John not revealing a deep contradiction between the political and economic dimensions of a single global regime?

Thereafter the text's nightmarish spiral through the destruction of immense systems of human and nonhuman life accelerates: Fire consumes "one third of the trees"; toxic poisoning takes out "one third of the life of the seas" (8:7), and so on and on. Of course the vision does not literally foresee climate change, nor yet the neoliberal capitalist form of the mating of economics and politics. Prophecy is not prediction. It does not foretell a somehow predetermined future. But it does read unjust patterns already so deeply entrenched in its present as to make their systemic iterations in unknowable futures all too probable.

In *How Will Capitalism End?* German sociologist Wolfgang Streeck helps update, in purely secular form, the contradiction. He finds current Western democracies undergoing a risky struggle between two constituencies not simply aligned with right and left: the "national state people ... and the international market people."[25] The tension comes to a head because capitalism "can only survive by constraint of its own complete commodification" of land, labor, and money. Yet it is motivated by utterly unconstrained, insatiable "growth." And there is no needed regulatory motivation or structure on the scene with the power to insist on limitation.[26] As the contradiction took its late-twentieth-century course, "the postwar shotgun marriage between capitalism and democracy came to an end."[27] Does that marriage and its collapse not faintly echo the whore-beast parable? Yet it would be altogether misleading to infer that the collusion of global capital with national politics has come close to ending in the twenty-first century. Rather, the takedown of democratic, ecosocially oriented regulation of corporations is itself key to conservative politics. That is hardly an assault on the global economy! In fact the right wing of US politics depends on the neoliberal globalism that it at the same time attacks.

The authors of the fundamentalist Christian *Trumpocalypse* (a term of praise) align "global capitalism" with all cosmopolitan efforts: such as the UN, interchange between world religions, open borders, and of course the ecological movement. So Donald Trump, the book declares in apocalyptic celebration, "is one of the few politicians who is at war with globalism. Most of the Republicans and Democrats, along with Obama and the Clintons, for all intents and purposes, are on the payroll of the wealthy corporate elite."[28] That claim may have some credibility. But the presumption that Trump had any political power apart from his extensive global business partnerships, alliances, and priorities has no basis in fact. And of course the role of conservative white evangelicals in keeping political Beast and economic Babylon intimately coupled remains indispensable.

So the nationalist/globalist partnership is not over in the US but rather has morphed into a particularly "virulent evangelical/neoliberal assemblage," in the language of political philosopher William Connolly. He demonstrates how "white evangelicals foment an accusatory spirituality toward nonwhites, ecologists, the media, migration, independent women,

CREEPS OF THE APOCALYPSE / 19

decolonial regimes, and intellectuals." In this they construe the market as "a vehicle of God's providence," while they hold the democratic state, even as they use it, "to be a bureaucratic titan."[29] So the tensive intimacy of Babylon and Beast keeps twisting into self-contradiction. The right-wing assemblage praises the present form of capitalism, even as it derides the globality of neoliberalism that *is* that form, and when it can attacks it by means of the titan.

Disruptive Novum

The complication, or co-implication, of democracy and capitalism only intensifies the spiral of ecosocial demise. The contradictions between the volatile temporalities of political polarization and of climate shifts, held in the continuous capitalist present that monetizes both, press toward greater emergency. As political theology makes clear, emergency justifies exceptionalism. So with emergencies racial, national, economic, the vicious spirals spin faster. The "spin" keeps the exceptional subject of the propertied present continuous—indeed sovereign. Times of crisis may simply reinforce the creep of the current form of financialized capitalism.

As Kathryn Tanner argues, "The more people are convinced of derivatives' capacities to tame the future, the more imprudent they become, taking more risks than they should, so that it becomes all the more likely that the future will bring catastrophic surprises." And "unanticipated catastrophic surprise closes off all possible options."[30] Note that such closure would characterize not the darkly *dis*closive apocalypse of J. Kameron Carter (or of John of Patmos) but the banal *fin* of a delusional infinity. In other words, the steady creep of the propertied present, confident in endless growth, conceals the recklessness of its gambles. To read the catastrophic potential of the propertied present as intersected in its illusory self-sameness by the speed-creeping temporalities of climate change and political polarization only underscores Tanner's economic analysis.

That catastrophic potential comes here edged with theology. Indeed, it is just at the edge, the *eschatos*, of Tanner's theological vision that another register of catastrophe is revealed. The vision exposes not just the reckless financialization but the religious delusions of mere rescue from time and its volatile indeterminacies. Here

> the future Christians expect retains a strongly negative flavor of potential disruption, something whose effects it would therefore make sense to try to nullify prospectively, and not just because Christians sometimes think that future might include damnation for

some. Even a purely benevolent end—universal salvation—retains a highly negative cast to the extent such a future will tear us away from what we remain in and of ourselves, sinners.[31]

In resistance to such redemptive dissociation from present materiality, Tanner's own soteriology comes into play precisely at that edge of time—whatever ends of whatever worlds suggest themselves. "Salvation would not simply await the resurrection of bodies to come but would be operative now to transform material lives for the better."[32]

Of course, even a theology or a spirituality of material transformation can serve capitalism. One passing example bubbles up. In Kathryn Lofton's narration of the merger of religion and consumption in the marketing of soap a century ago, "soap offered not only sanitation but explicit salvation." Pushing the Protestant merger of cleanliness and godliness, a reporter comically raved: "'There are millions without the desire to repent and be *laved*. We must continue to 'sell' the world on cleanliness.'"[33] Alien to such sudsy consumer positivism, salvation in its biblical sense never lacks a critical, "strongly negative flavor." It does not abstract life from the fray, nor persons from the bodies and the dirt of our shared life. No new heaven and earth results from individual purity or manipulable transition.

Tanner offers instead the "coherence of a whole new world to be entertained as an imaginative counter to the whole world of capitalism as it presently exists and pretends to be all-encompassing, to have no limits, nothing outside itself." Such a possible world "operates not at a remove from finance-dominated capitalism but by cutting across it, traversing it to disruptive effect."[34] With and without an explicit theos, expressively kataphatic or silently apophatic, does such a disruptive novum offers a possible clue, a hope against hope, against the falsities of optimism, progress, guarantee?

Such an embrace of the negative, not in a manipulable dialectic but as disruption, resonates with J. Kameron Carter's "black rupture." It is "at the limit of politicality" that his edgy *eschatos* cuts across the present. There "the surreal—the subreal, the submerged—flutters as invisibly felt and is apocalyptically unveiled as monstrous, as a sacral blackness that incites volatility."[35] As black rupture opens into black rapture, the propertied present pales and shakes. Of course, this *apokalypsis* of race dynamics does not unveil a generic Christian "new world." But neither will it dissociate from the countereconomics, counterpolitics, countertheology of ancient prophetic eschatology.

Apocalyptic unveiling in our time and in US space doesn't happen outside the spatiotemporality of a racialized modernity in which I for one forfeit all innocence. So of course one may creep off into a silence that no apophasis excuses. Before an *apokalypsis* that no revision assuages. Rupture never guarantees rapture. And yet economically and ecologically, *oikos* imagined otherwise might dis/close, in Carter's words, "a zone of festive dwelling."[36] Such dwelling is hardly dissociable from the dream of urban newness that concludes the old Apocalypse. With its cross-species eroticism (bride/lambin ironic juxtaposition to whore/beast), the vision of New Jerusalem celebrates a radically novel spacetime of dwelling, all twelve of its gates festively open 24/7.

And yet in the meantime, this mean time, great gates of possibility seem to be creaking toward closure.

Salvaging Apocalypse?

Might we agree that the triple temporality of the present—ecological, political, economic—does not assemble any merely predictable future? Even though as you read the tense present of an unpredictable degree of ecosocial catastrophe all too predictably continues to kick in? The ineradicable indeterminacy of any moment blurs with an unspeakability that at its theological depth means not horror but mystery. Apokalypsis and apophasis, so opposite in mood, won't here break apart. Even so, the unspeakable horror of the apocalypse swerves into its overimagined and underrealized hope for a future no less difficult to name. That promising future hides in an apocalyptic apophasis. So then the unclosed margin of indeterminacy does mean at least this: Catastrophe can become catalyst. Climate crisis with its socioeconomic consequences carries a potential for disruption that movements of resistance on their own can hardly match. Yet we can have no certainty that heightened ecological emergency will somehow provoke the emergence of (for example) a dark green democratic socialism. The dangers refuse to stand down: not just of the rejection of responsibility by those reaping profits from business as usual, but of some version of climate fascism claiming emergency power.[37] Then there are the risks posed by the last-ditch mitigations and big technofixes. And as the fixes fail, with possibly horrific side effects, we face the dangers of humanly—nationally, racially, sexually, tribally—brutal adaptations. On a burnt, baked, and flooded planet with some gated communities for the self-designated exceptions. "New Jeru" for the few.

So what possible hope (oh, that discredited notion) might keep us not doped but creatively struggling? What glimpses of possibility will press us into polyrhythmic solidarities, maybe even able to outpace the triply creeping dooms of economics, ecology, democracy? Surely such hope carries a soteriological intensity. That does not mean it comes down to intervention and salvation by an omnipotent Other, let alone to a final climax. Salvation might redistribute its agency more democratically, its matter more ecosocially, its sacrality more relationally, and for many less theistically. Salvation may then etymologically ally itself with "salvage."

Salvage happens to be the name of a British "quarterly of revolutionary arts and letters." A recent issue sports as subtitle: "Towards the Proletarocene."[38] The journal's "salvage communism," characterized in the words of novelist (and journal co-editor) China Miéville as an "apophatic Marxism" freed of all Stalinizing dogmatism, holds in political conjunction the depredations of capitalism, racism, and "as we race past tipping point after tipping point," climate change. "That is to say, global proletarianisation and ecological disaster have been products of the same process. The earth the wretched would—will—inherit, will be in need of an assiduous programme of restoration."[39] One need not convert to Marxism to take in Miéville's disruptive poetics, as he meditates in Suffolk—with "its lines of dead trees, lichened concrete in the bird sanctuary, drowned houses off the coast" are "ruins by design. The policy is called 'managed decline.' A nationally sanctioned becoming-eerie."[40]

Hope amid such systemic creepiness cannot be to avoid great crisis. "To hope against hope is not merely to contest all the dreg-like hope unearned: it is prefiguration. It is to live with an eye on the horizon where hope will be no longer needed."[41] And in the light of that prefiguration to salvage, to recycle discerningly, that which can and should still be saved. Might hope thus fold its futures into such a fulfilling *oikos* of hoped-for dwelling? A New Jerusalem inviting no religious or political certitudes? Such prefiguration does not mean that we are progressing toward it: "Interruption could hardly be more urgent."[42] Rupture opens possibility now—and does not wait to reach any horizon. After all a horizon only exists by receding. The prefiguration transfigures the present, which, dispossessed of its properties, opens to the temporalities of its tenses: a present contracting in itself tragicomic remembrances of what has been, even while imagining what is yet to come, even now becoming. Its present does not escape the tenses of past and future. Indeed those tensions of time itself are intensified by the creeps of the apocalypse. The contradictions between the possible futures churning up out of the conflictual past will keep threatening to overwhelm the present. Yet rather than surrender to impossibility or paralysis, we might salvage even the contradictions, the disappointments, the hopelessness—and transmute them moment by moment into a mobilizing complexity of time-tempos. There the Marxist utopia and the biblical New Jerusalem do a circle dance together.

Planetary Kairos

In this polyrhythmic now, possibility foments the new—not the old newnewnew of endless consumption, selfsame in its dissociative difference, but an earthy freshness that materializes now and here. Salvaging is not a matter of clinging to the ruins of the past. The operative prefiguration is neither a refiguration of the given nor a prediction of the future. Its novum arises not as exception but as *inception*.[43] In other words we might learn to salvage from the past whatever—however impurely—can be recycled renewingly. In the polyrhythms of labor, lament, love. And of hope.

Can the elemental convulsions of planetary time now open up,(*apokalypsis*, another temporality, far from The End of Time, tuned to the volatility of the current climate, material and political? Might its assemblages salvage from their determinate history the possibility of habitable earth futures—*in time*? Hope for that possibility lives free of the progress optimism of capitalism. It may remain difficult to distinguish from ecopolitical pessimism. But the difference matters. It materializes in this salvaging that is the very work of ecology, vastly prehuman and imperatively now-human. It lets us imagine and so initiate—in rupture, in rapture— timely works of collective creativity. And of such creative process, let me stress all too theologically: Creation is not ever from mere nothing.[44]

Some dark depth of energy, some pulsation of pneumatological wings over the rhythm of ocean, is always already in play. Inception comes not as the omnipotent performance of an *ex nihilo,* not even when secularized as revolution. It revolves, recycles the potentiality of the past as present potency, thus strengthening the *radix*, the rooted earth-time, of honestly radical revolution. In that ground it cuts off no ancient source of justice, peace, and new creation. Its turbulent depth supports the needed breadth. That breadth becomes practical in the assemblage of a public wide enough to salvage the planetary habitat. Transformation then carries glimmers and graces of old prophetic soteriology—salvation not as supernatural flight but salvaging of world. The prophets meant to activate and to liberate, not to discipline and postpone.

If then we salvage some theological sense of salvation itself, the haunting hope—pulsing upon the face of the deep—of new creation may find spiritual reinforcement. It finds spirit—with which to call up seculareligious assemblages, lively in their intersections. As Marcia Pally demonstrates, for a new economics and politics, "we need a way back to the evolutionary, ontological and theological principle of distinction-amid-relation."[45] Solidarity does not need us to come together in some solidified unity, ontological or social. It may require, it may stir, and suffer, immense differences of priority. It does not wait for a unification of the desired versions of political equality, economic justice and ecological restoration but goes ahead and practices a pluralizing entanglement of our histories in our futures. Amid the triply creeping temporality, solidarity arises not only in the simple "against," holding out for some miracle of redemptive inversion. Sometimes it can only salvage scraps of potentiality from inadequate gestures, well-intended compromises, unpracticed theories, broken promises. It starts always now, again, from the chaos, the detritus, in the improvised polyrhythm of our spirited if shadowed planetarity. In this spirit it can crack open the actual opening within the speed-creeping apocalypse of ecology, economics, politics.

At the same time, the transdisciplinary *oikos* of such theology continues, along with much liberal education, its own not so slowly creeping demise. Such fragile institutions tell their own lamentable, laborious, and occasionally lovable stories. And despite the vulnerabilities, the speed of our theory and the creep of our practice continue to pulsate with the questions of climate, capital, and democracy. But then is every such theological effort doomed to reflexive curation of the apocalypse? Perhaps. And so we must keep reinforcing the inceptions, the dis/closures, that put the lie to The End.

The disruptive moment of this planetary *kairos* of last chances will enable a widening solidarity, breaking out of the marketable modules of faith and knowledge. And at this time, this time that stretches from me writing to you reading, the contradictions of economics, politics, and ecology may yield to an earthwide temporality. Whether creeping or galloping, pausing, trotting or leaping, this moment depends on perilously new possibilities opening into its spatiotemporal indeterminacy. In that volatile dis/closure, improbable futures still stir, yet to be salvaged in the inception of their polyrhythmic present.

2 / The "We" of Catastrophe, the Throb of Cosmogony

ECO-THINKING WITH SYLVIA WYNTER

"We"? Sylvia Wynter interrogates that pronoun for its deceptive overgeneralizations.[1] She famously exposes the habituating monopolies of its transition from *Man(1)*, medieval and Christian, to *Man(2)*. He—*the latter one*—presents as modern, secularist, neoliberal, and abidingly white. And in the face of this long *his*tory, confronting what she calls "the overrepresentation of Man,"[2] she manages to reclaim the "we" for another possibility, for the chance, neither guarantee nor fantasy,

> that therefore, we no longer need illusions—such as those which now inter alia threaten the livability of our species' planetary habitat—in order to now remake, consciously and collectively, the new society in which our now existential referent "we . . . in the horizon of humanity" will *all* now live.[3]

In "The Ceremony Found," Wynter arrives at that chance by way of the difficult question posed in another of her later publications: "The Unparalleled Catastrophe for Our Species?"[4] From her Jamaican point of view she contemplates nothing less than what might "make possible for the peoples of contemporary post-Mandela South Africa, as well as our also Western and Westernized global selves, to now collectively give humanness a different future."[5] Indeed her writing may be read as one of the most important disclosures our species-we has produced of the specific conjunction of racial and economic world orders with ecological degradation and climate change. In this brief meditation I want to reinforce her work's capacity to animate the possibility, indeed the performative embodiment, of humanness as, after all, embracing the entire species. For only so—beyond the blood-stained and white-bleached subjection of all to some—does her existential *we* have a chance of grounding the solidarity necessary to meet the "unparalleled catastrophe for our species."

Her meditation on the South African possibility was provoked by a deep dive into the Blombos Cave on the coast of the Indian Ocean. She recounts that artifacts 80,000 and then, deeper inside the cave, 100,000 years old, were discovered (some instruments, some red ochre dye, a hint of art). She finds them illustrating her hypothesis on the human origin, which she names the "Third Event." It succeeds the "First Event" of the birth of the universe and the "Second Event" of the birth of life. Her Third Event consists of the birth of the human as *Homo narrans*. It reveals a cosmogony of "symbolic life terms," of community, of a "genre-specific referent-we, its us/not us," and of a "ritual-initiatory transformation." In such ritual, subjects "are all now reborn of the same origin story rather than of the womb."[6] And for Wynter this supports the elementally human interplay of story with biology. Her "bios/mythoi" dyad carries her creative resistance to either biological or monomythic reductions of the origin of the human, let alone to its rendition as "secular *Man*(2)'s *Homo sapiens/homo oeconomicus* in genre-specific biocentric bourgeois terms."[7] For her the bio/mythoi, precisely in its cosmogony *of* the human, never reduces *to* the human.

In "The Ceremony Found," Wynter argues that from the point of human emergence in Africa, the role of cosmogony consisted in holding our "eusocial, inter-altruistic . . . replicator DNA code" in unconscious subordination to the narrow limits of a particular social code. Indeed, one might say she provides a cosmogony of the Blombos cosmogony, reading its point of ancient origin from the point of view of a *present* possibility: cosmogony to the second power? For the Third Event laws that have functioned "outside our conscious awareness" may now become conscious.[8] By this she signals the surprising possibility of giving "humanness a different future" by offering it a fresh, indeed, an originative, and now conscious, account of its origins. This is no small matter: it requires the extension of the "then secularizing referent-we" to "a *propter nos homines*" ["for us humans"] remade to the now whole species-oriented "measure of the world."[9] Such a becoming would finally demand the exposure and exceeding of the deformed *propter nos* of the globalized, modernized, and whitened Western self, the Man that vast proportions of humanity can only marginally instantiate.

With its possibility of an alternative future, Wynter's meta-Darwinian species-inclusive account poses no hope of the sort that thinking people with good reason swat away as self-deception. Reading her, I realize not only that the crisis of climate change in its unprecedented breadth of interlinkage with every systemic injustice will require a vast solidarity among "us" humans if it is to be addressed. We know this already. The concept of "intersectionality" (not part of her terminology, but deeply kin to it, first formulated in an anti-racist context by Kimberlé Crenshaw in the '80s) has become indispensable to the articulation not just of the multiplicity of issues but of their interdependence. Climate change will land most brutally on those who have done the least to cause it, largely people, and peoples, of color. Wynter's nuanced intercalation of race, gender, sexuality, and economics with (more recently) ecology certainly deepens attention to this global web of challenges. But she offers something further. The coming to consciousness, her "autopoetic Turn/Overturn,"[10] does not just interlink the issues of that untoward list. It does more than gesture beyond competing and self-dividing social movements. It also potentially supercharges their intersectionality. The turning of the tables, the turning of history's direction, means the overturning of the global status quo. In other words it calls forth a "we" that might really arise, that might materialize in a great "otherwise" to the currently catastrophic direction. In consciousness of the profound interplay of the white/Black, the rich/poor, the hetero/homo and even still the male/female divides in all of their coordination with modern rationality/irrationality and so with order/chaos, now exposed and addressed, new forces of agency may really be emerging across the world.

No longer opaque to itself, such a self-aware "we" might yet energize a "species-oriented" solidarity strong enough to expose the neoliberal dogmatics of growth for what it is—the growth of terrestrial catastrophe. And so to interrupt it. *We* can demand the replacement of the measure of profit with the "now species-oriented 'measure of the world.'"[11] Thus by way of the Turn/Overturn Wynter would lift the first-person plural into the "*fully emancipatory* terms" of an "unprecedented Second Emergence": an uplift certainly not guaranteed but *able* to meet the "unparalleled catastrophe for our species."[12] At no turn of her argument does the hope Wynter generates degrade into mere optimism.[13] Its energy of actualization persists only through its depth and its darkness.

Code Made Flesh

Admittedly, from the perspective (the word, the mythos) of theology I approach the question of the "we" somewhat differently. That discipline participates in a religious "we" that Sylvia Wynter would no more embrace as such than she would espouse *Man*(2)'s secularism. Nonetheless her prose does, as we shall see, flash hints of religious mythoi. I will note ways that a certain theological engagement can strengthen rather than fragment the emergent "we." Such a theological viewpoint must of course presume a self-critical Christianity. Its theology has long been at work, on a vast manifold of fronts, to emancipate religious and also secular publics from the theocratic residues of *Man*(1)'s supernaturalism. In the modes of Black and Latin American liberation, feminist/womanist, LGBTQIA, ecological, and process theologies, the half-century-long press against the aggressive socio-symbolic remainders of a pale and patriarchal Father above has been primarily directed against Christian conservatism. But in its commitment to liberative biblical motifs and its critique of modern ideology such theology has always also needed to push back against reductive secularisms—and their deceptively secularized theologisms. Vis-à-vis those secularizations I may underscore a formulation of the editors of the book inspired by Wynter: "*Ceremony (Burial of an Undead World)* aims at unearthing the theological structure beneath the frontiers of capitalist extraction and the processes of conversion that enable and fuel capital accumulation, delineating its essentially sacrificial economy."[14]

The reverberations of theological tropes both negative and positive in Wynter's language therefore enhance its potential for a rigorous and inviting cosmogony—a potential that can live only if such resonances are not repressed. For instance, she repeatedly refers to the gathering of the multiple peoples of the earth in the now possible "we" as a "new ecumene." With her scrupulous attention to verbal nuances, that multi-religiously charged trope is hardly accidental. Not that the social formations of her *oikumene* would depend upon churches, temples, mosques, or other religious institutions, the conventional publics of ecumenical engagement. The word originally means simply the "inhabited" (world), from *oikos* (dwelling place). Yet it is hard to imagine her excluding from such a co-dwelling the immense and widely nonwhite swath of those who inhabit Judaism, Christianity, and Islam—at least inasmuch as they themselves embrace some version of a planetary *oikumene*. Indeed, movements toward theological ecumenism largely work hand in hand, locally and globally, with the eco-social justice arms of the multiple religious "dwellings." And let us, while we are at it—we fellow instances of *Homo narrans*—always note that *ecology* derives from the same Greek *oikos*. As Wynter prophetically signals, the capacity of the earth to house us, the materiality of our planetary dwelling, is now at stake.

A similarly theological implication haunts Wynter's adaptation of the terminology of Aimé Césaire's "new and hybrid science," in his 1946 articulation of the "Word as code."[15] Already that capitalization cannot fail to echo the *logos* of the fourth Gospel. Wynter unflinchingly amplifies this

Christological reverb when she complements the Word as code with what she names "the telos of the Ceremony Found's *New Studia*": "the code-made-flesh."[16] Surely this enfleshment is not just permitting, it is poetically unleashing, the background code, the noise, the choirs, of the ancient Incarnation. Not that her meaning can be simply translated back into John 1:14: "And the Word became flesh and lived among us." She is no closet evangelist. Besides, if John's gospel had relevance in its ancient context, it was taught with the timeliness of a code that would require sometimes radical updates. And still—perhaps never more so—does.

What was that Word—Logos—encoding two millennia ago? Nothing other than the Hebrew *mythos* of creation, in a precise echo of the creativity of Genesis 1:3: the divine speech act ("And God said 'let there be . . .'") that opens the First Testament. John 1:3 thus ceremonially iterates the ancient cosmogony for the Second Testament: The Word [Logos] "was in the beginning with God. And all things came into being through [the Word] and without [it] not one thing came into being." So the (then) new mythos of the early Christian Logos-as-code did not mean to supersede the ancient Hebrew cosmogony, but rather to update it with an unprecedented enactment of embodiment: the revelation of the code-made-flesh. Its telos? The wider legibility of a sacred code now read to be embodied in everything, in every becoming creature of the cosmos. Note that the expression of the cosmic *word* in and as *flesh* reveals the very *opposite* of the already classical dualism of the West: and so also the opposite, as Wynter nails it, of the "Spirit/Flesh order of value of the Christian-medieval order."[17]

In the ancient cosmogony of Genesis and its Johannine echo, is it perhaps possible to hear still pulsing the experience Wynter narrates, thinking back to the yet far older South African cosmogony, when humanity "discovered in fear and rapture the throbbing newness of the world"?[18] She is transmitting those throbs into an "ecumenically inclusive call for a 'new humanity.'"[19] Does Genesis 1 by contrast seem all too top-down and orderly in its sequence of creation?

Let me hint here at a wildly different reading. It requires that one really *read*, rather than habitually repress (as nearly 2,000 years of allusions have done) the second verse: "the earth was a formless void and darkness covered the face of the deep, while a wind from God swept over the face of the waters." (That is the New Revised Standard Version translation.) But the Hebrew word translated as "void" does not signify "nothing"— it belongs there in the phrase *tohu va bohu,* meaning "formless and disorderly." There is no textual warrant to void, let alone to demonize, that "darkness on the face." And the "deep" translates the Hebrew *tehom,* signifying the chaotic waters of origin. As for the primal "wind" (*ruach*), it is not something sent down by a God up there but *is* God, is the Spirit itself.

My theological point: Biblically there is creation only from the waters of chaos. Not "from nothing." The Christian assumption of *creatio ex nihilo* is standard, doctrinally orthodox—and, as all biblical scholars know whether or not they admit it, it represents a postbiblical and rarely questioned misreading. It has worked to create the bios/mythos of the Creator of omnipotent unilateral power. The Hebrew text suggests a very different bios/mythos: a calling forth—"let there be"—from the bottomless depths of a womb-like, watery source. Not from nothing, nor from mere disorder, but from the creative potentiality of the formless *tehom*.

Hear the difference? The primal chaos, as scriptural scholars almost fully concur, somehow preexists our particular universe—which says something significant about the divinity working in and with it. The Johannine creation recap can be read either way: To hear the anticipation of a Christological Word in the primal speech of Genesis does not render its creativity ex nihilo; yet the Logos has largely functioned to repress the ongoing pulsation of those dark waves that preexist the order of the creation—and are not cited in the Gospel. I won't preach on about this theological structure here. But I admit to having written a book about the *creatio ex nihilo* and its possible alternative, the *creatio ex profundis*.[20] The point here is to lend theological reinforcement to Sylvia Wynter's insistence that the racialized binary of white/black correlates with other binaries—of power/submission, spirit/flesh, light/darkness, translated in modernity into "the rational/ irrational mode of Order/Chaos."[21]

If then we read the biblical code words of creation as calling creatures forth from rocking, darkly creative waves of chaos, the whole order of *Man*(1) begins to shake. And resting upon it, *Man*(2)'s hyperorder will have to repress its *actual* religious background even more aggressively—one reason for the crucial alliance of secular neoliberal economics with white right-wing Christianity. Ironically, fundamentalist Christianity makes for an effective repression of the biblical energies of creation, of creativity. Man(2) apparently needs reactionary religious backup during this time when the order of creation itself—our habituated world-habitus—comes into question, when the too-long-denied disorders of our civilization come back not just to haunt but to flood and poison and burn us. Us the species. The primal creativity hinted at in Genesis, with its chaotic indeterminacies—open-ended potentialities that might have resourced and refreshed our species—are getting blocked theologically and materially.

And nonetheless, or all the more so, we the species, we who identify as species, struggle to evolve socially, even cosmically—and of necessity consciously. In the conspiracy of a collectively mindful creativity. Which is to say, of Wynter's Autopoetic Turn. For in this theological reading, the creator does not operate with the sovereignty of *ex nihilo*. Rather, the word as code calls, it invites—"let there be"—and only so enables the autopoesis, the creative emergence of creatures interlinked in their ever-becoming differences. And in the human creatures, liberating forms of religion and spirituality, never imposed or required, may lend motive force—and flesh—to the Turn/Overturn.

A Cosmogonic "We"

It is not, therefore, that such a Turn is no longer possible. But the scale of possible—and needed—transformation does signal improbability, due to the global scale of the repression, the commodification, the destruction. And that uncertainty now carries cosmological resonances at once ancient and futural. So the global grip of racialized capitalism requires a planet-wide response, charged by a wildly pluralist spirituality. The ancient Blombos Cave cosmogony remains revelatory. And beneath the official dogmas the First and Second Testament openings contribute fresh cosmogonic encodings of the meaning of our species' life on the earth. But ancient glimpses are, of course, insufficient qua cosmogonies for the imperative that Wynter voices as the "unthinkable yet looming possibility."[22]

Given Wynter's fierce commitment to the *bios/mythoi* dyad and so to teaming natural science with the sociogeny of the Word, her refusal of mere biocentrism requires of our species not a repression of biology or any other science but scientific liberation from the orthodox secularism of modernity. Then the sciences can work in principled solidarity with the genres and cultures of our species' poetics—including, in this *we*, varieties of spiritual and even theological practice. Such a transreligious, transdisciplinary, indeed transcontinental upsurge of solidarity may help *us*—as a mindfully expanding we—interrupt the movement toward our own extinction. And so the ancient future of her cosmogony both requires the revolutionary Overturn and inspires the visionary Turn.

Wynter's cosmogonic code does, however, invite further reflection on the material cosmos, on the relations with and between creatures nonhuman as well as human. I will in what remains suggest a discursive pathway that can work to strengthen the cosmogonic solidarities needed for the ecosocial leap of our evolution. There does exist, off the radar of the intellectual mainline, at least one full-blown cosmogony that addresses this need. There are multiple resources. But this one was delivered a century ago in *Process and Reality: An Essay in Cosmology*, delivered as the Gifford

Lectures in 1927–28 by Alfred North Whitehead, until then known as a great mathematician (and teacher of the logician and atheist Bertrand Russell).[23] Encountering the enigmas of relativity and especially quantum physics, Whitehead shifted into philosophical cosmology. For he recognized that the implicit worldview of modernity, in both its theoretical reaches and its common sense, could not accommodate the universe that was beginning to disclose itself. Modernity continued to transmit the mechanics of self-enclosed subjects and their separately objectified others. Whitehead wrote out a cosmos in which all participants exist only as radically interrelated processes. Not just humans but all creatures here decode as dynamic processes of mutually entwined genesis, no longer fixed substances but pulsating events of becoming. In his scientifically rigorous reimagining of matter there appeared delicate but startling glimpses of a spirit exceeding secular reduction. This cosmology might press Wynter's "we" in its primarily human horizon from two sides: toward the indiscernibility of any sharp boundary between "us" autopoetic humans and the rest of us animals, earthlings, creature; and at the same time toward the recognition of a theological dynamism in each of us. I want to suggest that these pressures collude profoundly with her challenge and alternative to capitalism's autopoiesis.

What is called process thought emerged in various experiments in application of Whitehead's dense cosmographic code. Though rarely embraced by the simply secular modern academy, these developments remain vibrant and diverse. In the present context I would especially note the brilliant work connecting race, gender, and matter in such process womanist thinkers as Karen Baker Fletcher, Carol Wayne White, and Monica Coleman.[24] Over half a century ago, process *theology* had emerged, guided by John B. Cobb Jr., developing the intuition of a deity neither in control of the universe nor omniscient of its outcomes. Indeed, Whitehead's cosmos has no linear beginning or end, no single *creatio ex nihilo* or predetermined endtime. Its God is entwined in process with the cosmos, in and with all the becoming creatures, at all times. If *Homo sapiens* stands out, it is not that we are exceptions to the cosmic code; it would just be that our species seems to be the only one on this planet self-conscious of our relation to the world. Able then "to unmake and remake" that world—but only in interrelations lived out, in responsible awareness or in reckless disregard, as part of the diversity of the species and elements of our earth. From the process perspective, the (largely white) minority of *Man*(2) that thought to control the making and unmaking have lived in a delusion that is coming to a head, threatening us all with a final unmaking.

Not by accident was Cobb among the first theologians to expose the depth and urgency of the looming ecological crisis: *Is It Too Late?* is the title of his prophetic environmental book of 1971.²⁵ Later came his full-scale critique of neoliberal capitalism, *For the Common Good: Redirecting the Economy toward Community, the Environment, and a Sustainable Future* (1989), co-authored with economist Herman Daly.²⁶ Given the latter's inevitably marginal status within his own discipline, here is a promising sign: As I write this piece, *the New York Times Magazine* has just published its lead article on Daly's ecological alternative to the neoliberal paradigm.²⁷ And Daly subtly avows the importance to him of a theological motive. Perhaps further crises of climate can motivate more such transdisciplinary collaboration and public recognition.

Process thought in this century largely transmits itself, often without God-talk, through ecological teaching and activist networks.²⁸ Religious communities and spiritual motivations syncing with scientific and secular publics remain key to any cultural transformation—any Turn/Overturn, any burial of the decaying but change-resistant "undead world." And, of course, such a radical evolutionary leap is not a matter of waiting around for the right revolutionary opportunity. For along with ongoing ecological destruction and its human costs, cosmogenesis persists. Opportunities for regeneration, for generative transspecies creativity, do not wait, they beckon. Or in the process theological sense, their possibilities "lure."²⁹

A Poiesis of Blackness

One can read a cosmogony of interdependent becoming as a pan-poetic vision—every creature is, more or less, for better or worse, a process of poiesis—both in the sense of sheer "making" and of a primacy of aesthetic desire. The process-relational cosmogony offers itself to our species as indeed a "measure of the world," in its immeasurable macrocosms, its sociogenic mesocosms, its intimate microcosms. And, therefore, process thinker Jon Ivan Gill is calling forth—in the spirit of the "hip hop mode of becoming" and its "Next Universe"—an "aesthetic religion," brilliant in its "aesthetic theopoetics." *Underground Rap as Religion* pours Whitehead's cosmology into the "multi/race/less/ness" of an originative, polydox, and rigorously, rhythmically unfolding theopoetic process.³⁰

Such poiesis remains lively in theory as well as in art, for it submits itself to continual experiment and testing, to intersectional elaborations and collaborations. It worries not about the multiplication and overcomplication of intersecting issues but about the oversimplifications of "the undead world." Thus the racializing dynamism of globalized systems of evercolonizing capitalism also requires, and indeed receives, ever more explication within theological conversations—at least among those committed to ecosocial justice. So for another profound poiesis of the Black radical tradition in religion, J. Kameron Carter exposes the radical connection of racial capitalism to earth-colonizing religion, while insisting on the alternative: "a poetics of religion as such, a poetics given with and in black religion and the blackness thereof, given with and in black religion's poetics of flesh, with and in the *mater,* the matter, the *material* signs or the semiotics of dispersed life."[31]

In the poiesis that Sylvia Wynter performs, in the gorgeous multitonality of its Blackness, that materiality finds itself mattering more than it could without her. And so this meditation is offered only in grateful celebration of the ceremonial freshness of her voice—and of its ever-yet-becoming *we,* turning and overturning the world.

3 / Political Theologies at War

A VIRTUAL TALK WITH STUDENTS IN UKRAINE

I have not gone through any trauma like you Ukrainian students have been experiencing.[1] Russia has crashed into your lives, interrupting everything. I greatly admire your organizing this virtual conference, with the leadership of Kseniia Trofymchuk, in order to persist with your theological studies. No matter what. This is surely a time that tests your faith, that may stir up radical doubts and deep despair, that raises the most fundamental questions. Fortunately theology, unlike most academic disciplines, invites those questions. And its answers do not arise apart from the voices of *your* experience, *your* uncertainty, *your* truth.

A crisis like this sucks people of faith right into the old, old query—how can a God of love let such horrors happen? To me? To the world? How can this be part of God's providential direction of history? Is it some sort of divine manipulation for our ultimate benefit, or merely the indifference of a distant monarch? Or of an impersonal infinity? These are questions of theodicy—the problem of the justice, or the justification, of God in the face of evil. The questions presume a standard view of God's power as omnipotence, as in some sense in control of all things. But they also presume some version of human choice, sin, and responsibility. So the driving question of theodicy comes down to power. If God has total control, if God is truly omnipotent, then evil is either permitted by "Him" or directly willed. Therefore, unless He does will this war, why hasn't He discreetly intervened to stop it? He could have given Putin a heart attack or a change of heart, couldn't He? But (for His own inscrutable reasons) He chooses not to.

And so, inevitably, the intimately disturbing questions of theodicy fold into the broader inquiry of political theology. What view of divine power operates in our theologies? How has that view of power been shaped by political views of sovereignty—absolute and relative? Conversely: How does a particular theology of divine sovereignty shape secular power? How does it shape broadly held views of political sovereignty? To be specific: We cannot in our theological thinking dislodge the question of Putin's abuse of power from that of the conceptualization of divine power. Whether or not he is consciously emulating an image of God is not decisive for political theology. It attends primarily to how political power is deployed. How is political force enacting—in modernity largely unconsciously, habitually, expediently—formative theological presumptions of power? Power may be more autocratic or more democratic in its exercise of state sovereignty. Are alternative concepts of God in play in that difference—a more authoritarian or a more egalitarian divinity?

That choice is unambiguous for Carl Schmitt, whose name is forever branded on political theology. Only in the exercise of a unilateral sovereignty is divine power legible as such. In this frame "God" means little more than absolute rule. And Schmitt reads sovereignty, crucially, as the supreme exception to all other kinds of order, power, or influence. Sovereignty therefore signifies the exercise not merely of the rule of law, but of the *exception to* the law. Hence the now over-familiar proposition of Schmittian political theology: "Sovereign is he who rules in the exception."[2] The sovereign has the power to break the law and knows when to do it, which is to say, when to transcend the law. Therefore, the sovereign is the one who has the right to impose the state of exception (*Ausnahmezustand*), otherwise known as the state of emergency (*Notstand*). Writing in the interbellum context of Weimar Germany, Schmitt found the new democratic polity weak and chaotic, its fragmenting individualism undermining the responsibility of leadership. The alternative: the sovereign exception. That logic was enacted in Hindenburg's 1933 declaration of the state of emergency that his Chancellor Hitler swiftly rendered permanent.[3]

With the identification of sovereignty as the power of the exception, as a singularity that interrupts the chaos of democracy, political theology in its Schmittian formulation lends a modern blessing to unilateral power: not only to fascism as such, but to a broad historical variety of authoritarianisms, of autocracy, imperialism, colonialism, totalitarianism. The logic of power that Schmitt reveals and reinforces reads in each case as a *theo-logic*: The logic by which the power secularized as sovereign exceptionalism is none other than the power of divine sovereignty—the power of the ultimate exception. This exceptionalist status, metaphysical or supernatural, no doubt characterizes the deity presumed still by a majority of Christians, indeed of Abrahamic believers, whatever their politics: the

God who is the omnipotent creator and ruler of the universe. From this point of view, the rulers of the earth, of its nations or its empires, may be read as relatively responsible or as dangerously arrogant in how they reflect that power in the name of the public good. But it is a version of that sovereign all-power that they are mirroring. So then what about the loving, responsive face of God?

It is not the case that with this broad monotheistic presumption God's love—indeed, for Christians the proposition "God is love"—is ever denied. Rather, it tends in practice to be presumed, privatized, and lent as a friendly supplement to the worship of the omnipotence. In that practice one learns to love—at least when it comes to the public sphere—those who are on the "friend" side of one's presumed friend/foe binary. As Schmitt made all too clear: "The specific political distinction to which political actions and motives can be reduced is that between friend and enemy."[4] That enmity keeps relations sharply differentiated between those who count as genuine subjects and those who are framed as the others, objects to the subjects. A sovereign subject can be said—the English verb form is revealing—legitimately to *subject* the other. In effect, to objectify and dominate, to subdue and control.

As long as the nature of divine power goes unquestioned, why would secular autocrats not continue to wrap themselves, however implicitly, in that godly glory? Why wouldn't they draw upon that legitimation to imply that, if they rule with exceptional power, it is because they operate in the image of God? That implication may be largely secularized, operating as subliminal prototype—as likely the case with Hitler, and more so, with Stalin. But in the recent and disturbing wave of autocratic movements around the world, the political theology is not hidden.[5] (Not even in its recent Indian fundamentalist, Hindutva, version.) The example of Putin's erstwhile friend Trump is a case in point. He makes no pretense of a serious religious practice, let alone of a sexual morality befitting his conservative white Christian label. But he has successfully bolstered the fundamentalist agenda, especially around LGBTQIA and women's reproductive rights. The white Christian right, which constitutes about a third of the US population, got and stays on board, 1.6.21 hearings and all—Trump no matter what.[6] A genuine human subject is assumed to be a Christian one, with the right to *subject* others to their morality. And failing that, to treat them as foes.

In the case of Putin, a more disciplined and secular persona dominates. But nonetheless a certain theological understanding remains indispensably in play. Before preparing for the present conversation, I had not realized the force and indeed the distinctiveness of his political theology. I assumed he was making politically expedient gestures toward Russian orthodoxy, thus reinforcing the theocratic support of Patriarch Kirill. Certainly the power of the symbol of *russkii mir* (Russian world) draws upon the history of Russian Orthodoxy, with its church conducting a golden glow, like that of its gilded icons, into imperial politics.[7] Yet it turns out that Putin has been cannily working a political theology of sovereign might all along. And with the invasion of Ukraine, he has exercised its prerogative to establish the state of emergency indefinitely. I learned of the influence on him of one Ivan Ilyin (1883–1954). I learned of this idiosyncratic Russian philosopher in exile only upon reading (like many, since the invasion) historian Timothy Snyder.[8] It turns out that the theology in play is odd and intriguing in its own right, indeed in a sharply nontraditional way. This pertains to Ilyin's account of the relation of power to love. What is first of all startling in his notion of God is that it is not at all the classical and orthodox—or Orthodox—God of changeless perfection and all-controlling power. This is not the God of a straightforward (or straightforwardly Schmittian) political theology. Rather this is a *fallen* God. Before any Edenic episode, God has fallen in the very act of creation—fallen into fragmentation. This divinity has been compromised by the diversity, multiplicity, and changingness of the world.

Ilyin finished a dissertation on God's worldly failure just before the Russian Revolution of 1917, and soon thereafter went into exile. *God's* imperfection long precedes that of Adam and Eve. It follows, Ilyin writes, that

> modern society, with its pluralism and its civil society, deepened the flaws of the world and kept God in his exile. God's one hope was that a righteous nation would follow a Leader into political totality, and thereby begin a repair of the world that might in turn redeem the divine. Because the unifying principle of the Word was the only good in the universe, any means that might bring about its return were justified.[9]

Ilyin came therefore—affirmingly, as Snyder demonstrates—"to imagine a Russian Christian fascism." But its autocratic power would be understood as the life force of the "spiritual organism" of Russia—the only unified and unifying nation of the Earth. In its organic unity Russia would ultimately overcome the otherness of difference itself, of all the divergent, fragmenting others. Only through this unifying force could the good in the universe, indeed the goodness and unity of God Himself, be restored. This is no casual political theology that Ilyin deploys in his divergence from standard authoritarian or democratic philosophies. Ilyin's political logic, according to Snyder, helped Putin transform the failure of his first period in office, the inability to introduce the rule of law, into the promise for a second period in office, the confirmation of Russian virtue. If Russia could not become a rule-of-law state, it would seek to destroy neighbors that had succeeded in doing so or that aspired to do so. Echoing one of the most notorious proclamations of the Nazi legal thinker Carl Schmitt, Ilyin wrote that politics "is the art of identifying and neutralizing the enemy."[10]

Whether he actually read his contemporary Schmitt remains uncertain. Indeed, David Lewis finds it unlikely. After Ilyin, there has also been much direct Schmittian influence in post-Soviet Russia.[11] But Schmitt and Ilyin share the view that democratic elections institutionalized the divisive evil of individuality. "The principle of democracy," Ilyin wrote, "was the irresponsible human atom." Counting votes meant merely to succumb to "the mechanical and arithmetical understanding of politics."[12]

Of course, we might largely—even democratically—agree that democracy risks institutionalizing the atomization characteristic of a problematic individualism. And indeed there is much to criticize along these lines in the electoral process, even beyond bringing Trump into power. And, of course, his power was hardly dedicated to the protection of any difference but its own. In state after state, his campaign went about doing its best to undermine the electoral process and miscount the votes. And not without Putin's purveyance of savvy Russian technopolitical assistance.[13]

What then of Ivan Ilyin's influence on Putin? In an article in *Moskovskiye Novosti* on February 27, 2012, Putin cites and expands upon Ilyin's vision: With him he imagines that "Russia as a spiritual organism served not only all the Orthodox nations and not only all of the nations of the Eurasian landmass, but all the nations of the world."[14] According to Snyder, "Putin predicted that Eurasia would overcome the European Union and bring its members 'into a larger entity that would extend 'from Lisbon to Vladivostok.'" So it is evident that the political theology at play in this version of spiritual organicism—that of an organism whose others become subject to one unifying same—has dominated Putin's relation to Ukraine from the start. "For the first two decades after the dissolution of the Soviet Union, Russian-Ukrainian relations were defined by both sides according to international law," writes Snyder, "with Russian lawyers always insistent on very traditional concepts such as sovereignty and territorial integrity." When, however, "Putin returned to power in 2012, legalism gave way to colonialism." Since then, Russian policy toward Ukraine has been remade on the basis of Ilyin's principles. Putin's vision of a Eurasian Union thus presumes that Ukraine would join. "Putin justified the effort to draw Ukraine into Eurasia by Ilyin's 'organic model' that made of Russia and Ukraine 'one people.'"[15]

One may find a bit ironic, given this dream of homogenization, that when Ukrainians in late 2013 began to build a European future for their country, Putin warned of a "homodictatorship." Of course, this is a very different "homo": He was deploying the sovereign homophobia ever useful to *actual* dictators. With strong support from Patriarch Kirill, he is able to blame both the EU and Ukraine for Russian homosexuality.[16] So same-sex love—deployed as the supreme example of the "unnatural"—is polemically fused with the unnatural, inorganic independence of Ukraine. I bring this up also because of the importance of homophobic cues for the US Christian right wing. And I suspect no American can forget the 2009 photos of Putin riding not bareback but bare from the waist up—a naked display of "organic" heteronormativity![17]

The Russian subject is invited to consolidate itself under this manly force, in relation to which not just LGBTQIA people but even the straightest of women can only be *other*. Such masculinist suppression of diversity remains key to the unified subject who subjects its others as objects. And it also sustains the patriarchal political theology in play—and with it the particularity of Russian organic unity. Let me clear that I do not mean to cast aspersions on the formal "Patriarchate" of Eastern Orthodoxy, hardly more masculinist historically than the other Abrahamisms. The organicism of homophobic homogeneity, as on the white US religiopolitical right, here conjures a unitive political power. As ethnicity and sexuality are forced to fuse, detestation of queer difference fortifies *theological* enmity against Ukrainian difference. (Religious authority has ever been tempted to scapegoat sexual difference for the sake of unity.) For scholar of religions and cultures Richard Foltz, the Patriarch became "explicit in framing the Ukraine invasion as a form of holy resistance against an alleged LGBTQ+ threat emanating from the West." As the Patriarch put it, Ukrainians, by supporting gay parades, forcibly impose "a sin condemned by divine law."[18] For the Patriarch, the war for Ukraine is "a struggle that has not a physical, but a metaphysical significance."[19]

The "Russian world"—*russkii mir* [20]—of straight oneness may tempt its critics to an *anti*-organic discourse. Indeed, much progressive and postmodern thought is already critical of any discourse of "the organic," as of the "natural," because of its repressive uses. But note that the brotherly Russian organicism of unity is unrelated to the material diversity that constitutes the actual organic life of nature. Of course, much Protestantized Western Christianity also carries its own currents of anti-naturalism. We will touch upon the *matter* of theological cosmology shortly.

First, however, let us return to the fragile question of love in relation to the homogenizing theopolitics of *russkii mir*, indeed of any empire. It is hard within any even nominally Christian context fully to silence the gospel priority of love of the neighbor. How does any version of Russian Christianity exclude from its reach, for instance, the neighboring people of Ukraine? As Jesus inconveniently made clear, even, or especially, the relation to the most difficult neighbor, the enemy, demands love. This is clear to many practitioners of Russian Orthodoxy, of course, as so many have with courage publicly testified.[21] And as to the question of enemy-love, one must always repeat: This does not mean to *like* or to *agree* with your enemies. The imperative means first of all to respect their co-humanity. And so it calls for some avowal of the likeness and interrelation between you and other members of the species. The loving subject does not *subject* the difficult other, but invites its otherness into relationship: and more precisely, into mindfulness of the relation already in play. Are we not already somehow part of each other's world, and so part of each other? So to love the other as the self: We love the other not as the same as ourselves, but as interdependent with ourselves and creatures of the same creation, even of the same creator. We may have real—destructive, even malignant—enemies, as I read the gospel imperative, but the friend-enemy distinction is never *absolute*. To love that enemy is to remain open to the *possibility* of reconciliation, forgiveness, even friendship. However improbable. In other words, the gospel gets routinely sabotaged by political theologies of friend versus enemy.

Ilyin did not ignore the political challenge of Christian love. He believed his own politics solved its contradiction by translating love into homogenization and interrelation into unifying totality. "It did not matter whether one individual tries to love another individual. The individual only loved if he was totally subsumed in the community."[22] Community now reduces to unity. In this totalization, to be immersed in love is to struggle "against the enemies of the divine order on earth." So on that basis Christians may, indeed at times must, apply collective violence in the name of love. But more: Anyone who failed to accept this reasoning was himself an agent of Satan. As Ilyin put it: "He who opposes the chivalrous struggle against the devil is himself the devil."[23] Hence for Putin the nobility, indeed the sanctity, of the struggle against the EU and NATO remains unquestionable. His demonization now, with hyperfocus, of Ukrainian democracy and of all who support it follows logically from the demonization of those who do not share his demonizations. Then we cannot avoid recognizing in his meta-demonization its own form of the demonic—as that which operates precisely by demonizing the other.

Speaking theopolitically, a love that avows its interdependence with its others does not deny the reality of evil and therefore of enmity. At the same time it does not admit of absolute good or pure evil as the basis for any responsible ("good") political struggle. Interrelationship keeps morality messy at every level. The embrace of interdependence performs the alternative at once to ontological independence and to any mere dependence. It offers, therefore, the alternative both to a simply fragmented plurality of subjects and to the assertion of totality over dependent subjects. We cannot repeat often enough: The delusion of independent subjects over against their separate others is not solved philosophically or politically by the opposite delusion, that of unity. The real difficulties of political difference and plural sovereignties do not manifest in separate units, let alone cash into unifying totalities.

Ukrainians, in other words, face the terror of an applied Russian metaphysics of totality. And precisely because that One is a delusion, it depends on the backup of a political theology of the exception—qua exceptionalist superpower. Its vision of Russia as spiritual organism does not actually live *organically*—if that means to grow with the internal integrity and interdependent difference resembling an actual organism. So the (Ukrainian) other must then be subjected to the absolute sameness of *russkii mir*. Must in other words cease to be *other:* not to become "friend" as full and interdependent subject but to get "totally subsumed."

It remains significant that in the operative political theology something different from omnipotent perfection and its secularization is at work. The Putin/Ilyin alternative may have traction, we were suspecting, because the political theology of mere top-down divine sovereignty has so routinely proven unconvincing throughout history. Personally and politically, that standard theodicy remains—for thinking people of any or no religion throughout modernity—quite recognizably inadequate. I wonder (and this really is a question) whether the sense that God *depends* on Russia for redemption has added a fresh and attractive force to Putin's imperialism. Of course, Ilyin's claim that God made a youthful blunder in His creation of the world sounds too heretical for Putin to be as forthright about it as Ilyin. But it seems that this theology is working for Putin indirectly and powerfully. And if so, might it be because we can read here some real insight flavoring what appears, especially in its nationalist deployment, as a ludicrous distortion?

The distortion is delivered by the Manichean notion that the finite world is one great fallenness, a terribly flawed, indeed for Ilyin an ugly, creation.[24] And that is why he argues that only Russian unification can redeem its creator. The twistedness of such a logic appears not just in the ploy of passing judgment on God and then—by way of one's preferred superpower—redeeming Him. The absurdity is managed by a surprising avowal of the arbitrary: "Fascism is a redemptive excess of patriotic arbitrariness."[25] The rendering patriotic of the Russian concept of the "arbitrary"—*proizvol*—is key. At the same time cosmological fallenness underlies the whole metaphysics, producing a worldview uninterested in the beauty and creativity of the creation, or in the inherent worth of the material universe. It mistakes the (very real) limitations of the world for the world itself. And so it answers the fallenness with its totalizing notion of "organic" oneness, lacking in any appreciation for the actual evolution, achievement, complexity, and splendor of the living planet—indeed of the creation and its unfathomable variety of creatures.

What real insight might lurk in Ilyin's theology, granting it its hook of persuasive power? Possibly the following: Perhaps there is indeed an elemental interconnection of God and world. This would not require a notion of God as inherently fallen, messed up, a lousy creator needing redemption by creatures. It could, however, mean that God is indeed interdependent with the world, that the creator is thus dependent on creatures for the material actualization of creativity. And perhaps even of love. If such is the case, then what we dub the creation might signify a living process of divine calling, creaturely response, and divine reception of the response. What we call God would then indeed be enriched by the unfolding of the creation. God would not "need" this world in order to *be*—even to be in an unimaginably full sense. But if God's creativity is not static, is not some once-for-all self-enclosed power-perfection, s/he/it/they might need the creatures, with their unpredetermined or even free responses, for the realization of that creative potential. That indeterminacy approximates the Russian *proizvol*. And creativity would then be enriched by—not dependent on but interdependent with—each becoming, creative or caring gesture of every creature.

So there: I have introduced you to process theology. Based on the "philosophy of organism" of Alfred North Whitehead and his century-old *Process and Reality*, it has been deeply supportive of my own theological intuitions.[26] Its universe takes place as an open and live process of becoming. Every creature, down to each quantum, *becomes* moment by moment; each comes to be, at each moment, in feeling, "prehending," taking in all that makes up its universe. Each creature counts as an organism. And each integrates all of those relations with a certain indeterminacy: a freedom, not to be independent of any of its relations, but to interpret them. However slightly or dramatically. For better or for worse. And God? God is there in each one as the "lure to becoming"—offering a possibility at that moment for some fresh integration. A possibility that the creature actualizes, if at all, in its own largely unconscious terms.

Each creature, even the officially inorganic, can therefore be called an organic, spatiotemporal integration of differences. So no two creatures in the universe are ever exactly the same. An organism lives by integrating innumerable creatures within itself from its unique perspective, and so exists only in a becoming interdependence with the creation beyond itself. No fundamental homogeneity of any organism, let alone of any system or world, is possible. Not for a moment. And evolution is about the development not of more *independent,* separate creatures; and also not of more passively *dependent* ones, but of ever more complex, sensitive, and intense *inter*dependencies, whole assemblages, networks, spacetime worlds of relations. All prehended materially, however unconsciously, vaguely—in each individually becoming creature.

So then God is also in a certain way interdependent. Such divinity is not God in abstraction or in separation from you, from each of you, from your experience, at this moment. For if God is in any meaningful sense alive, s/he/it/they in some unfathomable way experience every experience in the universe. That does *not* mean God's existence depends on any singly or in combination. But God's eternity in this vision does not—existentially—come down to a static perfection. Nor to a distant or changeless absolute directly or indirectly in control of everything. This is not God who controls, who intervenes in the process, or predetermines the outcomes. This one signifies the impetus to novelty, to *difference*, and so to greater intensity of experience. All our experiences get somehow integrated into this deity's life—not in a smooth and simple oneness but in an infinitely complex harmony. After all, even the traditional theologies of the Trinity disrupt, often uncomfortably, any notion of homogenous unity. Yet this process vision does not imply that God is imperfect. Perfection no longer means static changelessness. Divine perfection, or fullness, finds realization moment by moment. For God is in process, in relation, in becoming. Not in control but in love.

And so back to the opening question of theodicy: On the basis of such theocosmology, it gets answered in a fresh way. God is not causing everything that happens to happen. Not because God *chooses* not to intervene but because God is not that kind of being. *God Can't* (the title of a highly accessible work of process theology).[27] And only so has this God called forth a universe of creatures interdependent with each other and with her/him/it/them. God wills the good, the beautiful, but God's will does not *trump* the indeterminacy, the freedom, of the creation. Much happens against the will of God.

In other words God cannot be blamed for the tragedies. The wars. All the traumas of our history. Of Ukrainian history. We are all singly and collectively responsible for our decisions. For whether we tune to that divine call. For whether we feel it, actualize it in our own becomings. That is the sense in which God depends on our choices for the well-being, the shalom, of our world. Our choices affect—in some way, some art we can only imagine—the divine experience. Which then with imperceptible cosmic nuance flows back to affect our own. Hence such metaphors as grace, judgment, wrath, love . . .

From this process-relational point of view the Ilyin/Putin political theology captures enough of a fresh truth—enough to be *truly* dangerous in its distortion. It recognizes rightly a certain dependence of God on the creature for the realization of divine possibility. But from a process point of view (let alone a biblical one) it is misleading to suggest that the creation is or was itself the fall. Or that God needs therapeutic rehab; or that one species on one planet, indeed one white and northern portion of that species, is responsible for God's redemption from chaos. And from the view of a process interdependence, the even uglier distortion would be this: that such a return to perfection would take the form of a homogenous unity, an exceptional imperial order imposing oneness. That any unitary power over the world could become the redemption not just of the world but of God. Such exceptionalism eradicates the challenges of creative difference, the gifts of multiplicity. And so its russkii-mirish unity becomes a great mockery of love.

For process theology, any human exceptionalism dissolves into creaturely intersectionalism: No singularity takes place in abstraction from the endlessly interrelated differences of its world. Rather than seeking unity at the expense of difference, interconnection enhances diversity. But not only creaturely exceptionalism is deconstructed. Whitehead makes this theological claim, still shocking to some: "God is not to be treated as an exception to all metaphysical principles, invoked to save their collapse. He is their chief exemplification."[28] This means, as suggested above, that God supremely exemplifies the principles of relationality in becoming. God therefore enjoys and suffers life with us. This theologism, a real theologem, resonates with a certain Christology. Consider the thousand-year-old difference between the notion of Christ as the divinely foreordained *exception* to the human condition, his crucifixion paying off our debt of original sin, and of Christ as the loving *exemplar* of the human, suffering with us on the cross: This was the great medieval contrast between Anselm and Abelard.

So you see how process theology lends itself to a political theology of democracy, in which sovereignty cannot be forged or sustained as the exception. Rather, it would be exercised with persuasive rather than coercive power, in its networks within networks of undisguised interdependence.

Emergencies must be met within the parameters that exemplify—hopefully with adequate foresight and therefore needed flexibility—that interdependence. We have, however, to do, in the (in this case Russian) exceptionalism of empire, with a political theology of a oneness, in which a single power subjects its others to unifying rule. Of course, autocracy rather than democracy enables such unity. The evil West is seen as above all guilty of diversity, with all of its chaotic atomization. And at the same time, somewhat paradoxically—as David Lewis stresses in *Russia's New Authoritarianism*—the West appears as guilty of seeking to unify the world through global capitalism. He demonstrates the significant influence of Schmitt's notions of sovereignty under Putin.[29]

Indeed, the West is guilty of much such evil (which as an American, even in this conversation with Ukrainians, I must underscore). The US in particular surely does strive to unify the world through the force of global neoliberal capitalism, in which imposed and unjust dependencies are camouflaged by the myth of individual independence. It thus *commodifies* difference rather than simply repressing it. And yes, in the midst of this globalization, and in the name of democracy, it atomizes the world into economic units. That commodification is eradicating difference, as in the diversity of species, as we speak, driving climate change, and posing unprecedented ecosocial threats to the future, especially to the differences represented as nonwhite and nonelite. As this Western-based global capitalism is not directly imperial, it is meaningfully called neo-imperialism. So there seems to be some strange mirror play happening between the regnant economic neo-imperialism and the revival of Russian imperialism, also often called neo-imperialism.

The *russkii mir* of good Russia against evil West may rightly expose the danger of Western individualism, and denounce the false atomization of the human and of the world into independent units. But it seems thereby to have turned a real problem into an apocalyptic pretext for Russian intervention. Putin articulated this exceptionalism early in the Second Chechen War: "Russia is really standing at the forefront of the war against international terrorism. And Europe ought to fall on its knees and express its great thankfulness that we, unfortunately, are fighting it alone."[30] Thus there is significant discussion of the role of Russia as the *katechon*, "the restrainer," which redeems the world by holding back global terrorism. That Pauline symbol plays a profound role in this century's Russian conservatism.

An influential manifesto of Russian conservatism prepared by Mikhail Remizov's Institute of National Strategy in 2014 talks of "the traditional conception among Russian conservatives of the role of Russia as *Katekhon*—the 'Restrainer' [*uderzhivaiuschii*], preventing on the one hand, global anarchy, and on the other global monopoly and hegemony, both of which . . . risk apocalyptic consequences."[31]

As Lewis demonstrates, "This sense of Russia acting as an isolated, misunderstood bulwark—the *katechon*—against chaos and barbarism became a regular trope in official [Russian] foreign policy discourse."[32] Putin's foreign policy, in its opposition to anarchic liberalism and hegemonic "unipolarity," would indeed shift from the falsely independent subjects of much Western democracy. Yet it does not seek to restore *interdependence* but rather to effect a brotherhood of totality. Its *katechon* seeks the subjection of difference to an imposed Eurasian unity. And so to a neo-imperial political theology of holy Russia.

The political theology of the sovereign One suppresses rather than releases the creative interplay of subjects and their others—the interconnectivity of others *as* subjects with each other. Politically, Ukrainians are experiencing the violence of that suppression in the form of a global tragedy suffered at home, a tragedy that as I write also threatens worldwide consequences. The levels of sacrifice endured across Ukraine may indeed seem through a Christian lens to cast an immense shadow of the cross. Not—to return to the discourse of theodicy—because God wants or is causing (you) Ukrainians to suffer for the sake of some ultimate good. Surely, if the Christian metaphor of God refers to anything real, it is a God who wants you to flourish. To find love and joy in your present lives. And that means for you as Ukrainian subjects, to be able to embrace your differential interdependence with each other and with all the world. It means also to feel yourselves as always already held within the One in whom all creatures live, breathe, and have our being. And as One, that divine power cannot be in contradiction with divine love. Without a correlation, a relation, of noncontradiction between divine attributes, that One has no meaning.

Love does not coerce. So the correlate power is the power of love. Such power can only be persuasive, not coercive.[33] That love cannot signify a totality that subjects us so much as a difference that connects us. And when we call it One, we remember that is not simple unity but rather complex Trinity. The divine unity is inherently multiple: plurisingular. The Trinity offers the great parable of interdependence, and precisely therefore not of totality—of relational difference, not of homogenous unity. Love is empty without difference. It feels its relation to the other as internal—it senses its interdependence with the other.

When, however, difference dissociates from its entanglement with the other, it readily turns to enmity. Then the love verges on the impossible. So it is not for me to say that love of the enemy remains existentially or politically meaningful for Ukrainians now. Of course, you all remember the humanity of particular and of countless Russians. (Even I—I think of a Russian colleague, a writer in Moscow. He was becoming a long-distance friend. He may have attended too many protests against the war; his email address no longer functions; I can learn nothing; I ache for him.) From my comfortable vantage point I cannot preach love of the enemy as an imperative. I just want to keep it in hearing. Nor can I push in such a situation for any Quaker or Gandhian or MLK practices of nonviolence. They were resisting different forms of aggression, in altogether different contexts. I can only presume that the difficult notion of love calls Ukrainian Christians to help in discerning what forms of negotiation and compromise are needed; what outcome is nonnegotiable; what distinguishes justice from vengeance; what might support some new version of interdependence between the two nations; and what healing at the level of individual, church, community, and nation you would foster.

And we retain a longer-term vision—not of a political theology of unitary brotherhood, that of Russia or of any of authoritarianism, East or West. Nor of the global capitalist unity for the benefit of our elites and at the expense of the Earth's very habitability. The democratic alternative to autocratic oneness might be, perhaps can yet be, not universal neoliberalism but what Arturo Escobar calls "pluriversal politics." As he frames this rigorously pluralist strategy for the Left, struggles for autonomy, territory, and communality "require an explicit ontological framing that advances the principles of interdependence and relationality."[34] This framework would not come down to a single sanctified political form. And it would in diverse locally vibrant ways combine elements of democracy, socialism, and environmentalism. Its religious inspiration would manifest not with the autocracy of some quietly secularized theocracy—but in the spirit that pulls democracy toward an egalitarianism of entangled differences. It would find organic cohesion not in any imperially universalized unity but in the pluriverse of the living planet.

Read theologically, a pluriversal politics might actually tune to the calling of the *basileia tou theou*. A kingdom not of this world *as it is*, nor a realm postponed unto a fantasy hypertech future, or a supernatural New Jerusalem. Its new earth and heaven would emerge very much in and of this world, with its soil, its atmosphere, its cities, in a renewed creation: this world that what we may perhaps still call "God"—released from our despairing theodicies and archaic theocracies—is still inviting us all to become. Not making it for us. That isn't the way love-power works, is it? It cannot. But with and in and through us. All together.

In the meantime your suffering still verges on the unbearable. Yet you chose to reach across the earth for this conversation. You are enacting your own creative embrace of transnational, transcultural potentiality: your own pluriversal theology. In and through this tragedy you embody a political theology—mindfully, not manipulatively, theological—that all of us earthlings need.

Along with the camellias. In the words of the Ukrainian poet Lyudmyla Khersonska:

> I planted a camellia in the yard.
> I wanted to be a lady, not a war-ravaged rag,
> To cast down my lashes, let fall a light glove,
> Put on red beads, patent-leather boots,
> I listen: there are explosions,
> Does someone stomp the earth . . .[35]

4 / Apocalypse After All?

CLIMATE, POLITICS, AND FAITH
IN THE POSSIBLE

The hyper-crises of the world pulse rhythmically now between our daily background and our elective foreground: threats to democracy, wars with global menace, a pandemic, and sharing the headlines all too rarely, while quietly engulfing all the other threats, the steady alteration of the planetary climate. On the one hand, we tell ourselves, yes, the crisis is serious, but "not the end of the world."[1] Such a reassuring banality, hovering between denialism and realism. Yet we also feel the opposite tug, as in an editorial in the *New York Times*: "Across the ironized hellscape of the internet, we began 'tweeting through the apocalypse.'" Amanda Hess thus sums up the scene with Dantean drama:

> Often the features of our dystopia are itemized, as if we are briskly touring the concentric circles of hell—rising inequality, declining democracy, unending pandemic, the financial system optimistically described as "late" capitalism—until we have reached the inferno's toasty center, which is the destruction of the Earth through man-made global warming.[2]

Tweeting through the apocalypse: that captures a broad cultural nihilism That nihilism also takes quieter forms—such as the rarely vocalized "it is too late." Does that creeping resignation now belong to your own inner voices, or do you keep it at bay?

Is the end of the world *nihilism* the only alternative to the spectrum of *denialism*? How about a third way, the uncertain path of a responsible *realism*? Let me suggest that we will not find that way by repressing the signifier of "the apocalypse." Apocalypse may be the most forceful metaphor in our vocabulary for expressing collective catastrophe, global doom, the Worst. But in neither its original context nor its ancient etymology does apocalypse signify The End.

The Greek word means literally "unveiling," used/primarily of the bride's removal of her veil on the nuptial night: a moment in the ancient world of supreme eros. And in its biblical deployment *apocalypsis* does not mean final closure but climactic dis/closure. Revelation to revel in. While John's Apocalypse certainly discloses global scales of destruction, nonetheless, its "battle of Armageddon" does not entail ultimate destruction or serve as a synonym of Apocalypse. The book, really the letter (so timely in its time) of Revelation, ends in great festivity, at, as it happens, a wedding—indeed a rather queer one, between a city and a lamb. In its context *apokalypsis* comes charged with energies of material incarnation, resurrection, new creation.

My point will not be, however, to offer assurances that human history will work itself out, whatever. On this I agree with Pope Francis: "Doomsday predictions can no longer be met with irony or disdain."[3] Neither is the honest alternative (as his eco-encyclical makes clear) to pronounce some end of our world. I find, rather, that struggling a bit with the prolific metaphor of apocalypse strengthens neither nihilism nor denialism, neither give-it-up pessimism nor happy-ending optimism, but—paradoxically—a certain faith in possibility. Not faith that better possibilities *will* be realized. But that they *might*. As Emily Dickinson hints: "I dwell in possibility, a fairer house than prose / More numerous of windows, superior for doors."

So why then dwell in, or on, the apocalypse? A creepier house than prose. Perhaps for this reason: We just are not going to stop hearing frequent public invocations of that metaphor—larded with literalism, often responsibly, often not. For that reason I wrote my twenty-first-century *Facing Apocalypse*—even though I had assumed that my twentieth-century *Apocalypse Now and Then* would surely be my one such project.[4] But global warming now guarantees apocalyptic symbolism recurrent headline status. Sometimes the precipitating catastrophe is barely perceptible. Just before I began that second project, the headlines of the so-called "Insect Armageddon" in Europe, and then of the "Insect Apocalypse" in both Americas, were buzzing in my brain.[5] Due to climate change and agribusiness chemicals, the insect population had plunged precipitously in the three continents studied. Since insects constitute the basis for the whole food chain, not to mention crop pollination. . . . The journalistic point was not the histrionics of too late—but disclosure of a catastrophic collective process, so that we might *face* it. Similarly the *Los Angeles Times* has featured headlines such as "A Climate Apocalypse Now: Climate Change Is Only Worsening the

Record-Breaking Wildfires, Heat and Air Pollution in CA and the West."[6] That was *before* the dramatic worsening of the fires over the following three years, also in Canada and western Europe. Again—the point is not: *game over* but *wake up*. The situation persistently exceeds the natural cycle of wildfires.

Catastrophe is kicking in for the long term. It does not add up (she repeats) to the end of the habitable world. But it *might*: without far greater international response to climate change. Which demands of course adequate US response. In the meantime the language of apocalypse can help garner attention. But at the same time it keeps automatically signaling to a broad public, religious and secular: Doomsday is near. So then why bother with the struggle to lower greenhouse emissions for the sake of a long term we no longer believe in? Better just bring down the cost of gas and get on with our lives now. So even when the term "apocalypse" is used with responsible intent, it promulgates irresponsible effects. It feeds the it's too late/it's okay cycle. So as apocalyptic metaphors spread, they multiply nihilist, denialist, and also realist rhetorics.[7]

For those of us who attend to religion and to its secularizations, whether we work within or without its institutions, it may now prove important to do what we can to fine-tune the public understanding of the apocalypse as such. To keep the discourse honest, we must first free the ancient metaphor from literal predictions and doomsday misreadings. That enables us also to recognize certain ancient resonances with present history. These resonances have an ironic edge: for they carry no straightforward present connection with two-thousand-year-old prophecies. Prophecy is not prediction. It is not about foretelling future facts. The biblical prophets discerned in their contexts deep patterns of civilization, historical patterns so powerful that they could not be overcome without immense and prolonged struggle—into a future for which the prophets could offer not descriptions but vivid poetry.

Faithfulness to the Bible means reading bi-contextually: in its context and in our own. In other words it reads the Book of Revelation with open eyes: *not* the eyes of biblical literalism, which conceals the ancient context. Biblical scholarship offers the corrective of recontextualizing the text in its ancient historical scene. But theologically speaking, the symbol of the apocalypse demands more: It requires reflection, critical and perhaps constructive, on the ancient symbolism in its *contemporary* relevance. Theology requires a practice of attending to the life of archaic symbols in our ever-shifting present contexts. To encourage such attention at once in method and in content I have sought out the approach of an *apocalyptic mindfulness*.

Denial or Nihil

Speaking of shifting current contexts... In February 2022 two apocalyptic tropes that I had done little with in the recent book suddenly galloped across the horizon: the first two members of the four-horse quartet of Revelation 6. The white and red ones. *Facing Apocalypse* had meditated on the second two: on the black horse of economic injustice, anachronistically evocative of global capitalism; and on the green horse of plague and attacks from wild animals—resonant, it turned out, with the timely crisis of the corona virus as well as of ecological imbalance. (*Resonant,* not predictive.)

Now, however, it is the white horse that has exploded into view, indeed onto our television or computer screens: the one whose crowned rider, wrote John of Patmos, "came out conquering and to conquer." And next to him gallops the red one, whose rider wields "a great sword, who takes peace from the earth." Conquest and war. How current. But no. Revelation did not *predict* Putin's invasion of Ukraine or Netanyahu's of Gaza—no more than the countless invasions since John wrote down his visions. Before Russia's military attack, the Ukrainian foreign minister had reasonably urged his people to ignore "apocalyptic predictions." But soon after the invasion international news sources were asking the question of the Ukraine as "a possible step towards the Apocalypse"—by which is meant nuclear exchange. In fact one 2019 article notes that Putin has spoken more about the nuclear apocalypse over the past fifteen years than any other national leader.[8]

Nonetheless, the gallop of the white and red horses does not portend any predetermined outcome. But as in their own context of the Roman Empire, the metaphors may be read in this one as unveiling catastrophic planetary patterns already advanced and threatening worse. With COVID still plaguing the world, there came conquest and war unprecedented in Europe since World War II; and these, along with nuclear threats, feed through Russian gas into the environmental issues of energy. And then come the hoofbeats from Israel and Palestine, that conflict soon reaching "unprecedented level of dehumanization"[9]—eerily unfolding on the terrain of the original Apocalypse, unleashing new-old global danger. Predictions aside, the rhythm of the hoofbeats has deep reverb.

The danger of nuclear destruction had been one motivation of my earlier *Apocalypse Now and Then,* subtitled a *Feminist Guide to the End of the World.*[10] And yes, with the irony of the *Now and Then,* I *did* mean to deconstruct the single-telos or end point, pessimistic or optimistic, of apocalyptic mythology. And its patriarchy. I wanted to interrupt the sense of history as a timeline with a determinate goal, whether through a linearized Christian eschatology, or its secularization in the form of modern Progress. Or then again, as in the case of right-wing US politics, of the two joined in expectation of an imminent end time strangely—or rapturously—married to an endless capitalist confidence.

In the United States, almost two centuries of Protestant dispensationalism live off of end-time predictions: always coming soon, then soon rescheduled. This US premillennialism had hooked into Hal Lindsey's *Late Great Planet Earth* fundamentalism that forged a Christian political right wing. This enabled the 1980 election of Ronald Reagan, who agreed with his friend Hal that the End would come through nuclear war (with the Soviet Union), and that it would come in their lifetime.[11] And they weren't young... and the president possesses the nuclear codes... so even though I am not a biblical scholar, I plunged into the Book of Revelation, with deep distaste for its determinist and its misogynist proclivities. I came to think that at least the nuclear version of apocalypse might be left in permanent safe storage. And I hoped for myself to leave the apocalypse—the metaphor and the text—in the twentieth century.

In the present century it was, as noted, the steady gallop of global warming that returned me to John's Apocalypse. Compared to nuclear exchange, what a quiet catastrophe climate change unfolds. But here's a grotesque fact: During World War II, the US dropped an atomic bomb over Hiroshima, Japan, wiping out 90 percent of the city. Last year, researchers say, the ocean heated up by an amount equal to the energy of five of those bombs detonating underwater "every second for 24 hours a day for the entire year."[12] *Every second.* Pause. Check the data yourself. And in the meantime the US religiopolitical Right uses the Book of Revelation to energize climate change denial. (If the Lord is coming soon, they say, why bother with environmental repair? And hey, even if global warming is real and means The End, then it is God's will...) In this way the supernatural endtime hope of the evangelical Right serves the super-*secular* optimism of neoliberal capitalism, in their shared ecological indifference. The otherworldly faith operates in cynical allegiance with the hyperworldly economic optimism that runs much of US politics—and the world.

On the other side of the political spectrum there is, as suggested earlier, a more recent enactment of apocalyptic determinism. It has quietly emerged on the Left, primarily in response to global warming. It is, unlike its opposite, scientifically informed. And it considers any connection to the Bible part of the problem. Less a position than a mood, this version of apocalypse feels we are too late to address climate change. And it thereby deenergizes its own ecological ethics.

So on the one hand, we have that *too late, why bother* nihilism. And on the other hand, the *we're saved praise the lord cum secular capitalist* denialism. Between the junk optimism of climate denialism and the paralyzing pessimism of climate nihilism, self-fulfilling prophecies of doom keep spiraling around our collective future.

Dreamreading the Apocalypse

Given such apocalyptic resonances, I returned to the Greek island of Patmos (in the Spirit, not the flesh, regrettably) and wrote *Facing Apocalypse*. Facing into this unveiling has remained eye-opening. There simply is no—simple—"end of the world" anywhere in the Bible. Many endings, yes. As there are in the world, which, for example, Brazilian anthropologists Déborah Danowsky and Eduardo Viveiros de Castro elegantly exhibit in *The Ends of the World*.[13] They are examining the multiple colonizations of Indigenous peoples in South America. And in the Book of Revelation, indeed in the Bible, there is no singular point of total and final termination. But it narrates several remembered and anticipated mass destructions, human and nonhuman. And because we won't in any foreseeable future escape such scales of destruction, actual and potential, more of us perhaps do need to spend some time with the metaphor, the metaforce, of the apocalypse.

In this climate-changing century, the threats to established democracies also persist and grow. On the US front Rita Nakashima Brock blogged this in early response to the January 6, 2021, insurrection: "As I watched news reports of the siege deep into the night, I had the unsettling thought that I was watching a national apocalypse unfold. Thoughts about apocalypse had been on my mind as the pandemic surged and George Floyd's murder captured global attention, igniting the largest social movement in US history."[14] Brock uses "apocalypse" with precision—as a crisis that discloses. Yet like most critical thinkers, Brock had generally resisted any use of apocalypse—in part because right-wing evangelicals use it to thwart challenges to their white male supremacism. Indeed, that edge of reactionary Christian apocalypse was key to the conspiracy cults like QAnon that helped fire up the January round of Trumpocalypse. (I thought *I* had made up that term—only to learn that *Trumpocalypse* was already the title of a 2018 book by McGuire and Anderson, two Trump supporters who coined it as praise!)[15]

As multiple human issues keep bursting into crisis—democracy, race, sexuality, Ukraine, Palestine—the eco-apocalypse gets (understandably) pushed into the background. Yet none of the issues can be separated from their material environment. Jacqueline Patterson, an African American civil rights leader, nails it from the race angle: "Economy, food, housing, transit—all of these are civil rights issues. And climate issues intersect with every single one."[16] Such *intersectionalism* unveils the extent of US white *exceptionalism*. Of course the complex and multiplying interlinkage of issues within issues can overwhelm. Hence, the importance of the scholarship that intertwines them, like Melanie Harris's *Ecowomanism*, Kathryn Yusoff's *A Billion Black Anthropocenes or None*, or Jeremy Williams's *Climate Change Is Racist*.[17] Or, attending to global poverty rather than US racism, the "integral ecology" of Pope Francis's 2015 encyclical. Apocalyptically speaking: The feeling of impossibility, with its shadow of nihilism, will remain tempting. At the same time, might these troubling intersections unveil—open up—the possibility of solidarities broad enough to make the needed difference? Not assurance, not guarantee, but improbable possibility? The *chance*?

Still you might ask: What does such revealing intersectionality have to do with the old Apocalypse? It did not foresee facts like neoliberal capitalism or its carbon emissions, crises of democracy, white supremacism, and so on and on. But if ancient prophets like John of Patmos read social patterns entrenched so deeply that they last way too long, they thereby shed light on how imperialism can turn into neo-imperialism, aristocracy into democratic class and race hierarchy. The book of Revelation narrates its visions of the patterns of civilization from the viewpoint of a barely imaginable alternative. Prophecy, we can teach, is a radical *dreamreading* of our civilization. Its transtemporal code, rendered in an oneiric poetics, conveys critical rage at the status quo—past and largely present. Its visionary attraction to a radically transformed future invites *our* dreamreading now.

Those patterns are read by John as the two beasts of sea and land, code for the global expanse and power of the Roman Empire; and third, as the so-called Whore of Babylon. She is code for Rome's version of global trade: hence the twenty-eight luxury commodities John lists as lost with her destruction—jewels, purple dye, wine, etc. . . . and lastly, human slaves (Rev 18). John calls merchants "the magnates of the earth." When in *Apocalypse Now and Then* I worked on this feminine image of Babylon, I was preoccupied with the sexism of John's symbolism. And certainly the misogyny of the image of a global prostitute must not be downplayed.[18] But in this millennium's round, I was more tuned to John's prophetic insight. That meant dreamreading his "whore of Babylon" as a systemic appetite so imperially greedy that it commodifies even its own flesh. How can one not fail to read his economic porn queen as the imperial ancestor of the lascivious desire globally cultivated now by neo-imperial capitalism? Of course—politics and economics have undergone great shifts in two thousand years, some promisingly anti-imperial, egalitarian, postcolonial. But might we agree that nonetheless a deeply persistent pattern of global power and transnational greed has brought us as a species to our present environmental edge?

On that *eschaton*, global warming is also dreamreadable in John's letter: The seventh seal opens after a dramatic pause. There is revealed: one third of the trees of the earth burning; one third of the life of the sea dying. Not far from present conditions? And amid the vortex of catastrophes, an eagle is grieving: *Ouai, ouai*! "Alas, alas to the inhabitants of the earth" (Rev 8). The inhabitants signify all the planet's living creatures. Not just human. In the face of mass extinction—such an ancient face—is the eagle already voicing what we now called eco*grief*? Soon the twenty-four elders sing darkly of the time for the destruction of those who destroy the earth (Rev 4:4): Not to be confused with a time for the destruction of the *earth*—however subliminally convenient to denialism or nihilism.

If this archaic tumult of symbols matters now, it is because something of its dreamy and nightmarish pattern keeps on materializing. I am not saying the text anticipated or is needed for climate science, or LGBTQI struggles, or work on democracy and racial justice. But perhaps more of us who are concerned with the public effects of religious symbols do need to meditate with the ancient apocalypse. So as to face its political theology, with the violence of its angelic hosts, its messianic anti-imperialism and its warning of a mounting spiral of planetary destruction. And so to take in also its imagination of that odd bride, the multinational, postcolonial urban utopia—the New Jerusalem.

Apocalyptic Mindfulness

In other words, I am hoping that an occasional exercise in dreamreading the apocalypse can help to surface potentials working unconsciously and collectively, not as timeless archetypes, not as fundamentalist stereotypes, but as ancient prototypes.[19] By keeping those metaforces conscious—prototypes both reactionary and revolutionary, destructive and constructive, sacralized and secularized—we begin to reconfigure their effects. With apocalyptic mindfulness. And perhaps this attentiveness will help us process our own ecological grief for what it is too late to save, and thereby free us from the cycles of nihilism and denialism. So that we might save what can yet be saved.

Isn't there a danger, however, that such dreamreading may tempt us to expect some version of the glittering New Jerusalem finally to come down from heaven? Well, yes, but surely not in any guaranteed or literal or futurist sense, not in the way of a top-down *novo creatio ex nihilo*. But the metaforce of apocalypse has been and will be able to enliven the *down-to-earth* hope of communal life, even urban life, transformed transnationally and renewed ecologically. Hope for planetary health human and so much more than human. But then this is hope that must not be confused with optimism. Optimism remains self-deception. As I write, the last eight years have been the hottest eight in known history. And even in a temporarily friendlier United States, our national exceptionalism pounds economically on. Despite Republican shrieks about Biden's green radicalism, "2022 saw the second highest oil production in US history."[20] And as you read, I suspect causes for optimism have not bountifully multiplied. Nor are they likely to do so now. But in this I am echoing a theology of hope: Christians are neither optimistic nor pessimistic. But we are hopeful.[21]

Glimmers of hope do peek modestly through the veiled New Jerusalem. The Inflation Reduction Act has moved the US in the right direction. Solar and wind are becoming cheaper than gas and oil in much of the world. Cost of batteries is down, making electric vehicles viable—there are long waiting lists for them, driving a rapid transition. Hundreds of billions of dollars are being invested globally in clean energy. And the following statistics are heartening: Before 2015 the world was on track to warm by 4 degrees Celsius by 2100. Now it is on track for 3 degrees. The best outcome is probably not possible, keeping it to 1.5 degrees and off fossil fuels by 2030. But keeping it under 2 degrees remains genuinely possible. And that would be broadly livable. "The good news is we have implemented policies that are significantly bringing down the projected global average temperature change," says the Canadian atmospheric scientist Katharine Hayhoe, an evangelical Christian who has gained a reputation as a sort of climate whisperer to the center-right. The bad news, she says, is that we have been "systematically underestimating the rate and magnitude of extremes." "Even if the rise is limited to two degrees," she says, "the extremes might be what you would have projected for four to five."[22] Apocalypse remains all too relevant—as revelation not of the end of the world, but of our civilization's precarious dance of last chances.

In the process, might the ancient apocalyptic vision sometimes refresh our struggles with a sip of its water of life? Water that its utopia insistently offers as "free of charge for all"? Free clean water—material and metaphoric— for all: another deep current resonance, especially in the global South. And Revelation envisions an urban civilization no longer dominated by military or economic might—in which the representatives of the nations all come riding peacefully together through the gates, ever open, of New Jerusalem. That image of multinationality suggests the *this*-worldliness of the dream. But as they ride, they are notably *not* accompanied by the four horsemen of

Revelation Six, signifying colonization, war, economic injustice, plague and natural imbalance. (Who knows. Perhaps those four colorful horses will toss off their riders and join in the peaceable multinational parade.)

In terms of theological horsepower, what does this all mean? Surely that Christians can push back against any narrative of a simple, absolute ending. The latter cannot be found in Revelation, nor indeed anywhere in the Bible. John dreamreads a nightmarish spiral of planetary destruction. But not The End. And out of the chaos come—in the language of the long tradition of Hebrew prophets—the new heaven and earth, the new creation, the new city. Rather than a brand-new creation supernaturally fabricated (the *ex nihilo* model) we may read it as the vision of a world radically renewed: revived by the conversion of our species to justice for all earthlings, to planetary healing. But the dream of New Jerusalem remains a dream of and for the future of *this,* our earthly, civilization, a dream of John's and, more distantly, ours: Otherwise why would it feature such structural continuities as kings and nations? "The nations will walk by its light, and the kings of the earth will bring their glory into it" (Rev 21:24). The metaforce of radical planetary renewal—not simple supernatural replacement—shines through the final scenes.

Might this intensively urban and fully terrestrial resurrection help now inspire reconnection with the whole of creation? Theologically, such work in and beyond the biblical text requires a refreshed sense of the creaturely/creative texture of our world. And of the dense intersectionalities binding all natural creatures to each other. Even to what a few creatures call the creator. If we only exist as creatures, that means we come to be in relation to the creator in and through our relations to the rest of the creation. No creature is an exception to the condition of creaturely interdependence, of fleshly finitude, of vulnerability as well as creativity. . . . And all creatures, indeed all of us in all of our relations, do not add up to the creator.

"God" remains the mystery that eludes religious mastery. That history of mastery has provoked many, perhaps most, thinking people to abandon the mystery as mere mystification. But we might refresh the mystery. We might dreamread the divine as the relation of all relations, as the intersection of intersections—in which we each live, move, and have our becoming. This deity would not read as supernatural in the sense of separate from nature but, as ecotheologian Sallie McFague signified by the title of her *Super, Natural Christians,* as *hyper*natural, the nature of all natures.[23] This is God not just *in* relation but *as* relation—which the other John's identification of God as love poetically pronounces (1 John 4).

As Augustine put it, "Wherever there is love, there is Trinity: a lover, a beloved, and a fountain of love." Then we speak not of God as the supersubject who subjects all, nor as an object on whom we can lay endless doctrinal propositions, but as a fountain always already pouring out in relation, pouring out relationship itself. A particular kind of relation. The love-relation. However, love is not a strong concept in John's Apocalypse. We must be clear: the apocalypse is not gospel. All the more reason to read it mindfully.

This mindfulness will demand some radical theologizing: such as shaking Christianity free of the root notion of the creation as a simple once for all beginning from nothing leading to a single, coming, supernatural conclusion. The messianic figure in the apocalypse declares, "I am the alpha and the omega." How to read that? I think this way: The I AM eliminates the linear distance between alpha and omega. It evokes the new beginning we can each and all together make now, always again now, in our own lives and loves, in face of—whatever endings we *face*. The doctrines, the metaforces, of creation and eschatology do not exist at the two extremes of a timeline. That *I am* is here, now, present tense, with us. Not to do our world-work *for* us. Not to intervene at some last minute and fix things. Yet I think I heard a childish voice in my head praying "please give Putin a heart attack." "Please just a bit less arctic ice melt." And that wish for God to intervene and fix gets met with another voice, an old voice of disappointment, of strained faith. The denialism and the nihilism don't just disappear.

In apocalyptic mindfulness, however, both of those voices in me get not silenced but answered—by a more honest voice. A voice that recognizes that God does not work through omnipotent interventions from above, no matter how desperately we pray. All-controlling power: That is not what God *is*. Not if God in the Christian sense *exists at all*. At the heart of the gospel divine power appears indistinguishable from love. So even if that heart is too quiet in the Apocalypse, lost in the noise of systemic violence and answering messianic armies, it keeps beating. Even as a love lost and mourned, but still insistently calling. It comes toned by sorrow at the love already lost by followers of Christ. "But I have *this* against you, that you have left your first love." The power of love does not act to control but to call. To inspire, invite, lure. . . . A bit of the erotic tug of the New Jerusalem?

The divine lure makes its appearance as a core concept of process theology. In this theological perspective (alien to the tone and finality usually conjured by apocalypse), God does not interfere and overpower worldly processes. God lures with an "initial aim" for each creature at each moment—a possibility that the creature may choose to realize.[24] A little bit, or more. Or not at all. Such possibilities often feel *impossible*. And faith in such possibilities does not mean they will actualize themselves. Whether they might actualize themselves remains, despite all denials, up to us creatures. Us, in all our intersections with our world, all our interconnections. The love at the heart of it all does not control. But flows, through that spirit-fountain. Prayer tunes itself to that love. It makes the actualization of the more loving possibility—less impossible.

The Song without the Words

This non-controlling power does not intervene, rescue, fix. It gives no guarantee but stirs something like what the eco-activist Rebecca Solnit calls "hope in the dark."[25] It is an affect that lets us, maybe even requires us, to face the danger. To face some facet, some echo, of apocalypse. As the great African American author and activist James Baldwin put it decades ago: "Not everything that is faced can be changed. But nothing can be changed until it is faced."[26] In other words we may not escape great challenges, some of them collectively traumatic. But we might together bear them, bear with them. In spirit. In community. And we do so in apocalyptic mindfulness of our planetary intersections. With the apocalypse mobilized *against* the End of Time, might our time twist open to more inviting possibilities—*in* time? Within the temporality of the mattering world? And in time to avoid catastrophes of the quite final sort?

In the meantime, our intersections will keep tangling us up. For worse and for better, for closure and disclosure. The overheated specter of apocalypse will not vanish. It can, however, help to unveil possibilities: dis/closures; openings into transformation. Even as it makes us face some big cruel realities.

Precisely in facing the intensifying fragility of our planetary life, a critical mass of us might come—just might—to embrace our creaturely interconnectivity: human and so much more than human, across multiple ways, religious and secular. Even as global warming connects us all damningly, can't it also heat up our global solidarity? The eros of our vastly shared materializations might stir new movement. Then through that ancient fountain of love flow fresh possibilities, alternatives to both the tweets of nihilism and the treats of denialism, alternatives made possible by an imaginative and only therefore responsible realism. The reality of an apocalyptic mindfulness connects us to each other, to the earth, to the eros of possibilities that might, just might, yet be realizable. In the dark of improbability, those possibilities sparkle—like the gems covering the walls of the New Jerusalem. Some appear as last chances. Yet they may signal real chances. Holy possibilities.

We will keep hearing the eagle's cry of lament for earth's inhabitants. But if we listen, we hear a different bird song too. So I end with another verse of Emily Dickinson's:

> Hope is the thing with feathers—
> That perches in the soul—
> And sings the song without the words—
> And never stops—at all—[27]

Part II: Power and Its Alternatives

What alternative is there to power? Elementally speaking, power is the energy of things exerting influence on things. Power is energy as influence. Nothing is not made of power, however minimal or massive, material or cultural, understated or dominant, sensitive or violent, individual or systemic are its energic effects on its world. And when power is not just human but political, it contends constantly with alternatives not to power itself, but to its regnant form. What is politics but contention with divergent possibilities—inviting or threatening—for the systemic exercise of influence? And so for the social flow of power itself?

When, therefore, it comes to politics, dominant systems of power arise by besting the alternatives, somehow using, incorporating, subordinating, or squashing them. If even a once aggressively dominant voice of power could avow that "politics is the art of the possible" (Bismarck), political power—however crude or monolithic its art—can never simply eliminate the pressing alternatives to the given: the possibilities that matter. For those possibilities promise, or threaten, to become actual. Indeed, the alternatives that press will have already partially materialized.

Part One considered a configuration of current power as it circulates through the life of the world politically, economically, and ecologically—truly planetarily. In so doing, it could not long defer the theological dimension of this project—or, well, of this world. For there is at this point no avoiding political theologies of power. Even centuries after most formal versions of Christian dominance have dissipated, no Western power can neatly erase either the deep history or the ongoing habits of its religious background. Modernity has largely defined itself in terms of its outgrowing a politics of overt Christian self-justification. And that evolution, speaking socially or democratically, usually counts for the good. But in the version of power currently menacing democracy itself, the crass secularism of neoliberal capitalism merges with the (no less crass) Christianity of the illiberal white US right. The global system of economic superpower profitably invests in the nationalism of right-wing religion. The first essay in this Part addresses this new force field of religion—this "Foxevangelical" form. How new is it? Its Christian antagonism provokes, of course, the antagonism of (not so new) secularism. But does a different reading of power, more agonistic than antagonistic, and also mindful of its own religious sources, offer alternative energies?

To tap the motivations of another sort of spiritual energy, reading the alternative notions of power in play takes on theological magnitude. So a meditation on the metonymy of divine power beckons. Most Abrahamic believers across the political spectrum have long presumed that God's power, being sovereign, in some way controls all and is properly called omnipotent. And, of course, it is that dominant theology of power, of divine power as omni-domination, which keeps the white Christian right so politically effectual. Genuinely democratic forms of power find no equivalent theological support in omnipotence, incongruent as all-control remains with ideals of egalitarian diversity. At the same time the existential anguish of felt incoherence between divine power and every form of human suffering continues to undermine the prophetic possibilities of social justice. Any cosmic spirit of love continues to fade.

Perhaps the systematic alternative long offered by process theology may now need to be heard more broadly. Alfred North Whitehead and his school offer as the alternative to dominance not simple powerlessness but an altered notion of power: as not control but influence, exercised not from above and outside but between and within. Indeed to re-engage the possibility of spiritual empowerment opens into multiple and ongoing experiments in rethinking divine power. Notions of divine vulnerability not just on the cross but across the cosmos begin to come into their own—beyond the cycles of omnipotence and impotence. God's weakness, folly, and insistence allude to the titles of three books of philosophical theologian John Caputo, all aiming at materializing the im/possible. And all along we may be teasing theology itself into theopoetics, a *poiesis* in which *theo* cannot be severed from its *eco*. So this Part in the end offers a reading of the poet Lucille Clifton's profound and succinct eco-poetics, as expressed in "A Black and Living Thing."

5 / Nationalism and a New Religion

FOXANGELICALS AND THE AGONISM
OF AN ALTERNATIVE

Off the fast track of journalism, writing the dynamics of the "current" poses quite a challenge. The present reflection, for example, first unfolded as part of a project under the heading of *Doing Theology in the Age of Trump* (2018), directed at the "threat of Christian Nationalism."[1] At this subsequent moment we may refuse to cede an *Age* to the name of "Trump." And we may question whether the category of "nationalism" is adequate to the ongoing US convergence of white supremacism, transnational capitalism, undisguised masculinism, and climate denialism. Does this nationalism's "Christian" nomenclature clinch the category? Dubious, given its multifarious and not all nefarious meanings. But it will do for this reflection. The point lies not with tired, righteous incredulity (including my own) at right-wing Christians salivating over a foul-mouthed bully who barely bothers with Christianity beyond the (nonbiblical) anti-abortion signal. No matter how well he embodies the answer to the question WWJ*N*D—"What would Jesus *not* do?"[2]

Let us rather consider whether a certain political theology can help to assess the role of what journalist Amy Sullivan denominated "America's New Religion: Fox Evangelicals."[3] Political theology traditionally analyzes the impact of religion on (secular) politics. So does it also go the other way and expose the effects of politics on religion? Key to the category of political theology as such remains the proposition of the German jurist Carl Schmitt: "all concepts of the modern political state are secularized theology."[4] This secular effect is exemplified above all by the derivation of the notion of political sovereignty from that of divine omnipotence. It imports not just the sense of dominion—the divine right of kings—but of exceptional, even miraculous, intervention.

Schmitt notoriously pits "the miracle," as the "exception," against the boring bureaucratism of bourgeois liberalism. He attributes the threat of communist revolution to the impotence of democracy, instantiated for him in the Weimar Republic between the wars. When in 1929 he posits that "the specific political distinction to which political actions and motives can be reduced is that between friend and enemy," he brushes off the all-too-evident Christian counter-position.[5] He insists that the biblical injunction to "love the enemy" has nothing to do with political enemies. "It certainly does not mean that one should love and support the enemies of one's own people."[6] This theological gesture surely reads as a case of political impact on religion, not vice versa. Having privatized that gospel imperative, the way is cleared to Schmitt's radical redefinition of politics itself: "The political is the most intense and extreme antagonism, and every concrete antagonism becomes that much more political the closer it approaches the most extreme point, that of the friend-enemy grouping."[7]

Schmitt defines "the enemy" as "the other, the stranger; and it is sufficient for his nature that he is, in a specifically intense way, existentially something different and alien."[8] The enemy need not be mounting an attack or threatening violence, indeed doing anything belligerent. So one grasps how such a concept of difference well supported the rendition of the Jew as unifying enemy for Nazism. For if the political collective comes down to identity through antagonism, the religio-racialization of a nearby Other—however peaceable—becomes key to producing the requisite enemy. The existential proximity intensifies antagonism. And so the close but alien *they* precipitates the friendship of the *we*.

Even in diametrical disagreement with Schmitt's politics one may grant this account of politics a certain descriptive credibility. Or at least, with its quietly secularized theology of autocratic power, of an anti-democratic style of politics. Its use of fear and loathing to unify an "us" against a "them" found its extreme form, and Schmitt's support, in the fascism of the 1930s. Almost a century later, the authoritarian voices of anti-immigrant right-wing movements have been winning long unthinkable levels of parliamentary representation in Europe.

At the same time, the persistent US power of "us" unified against unwhite others, both internal and immigrant, cannot be categorized simply as nationalist. Rather, it arises as the *leading* symptom of a disturbing international haze of *white* nationalist antagonisms. It calls to mind Hannah Arendt's eerie postwar warning of the role "white supremacism" would have in fomenting "a new fascist International."[9] In *What Does the White*

Evangelical Want, Tom DeLay analyzes how "white evangelicalism grounds itself in centuries-old patterns of white supremacy."[10] He warns that its contempt for everyone marked as outside, as—in Schmittian fashion—enemy, summons the "specter of fascism."[11] That specter blends the localities of white racism into a global political force, sanctified in advance. So DeLay warns that "the most dangerous faith in the world today is white evangelicalism, the most dangerous organization the Republican party, and the most dangerous arrangement global, neoliberal capitalism. Each gladly amplifies the most clearly catastrophic threat human civilization has ever faced, in climate collapse."[12]

In other words we (no Schmittian *wir*) face now an "aspirational fascism": that which William Connolly conceptualizes in his analysis of "the age of Trumpism."[13] This designation builds on his prior analysis of the politics of antagonism. This effective affect is enabled by a festering resentment. In its "ethos of existential revenge" the antagonism sustains what Connolly had earlier exposed as "the capitalist-evangelical resonance machine."[14] Drawing on the Deleuzian figure of the machinic assemblage, Connolly had proposed his resonance machine in particular relation to the early twenty-first-century US intensification of right-wing Christianity as it coils together in a "state-capital-Christian complex."[15] This assemblage, always economically embedded, certainly runs from religion to politics. But it circulates also from politics back to religion, thus strengthening, in his analysis, the right wing of Christianity itself. The machine's ability to unify significant portions of an economically disaffected white working class with the super-rich depends on a religious intensification: "The bellicosity and corresponding sense of extreme entitlement of those consumed by economic greed reverberates with the transcendental resentment of those visualizing the righteous violence of Christ."[16] The *they* of the *we* may shift. Divergent caricatures of racial and of religious difference come into play. But the unifyingly divisive strategy of antagonism persists.

Marcia Pally in her brilliantly succinct *White Evangelicals and Right-Wing Populism: How Did We get Here?* analyzes the partial but extensive merger of those two populations.[17] Probing its complex history, she argues that shifting forms of status loss, economic and way-of-life duress along with religious concerns have effected for this public a peculiar politics of "wariness of government." In a dangerous paradox politics threatens to unhinge the democratic constraints on government. "Thus, the very qualities that contributed much to American vibrancy—an anti-authoritarian government wariness and energetic community-building—may under conditions of distress, inform us-them worldviews: 'us' and 'our community' protecting ourselves from an interloper government and other 'outsiders.'"[18]

Particularly nonwhite ones. The wariness then intensifies the us/them binaries reactive to the "socially liberal, multicultural society." So a new political authoritarianism, hardly recognizable as such to its pious proponents, is energized by a righteous antagonism.

And in the face of duress social, economic, or ecological, that energy threatens to intensify. This cannot be accounted for in terms of a unilateral operation of conservatively Christian or apocalyptically fundamentalist theology upon politics. There seems to be a dynamic circulation between the impact of religion on politics and the impact of politics on religion, indeed in a circle vicious enough to produce a change, as Sullivan hints, of religion itself. Or of the meaning of religion. Does this circulation therefore express the unifying antagonism that we face in the dynamics of white Christian nationalism?

Guns, Fox, and Christmas

In her investigation of the overwhelming white Christian evangelical support for Trump, Amy Sullivan discerned a significant change in the character of the religious Right itself. It registers precisely in the versatile politics of friend versus enemy. She interviews Jonathan Martin, a popular pastor and author. "'It's meaningful,' Mr. Martin says, 'that scions of the religious Right like Jerry Falwell Jr. are not pastors like their fathers. There was a lot I didn't agree with him on, but I'm confident that it was important to Senior [Jerry Falwell] that he grounded his beliefs in Scripture,' Mr. Martin (who himself identifies as evangelical) said. 'Now the Bible's increasingly irrelevant. It's just 'us versus them.'"[19] And yet the claim of biblical authority remains all too relevant to that very antagonism.

What medium has enabled such a bluntly Schmittian metamorphosis—of the conservative religion feeding and fed by the politics? Both Testaments could always be deployed in support of political antagonism—"if they are not for us, they are against us." So I was surprised to learn that among avowed evangelicals biblical allusions have dropped precipitously. Indeed, one survey reports the startling finding that fewer than half of those who consider themselves "evangelical" now actually hold traditional evangelical beliefs.[20] Among white "self-identified evangelicals" the label "evangelical" now arguably functions more as a cultural than as a theological identification. African Americans, by contrast, are more likely to reject the term "evangelical" (in part for its cultural whiteness) even when they practice a firmly gospel-centered discourse. Race and political party appear more likely than religious conviction to determine how one votes. If, as Sullivan puts it, "'evangelical' effectively functions as a cultural label, unmoored from theological meaning," the importance of religious self-identification is not thereby diminished. But what then gives shape to the particular friend/foe binary that is replacing biblical belief within evangelical identity?

This is where Fox—with Friends—comes into play. Amy Sullivan centered on the example of "the War on Christmas," a long-time Fox News crusade. The Fox war against the purported war never took the form of a religious argument (about virgin birth, the status of the incarnation, or the need to redeem Christmas from commercialization). "In an irony appreciated by anyone who remembers the original anti-consumption, anti-Santa meaning of the 'Reason for the Season' slogan, Fox and allies like the American Family Association focused on getting more Christmas into stores and shopping malls." She notes that even after Trump's 2016 election, when Bill O'Reilly declared "victory" in the War on Christmas, "Fox News gave the supposed controversy wall-to-wall coverage and folded it into the network's us-versus-them, nationalist programming." So the regular Fox News viewer, churchgoer or not, absorbs "a steady stream of messages that conflate being white and conservative and evangelical with being American."[21]

Note that the *trump*hant (sorry, can't resist) conflation of conservative Christianity with capitalism depends for its force on the third vector, the affective field of white supremacism. The politically unificatory racism moves with an affective contagion Connolly calls "existential ressentiment." It operates "in practices of capitalist greed, religious exclusivity, media bellicosity, authoritarian strategies, sexual narrowness, and military aggression."[22] This constitutively American antagonism, with its dark foes—intimately African American, oscillating with intrusions of Muslim or Latin American—proves indispensable in firing up the new "friends" of Christian nationalism. After all, Fox News had reassured us that not only was the historical Santa white like the snow but that "Jesus was a white man too."[23] The mouthpieces come and go, the issues shimmy and shift. But as the primary purveyor of this political "we," conveying its daily charge of affective imagery, Fox News takes the lead in delivering the white Right political theology. Is it taking the place of traditional beliefs for that majority of self-identified evangelicals who no longer study the Bible? "A pastor has about 30 to 40 minutes each week to teach about Scripture," notes Reverend Martin. But the congregants have "been exposed to Fox News potentially three to four hours a day." Hence "Fox Evangelicals." Call them Foxangelicals for short.

The result, Sullivan suggests, is a "malleable religious identity that can be weaponized not just to complain about department stores that hang 'Happy Holidays' banners, but more significantly, in support of politicians like Mr. Trump . . . and of virtually any policy, so long as it is promoted by someone Fox evangelicals consider on their side of the culture war." She was especially surprised by the absolute importance of gun rights to most Fox friends. Here the primacy of antagonism blazes to the fore. The documentary film *The Armor of Light* testifies to the new fusion of guns with God.[24] Its protagonist Rob Schenck, another thoughtful evangelical leader, had come to prominence as a popular pro-life crusader. We watch him run into one long wall of resistance when he tries to teach his constituency that pro-life values require restrictions on gun access. He finds that his public has been daily and successfully taught by Fox that their way of life, indeed their *life*, is threatened by (Black) criminals, (Muslim) terrorists, illegal immigrants—killers gunning for them. Not surprisingly, he finds that for Foxangelicals, gun ownership trumps biblical teachings of respect for strangers, love of enemies, and welcome of aliens, such as the imperative of Deuteronomy 10: "Love the foreigner, for you were once foreigners in Egypt." And you've probably seen T-shirts and election posters emblazoned with "God, guns and Trump."

Christosecularizations

If it is true that Foxangelicalism has mounted something like a "new religion," it can never admit as much. That would take the "Christian" Right out of Nationalism. But we see here the potent effect of conservative politics on religion. It functions by conveying a loud new religio-economico-political assemblage in which the biblical theology that justifies the "we" has been—amid all the noise—quietly secularized. Very quietly, as secularism is something the Right needs to accuse the Left of. But this is a secularism that poses as religion, indeed functions as a new one. Theologian John B. Cobb Jr. has long distinguished between the "secular"—to which he counts most major "religious" breakthroughs—and "secularism," which is its own religion.[25] The latter refers to a dogmatically atheistic secularism, derived from modern liberalism and science. If Foxangelicalism can be called a new religion, it is the religion of a conservative secularism that masks itself as traditionally Christian and decries the secular (as, in its war on the war on Christmas).

It was, after all, as a theorist of the Right that Carl Schmitt was exposing the secularization of theology in all forms, conservative and otherwise, of the modern state. He meant to make a conservative Christianity more explicitly effectual within the political. The Schmittian political theology has been since the World Wars perhaps more apparent in the United States than in Western Europe. Through the Reagan amalgam of a new religious

Right with the Republican party it produced the political resonance machine of fundamentalism and capitalism. But it now becomes evident that the resonance goes deeper than the "beliefs" of conservative Christians. The machine penetrates to the gospel, the *evangel*, to root out its dissidently amatory good news.

The machinic character of the assemblage does not, to return to our opening question, work one way—from religion to politics. It circulates: from politics back into religion. And back again. The politics may be thereby uroborically swallowing its own religious tail. We might better call the Foxy substitute a religious movement, form, or supersession, than a new religion. The latter would misleadingly suggest a supersession of Christianity itself. Christianity, however, remains endlessly multiple, diverse, and self-contradictory. But in the specifically Christian guise of sovereign supersessionism is it sanctifying the secularization of its own most exclusionary we-they legacy? And so a supersession of the biblical—indeed gospel, *evangel*ical—basis of Christianity?

Foxangelicals, increasingly freed of the *evangel* itself (let alone serious New Testament scholarship), come well shielded from biblical debate and resistance. Therefore, they cut loose of the faint, lingering legacy of biblical arguments coming from the prophets of social justice, the gospels of public love, the acts of agapic communism, the divergently radical Christians from St. Paul to Martin Luther King Jr., from St. Francis to Pope Francis, feminist or ecosocial, Quaker or queer.[26] Such expressions of a religion of course exercise their own influence on politics; conversely, they do not themselves transcend the systemic presumptions of their epochs. And such Christian antecedents and expressions of progressive politics get over and over left in history's dust. Antagonism, it seems, can bind (*relegere*, root of *religio*) more efficiently than love; it provides a more politically unifying force of identification and belonging. At least temporarily.

Agonism and Hope

Regarding the current (well . . .) political condition, it may be tempting to underplay the affective contagion of its antagonism. As to the latter's face, Connolly has argued not that Trump is a Nazi, or a bumbling idiot, but the "relatively skilled rhetorician of a new aspirational fascism."[27] That potential for fascism spreads through rallies, tweets, smearing of opponents, "Big Lies," and the "bodily disciplines" of an aggressive, intimidating white alpha masculinity. If we also consider the Foxangelical channeling of the aspiration, missionary in its affective spread—the situation appears troubling indeed. So Connolly's answer to the antagonism appears all the more inviting—perhaps even realistic. Building on Chantal Mouffe's concept of "agonistic pluralism," he has dubbed it "respectful agonism."[28]

Agonism suggests struggle rather than mere enmity. We need not deny that the Trump/Fox amalgam functions as the enemy of an "us" who seek race, class, gender, sex, culture equality and emancipation. Its mixed public folds into Connolly's "critical pluralist assemblage," which includes multiple religions and spiritualities.[29] But while expressions of the dramatic threat to that progressive "us" may mobilize more effective national and international coalitions across our challenging differences—that opposition cannot unify and define us. The simple oppositionalism of antagonism cannot be *simply* opposed (without succumbing to a meta-antagonism). It can only be resisted by complexity—and thus intersectionally, strategically, self-critically countered. In an agonism tinged with avowed agony.

One is tempted to hope that in the face of climate catastrophe, Trumpism will have served—beyond the decencies of the Biden administration—to galvanize a new *us* of more revolutionary resistance. But such political desire sabotages itself as soon as it seeks to unify and purify, to reduce to the certainty of some One, our varieties of radicality and commitment, of identification and motivation. It then undermines the pluralism of the actual alliance we now urgently need. The requisite complexity of an intersectional web of solidarity does not brook mere opposition. The hope (against so many hopes) does, however, contain a democratically imaginable truth: Current catastrophe in its political register and its global ecology may serve, may already be serving, as the catalyst of a rigorously intersectional manifold. With the multifaceted pluralism with which Connolly would strengthen our fragile democracy, it may press past the regnant individualisms and exceptionalisms toward a genuinely shared, which is to say actually *social*, democracy.

If radicality translates from a single root into a spreading rhizome, our multiplicity of burning issues—race, class, sexuality, climate, and the open *etc.*—can cease to dissipate political responsibility on the Left. That pluralism also lets the many religions and their secularizations stay more cognizant of rather than competitive with each other. Then they work better together to fire up the national spectrum of an international ecosociality. Its embracing planetarity would be forged not in parallel or warring authoritarianisms, but in a wide and sometimes wild spectrum of urgently earth-toned solidarities.

If that spectrum is to become more than a mere specter of its own potential, we arise together not in mere antagonism against the enemy, let alone each other. We mind the irritability of our proximate differences. We arise in the agonism of our differences—as struggle not *against* but *with* each other, toward, yes, an actually common good.[30] So common that it attracts the needed solidarity of what Fred Moten and Stefano Harney call the "undercommons."[31] By way of such positive agonism—through disciplined resistance to antagonism, through mindfulness of our most difficult relations, and yes, through experiments in enemy-love—still malleable fringes of the conflicted, undecided, passive, or even opposed public may also be reached. Because of vulnerabilities of youth, or race, or sex, or class—here and there, we can effect unpredictable, possibly rapidly mounting shifts. Even religious actions (who knows, maybe even occasional WWJD marches on DC) might find new modes of impact. *Might*. Not a chance, not for progressives, if we lose sight of the deep indeterminacy of the world. Our religious, modern, and even leftist habits have often habituated us to barely conscious versions of certitude, even of determinism, which dump us in despair when our particular line of progress fails us. Rebecca Solnit puts the enlivening alternative—not optimism but hope—beautifully:

> Hope is an embrace of the unknown and unknowable, an alternative to the certainty of both optimists and pessimists. Optimists think it will all be fine without our involvement; pessimists take the opposite position; both excuse themselves from acting. It's the belief that what we do matters even though how and when it may matter, who and what it may impact, are not things we can know beforehand.[32]

What we do matters, it materializes—no matter what we know. And so a mindful uncertainty frees us from the wasteful circle of pessimism and optimism, even as it lets us collaborate with each other in our differences. Freed—hopefully—of the antagonistic certitudes of the political theology of enmity, we may—as a we—face rather than fear the unpredictable. That unknowability, in its instability, even in its chaos, then becomes an opening.[33] However agonizing.

Important for the present meditation, instability infuses Foxangelicalism as well. That such religion depends on the concealment of its own innermost dynamism—a secularist supersession of biblical Christianity—suggests not just its versatile, hyperfunded force but a fragility of self-contradiction. Nor does its overdetermined power free it from its vulnerable indeterminacy. It is sometimes encouraging to remember the ontological universality of the unpredictable and of the unknown. An element of irreducible indeterminacy apparently characterizes all cosmic materializations (quantum particles and party politics). Thus Connolly has found in Whitehead's cosmology of interdependent and indeterminate process clues to an embrace of the world as becoming. Those material clues hint at the political alternative to existential resentment.[34] For in the moment-to-moment self-actualizations of such an open-ended universe, neither the delusions of optimism nor the excuses of pessimism manage to shut out the effervescence of new possibilities.

What has such overdetermined indeterminacy to do with political theology as a current dynamic? How does it pertain to the effect of theology on politics—and always vice versa? To account for the religio-political cycle of the Right, perhaps we need more openly to inhabit the Left spectrum of political theology. But is it possible to agree that a constructive, not merely descriptive, politics must at a certain point surface its own *theology*? My *Political Theology of the Earth* represents one such experiment.[35] It recognizes in theology a force for secularization in the past and so also in the present. It reads the secularizations of an all-determining omnipotence—from theocracy to aspirational fascism—as a deep theological problem. It is a problem for which we in the Christian legacy bear special and confused accountability.[36] So then we work—often with great agonism—to amplify an alternative secularization, appropriate to a saeculum, an age, neither exclusive of nor defined by lived forms of religion.

Such an alternative would seek to extend the history of radical, theologically primed movements as narrated, for example, by Ernst Bloch in the three immense volumes of *The Principle of Hope*.[37] In his unorthodox Marxism he read a transformative hope as the secularized impetus behind all democratic and socialist revolutions. And he recognized its descent directly from the Hebrew prophetic tradition of anti-imperial dissent and of radical hope for the urban New Jerusalem, the cosmic new heaven and new earth. It is the ancient visionary answer to the history of determinist power. Of course, once, against all odds, in power, the visionary revolution often succumbed to antagonistic determinism. Other political theologies, repressive of the prophetic dissidence, repeatedly took the reins. So it remains a history only sporadically realized, of prophetic resistance and messianic imagination, as it pulses into the potentiality of the present.[38] Perhaps even this one.

As we foster the secularizations of an ecosocial faith we might then best, when solidarity enables communicative honesty, disclose its operative residues and reserves of religion. We may find then something not dead, not even complete, still weaving itself into the saeculum. What if we recognize in it the yet evolving contours of a theology, better yet a theopoetics, lacking from the start in certainty but rich in possibility? Its God-figuration counters the paternal ghost of all-controlling omnipotence with an endless, an incomplete, potentiality. An omnipotentiality. It comes darkly hopeful, almost illegibly inscribed as possibility that does not control but calls.

Calls to what? Well, perhaps and at least, to an ongoing struggle, a process prone to creative coalitions and unexpected breakthroughs. Theologically such process may find itself sustained, amid no matter what crisis, by a vibrantly unsoppy, cosmically overreaching affect. We cannot often call it love: The vulturous clichés wait to pounce. We have been naming it a respectful, a creative and coalitional, agonism. We might even call it an *amorous agonism*.[39] It can struggle with—*with*, not against—any relevant alterity, any engaging difference, inviting a reciprocity beyond antagonism. It opposes all that unifies merely through opposition: So its agonism respectfully, unyieldingly, repudiates the politics, Right or Left, of pure antagonism. In this it does not contradict itself, it frees itself to honest struggle—and to an avowed uncertainty carried with coalitional confidence.

Such honesty makes truth possible, even theologically, a truth that practices its politics not in certitude but in relation. A truth of love and hope. And the amorous edge of relation opens a planet-full of possibilities, rippling through the earth and the waters, into the atmosphere and off into—it All. If that edgy love is occasionally even now suspected of divinity, surely such a theos seeks not to impose its logos but in relation endlessly to materialize it.

The friendships possible in the politics of such solidarity are not defined by shared enmity. It performs an alternative friendship, kin to a very different Fox, the one who founded the Society of Friends. For such friends "truth doth flourish as the rose, and the lilies do grow among the thorns, and the plants atop of the hills, and upon them the lambs do skip and play."[40] Such solidarity retains a playful vulnerability amid the perils of interdeterminacy. And it might distinguish but finally not decide between such primary differences as secular and theological; as Christianity and the other Ways; as silence and the Word; as electoral politics and radical social movements; as national and international solidarities; indeed as human and nonhuman planetary systems; and yes, as politics and religion. So we resist not religious novelty, not christosecularization, but the untruth of a Christian movement neither avowing its novelty nor caring WWJ(N)D. And often enough, as in this essay, we resist it for the love of Christ.

In these latitudes of indeterminacy a political theology of amorous agonism remains determined to foster the ecosocial good of the whole public of the Earth. Yet its peculiar planetarity will appear overstretched and weak before the nationalist power of the Right, joined with world-consuming global capital, and daily justified by its Foxangelical network. Sometimes agonizingly weak. But precisely not defeated by this vulnerability. For our solidarity outgrows the "cruel optimisms" and paralyzing pessimisms that blind us to actual possibility.[41] If the political theology of the Earth keeps appearing, if *we* keep showing up in multiplying alliances and intersectional coalitions, does not even the chaos of our complexity reveal a potentially vast assemblage in the making?[42] Its ecosocial solidarity will be directed not first of all against an enemy but toward fresher possibilities—lilies amid the thorns. Able through proximate affection and contagious creativity to renew our world-friendship ever again, this unfolding assemblage of earthlings appears incomplete, endless, undefeated.

6 / Power, Theodicy, and the Amipotent God

Eloi, eloi, sabachthani: the last words of one whose life's perturbation of power resulted in his death.[1] However you work out your christology (if you have one), there remains perhaps no simultaneously more cruel and more familiar symbol of the powers that be, that were, than punishment by crucifixion. Christianities of social justice have long had to underscore the fact that the crucifying power was not the Jews, let alone God, but the Roman Empire. Of course, mutters John of Patmos: the enthroned beast of Roman rule and the "great whore" of its global economy. Since then, power has morphed into any number of systems, Christian and secular, imperial and neo-imperial, political and economic.

And yet the overfamiliar last words from the Mount of Olives resist reduction to systemic injustice. "My God my God why have you forsaken me?" At least according to the gospels of Mark and Matthew, those are the words. Luke's Jesus offers much more reassuringly, after forgiving the soldiers: "Father, into your hands I commend my spirit." John's says simply: "It is done." What is surprising is that Mark and Matthew retain the complaint of Godforsakenness—so alien to the gospel's meaning of "good news"—at all. It makes for such bad propaganda that, by historical critical criteria, Jesus might actually have said it. In this version, their words signify that Jesus did not expect this outcome; that he feels abandoned by his Abba. That he should not be experiencing this depth of torment, of humiliation. The disappointment runs intimate. Abba could and should have made it come out otherwise. Or at least been there with him, comforting, strengthening. I will not discuss now the easy standard answer—that it *did* come out otherwise. The resurrection! However you interpret the Easter symbol, it does not solve the problem here, of the actually unbearable agony. In this problem, indeed in the face of any horrific suffering, smolders the question of theodicy: How could a loving God *let* this happen—let alone directly, or indirectly, cause it? Therein lies the theological heart of the problem of power vis-à-vis the God of love. Let me suggest that without facing our own versions, intimate or systemic, of forsakenness, without grieving not just the specific unbearability in play but some accompanying sense of being abandoned, every restoration or renewal or resurrection may ring hollow.

Theodicy and Apocalypse

The question of theodicy has long found in process theology a key if controversial and open-ended answer. Indeed, David Ray Griffin crystallized the logic of the problem and of its resolution a half century ago in *God, Power, and Evil: A Process Theodicy*.[2] The operative syllogism: If "God" is *both* (A) all-controlling *and* (B) all-good; *and* (C) there is real evil; *then* there is no God. You can have either A *or* B with C, but not both, and still have "God." A God of all-controlling power cannot be truly good, indeed loving, and "let" evil, or needless suffering, happen. However: If God's power is not by nature controlling, but instead works by persuasion and cooperation, then it does not contradict God's love. Ergo, in the face of whatever traumas, God could just possibly exist.

And yet it is nonetheless important—even among process theologians—to let that anguished cry of godforsakenness resurface now and again. Otherwise our answer may become pat, abstract, detached from the fresh agonies of our moment. The gospel godforsakenness expresses an existential anguish, not a metaphysical fact. Indeed, as has become clear to me in teaching, if I move too smoothly to and through the process theodicy, it feels to some no better than atheism. They suspect (even if not saying so to the teacher's face) that it is process theology that has forsaken God.

So here is what I am wondering: How does forsakenness—specifically by the one named "My God"—play in the big, the apocalyptically charged, traumas of our time? That means, as I was writing, the local agonies of new wars, with the nuclear threat unresolved globally. And, of course, it means, over a longer "now," crises of global warming along with their exacerbation of social imbalances. These are not apocalypses in the sense of "The End of the World." The end of the world is at any rate not a biblical notion: *apocalypsis* means not closure but disclosure, revelation—of a catastrophic human pattern pushing *not* toward a simple The End, but toward worsening historical realizations, and set in "intensive contrast" to the greatest of earthly hopes.³ And for decades now, global warming can be relied on to provide a superb scientific illustration of apocalyptic symbols: Even the sober *Scientific American* has warned of "Climate Armageddon."⁴

Such usage, however, does not weaponize apocalypse as the End (as I ever repeat). Rather, inasmuch as it does carry a biblical resonance, it conjures the Dragon/Beast/Whore trinity of systemic power bringing on planetary catastrophe. In textual context, that includes such creepily resonant illuminations as the burning of a third of the trees, the death of a third of the life of the sea (Rev 8:7–9). The Roman power that in the gospels crucifies Jesus gets coded in Revelation's prophetic nightmare as the imperial power over sea and land; and it is empire mating with a planetary economy personified as hyper-seductive, set in a vision-list of her twenty-eight luxury products for global trade (Rev 18: 11–17).⁵

Fundamentalist readings usually presume that if nuclear or ecological catastrophe happens, too bad, but that is part of God's providential plan (born-agains will be raptured out at the last minute anyway). A far wider array of Christians also assumes that anything so huge must be in some sense divinely willed; and that even if such destruction and suffering is *not* the direct plan of God, God will have "let" it happen. In such theodicies, what sense of Godforsakenness plays out? And does process theology offer an adequate alternative, pastoral and political?

That Godforsaken Cross

Before leaping into process theological arms, it may be helpful to pause with another highly influential, politically progressive and ecologically oriented theology. Jürgen Moltmann, the leading Continental theologian, takes us right to the cruciform question of forsakenness:

> When God becomes man in Jesus of Nazareth, he not only enters into the finitude of man, but in his death on the cross also enters into the situation of man's godforsakenness. In Jesus he does not die the natural death of a finite being, but the violent death of the criminal on the cross, the death of complete abandonment by God. The suffering in the passion of Jesus is abandonment, rejection by God, his Father.... He humbles himself and takes upon himself the eternal death of the godless and the godforsaken, so that all the godless and the godforsaken can experience communion with him.⁶

Jesus's being truly human means that the fullness of the incarnation requires that he partake of the fullness of human suffering. And that means a suffering unalleviated by his faith—that is, the worst kind of suffering, a traumatism that feels helpless and hopeless. The divinity of Jesus forsakes the humanity of Jesus at the crucial moment, that cross-moment. This manifests for Moltmann how God's radical solidarity extends to "the godless and the godforsaken."

I hear in this confessional theology much that remains existentially persuasive—and process compatible. Certainly, process theologians would agree that God is just as attentive to the godless as to the godly. The divine lure may indeed call to "the godless" through their most acute vulnerability—precisely in their feeling of godforsakenness. And in so doing this God does not actually forsake them. Does that imply, as for Moltmann, that in Christ, God is deliberately entering into godlessness on the cross by revealing the absence of—Godself? Or might such a move feel, if not simply self-contradictory, a bit too performative? God *playing the role of absent father* so as to lure the godless? Does this not suggest a gesture of indirect but still omnipotent maneuvering of the situation? And if we then apply the experience of godforsakenness to nuclear Armageddon or to climate apocalypse—we might get the impression that God has also chosen to play out absence, abandonment on a horrifically global scale. The very earth nailed to the neo-imperial cross? *That* metaphor might work increasingly well. But surely not if read as strategic divine abandonment for the sake of ultimate communion.

Nor I think would Moltmann, who has been a leader among Protestants on matters of ecology, recognize a God who is crucifying the planet. He sharply distinguishes God's all-might from the "idolatry of power in world history."[7] God in creation self-limits: "The limitation of God's unending power is an act of God's power over Godself. Only God can limit God."[8] But "in the relationship of love, free spaces for the beloved develop"—hence God's creative power already holds within itself a "self-renunciation" of power. Otherwise, we would have to assume that God "determines everything" and is "responsible for everything, so the Almighty is also the accused in the theodicy question."[9] Moltmann builds on Kierkegaard's argument that God has created independence in the creatures. Not to have done so would have expressed a controlling rather than loving power. "So God's almighty power is his goodness."[10]

These are illumining moves on the chessboard of theodicy. Yet the reliance on the notion of God's withdrawal, God's self-renunciation, still tends to leave the sovereignty of controlling power intact. For it is because the omnipotence is inherently all-controlling that it must limit itself, that it needs to withdraw. Only God can limit God. There is no hint then of the way *creatures* limit God's power. So the specter of all-determining power lingers—along with its haunting theodicy.

Intimate Agony

Here—without exorcising the ghost of theodicy—the process theology of cooperative rather than coercive power may illumine the conversation. It allows one to embrace, indeed deepen, Moltmann's insight along with Kierkegaard's, that God's power *is* God's goodness. On this matter, process theologian Thomas Jay Oord has written powerfully (and cooperatively) that God's power cannot be a power of control or else it contradicts love itself.[11] God—the biblical one—actually *cannot* control outcomes. So then the power in play is not intrinsically controlling and needing to be somehow renounced—in creation, cosmologically; on the cross, christologically.

Unfortunately, however, the understanding of the one God in the Abrahamic monotheisms did and does *tend* toward versions of unlimited power, even if the scripture depicts no simple all-control. And even if that word "almighty" is actually a mistranslation of *el Shaddai*—"the Breasted One."[12] (You can see why patriarchy needed to mistranslate). And so the experience of Godforsakenness on the cross, whether it is the experience of the historical Jesus or of his disciples, might to most still suggest the last gasp of an interventionist hope. This despite its coming from one whose life had manifested the most profound cooperativity with the divine known and narrated in human history.

Does his last crucified outburst mean from a process perspective that Jesus was wrong? Perhaps not, unless one thinks he was pronouncing a proposition: "God has abandoned . . ." But no, he was asking an anguished question. And its affect seems agonizingly real. No one *feeling* such forsakenness is wrong. If Jesus felt that forsakenness, it means he registered the depth of his own powerlessness in that moment. He has been crucified by a politics that systemically forsakes and indeed replaces God. And his God does not, cannot, prevent human choices or politics. So perhaps the utterance does carry a last gasp of his own presumption, however subtle it was, of a logic of omnipotence.

Or from another angle: If there never was an absolute boundary between Jesus and his abba, if at some dark depth Jesus is not separable from the divine, he perhaps faces in dying a deep register of that intimacy. Then his own suffering cannot be separated from God's. Yet he remains (as the tradition presumes along with his divinity) utterly human. Maybe he is not feeling deserted by God as such so much as by the "You," the personal otherness, of the one from whom he is nonseparable. Non-difference can register as *indifference*. The closest can feel like the furthest. The infinity of this intimacy darkly flashes—the impossible. And in that moment the anguish is not relieved but amplified by such nonseparability. That incomparable indivisibility does not negate the compassion, the suffering-with, but deepens it. As Jesus's *own* pain. There is no minimizing that despair.

For serious Protestant theology it will remain important that in Moltmann God is no longer the Unmoved Mover but one who both moves and is moved. "The 'unmoved Mover' is a 'loveless Beloved.'"[13] Moltmann's alternative meaningfully resembles process theology's "Most Moved Mover" (Charles Hartshorne). With its hint of the Breasted One, this most moved deity who suffers with us no longer resembles a monarch or any controlling power. Of course, power in the political sense will always retain some edge of sovereign control. But when underwritten by theologies of all-control, the politics amplifies not the existential challenge of the cross, but an endless repetition of the logic the crucified one rejects. How then can we break the cycle of political theologies of control, as they can only trap us in a godforsakenness ever reinforced by further disappointment—and unrelieved by the supreme com-passion? And as they may render us helpless, pacified, even though we are not hanging on a cross but still able to make some sort of difference? Perhaps only by the breakthrough of the life that is at once the most moved and the most moving—all-control gives way to all-love. In which abandonment also is not a static state but an emotion, a motion, moved and moving, unstuck, unsticking.

The Power of Amipotence

Why not then borrow from Tom Oord a revelatory neologism? In *The Death of Omnipotence and Birth of Amipotence* he writes that "amipotence replaces omnipotence. It "combines two Latin words, *ami* and *potens*."[14] The *omni* transmuted into *ami*, friend, makes for a dramatic shift of meaning. In this amicability, however, God has not turned powerless: "Amipotence is the maximal power of love."[15] So it retains energetic potency, this amity, this love. Love's power, however, is uncontrolling, and "the Spirit's synergy with creation is uncontrolling love at all times and all places."[16] In Oord's sense of uncontrol, and revealed in the title of *God Can't*, God cannot just intervene, step in and stop the horror, give the world's dictators either a heart or a heart attack, convert the capitalists to saving the work of those days of Genesis 1, of those billions of years evolving the dazzling plenitude of life on earth.[17] That's not how it all, nor how the God of it all, works.

So a divine amipotence carries another meaning of power, of *potential*. It galvanizes *potentiality*, a potentiality manifest in every moment of every creature of the creation's life. This is God's power: to offer possibility for creaturely actualization; not a direct action that intervenes, but a directed possibility for change. The divine tilts the abstract infinity of pure possibilities toward the real potential for particular becomings. Here process theology develops the pure possibilities, Whitehead's "eternal objects," as the timely content of the divine lure, the "initial aim," in its individuated appeal to each becoming occasion. The lure of those possibilities initially aims the creature toward self-actualization, indeed, toward a *better* actualization than that of its antecedents. In its interdependence with fellow creatures, the creature responds—cooperating with the divine lure or not, a little, or a lot. It feels the others as potentialities of its own moment, and it may—or may not—be persuaded to collaborate with them in becoming. So those initially aiming possibilities, conjoined with the potentiality of the whole shared creaturely past, rely on the creature for actualization. In this open-ended cosmological creativity, process theology pretends to no ghost of all-determining power.

David Griffin made clear that God is rightly named "perfect." *And* such a God, as perfect also in power, lacks any monopoly on that power. God's sort of power cannot be equated with omnipotence, with all the power there is, or with a power to control all that is. Griffin reflects with Charles Hartshorne that "the ideal or perfect agent will enjoy the optimal concentration of efficacy which is compatible with there being other efficacious agents."[18] As Griffin crystallizes the operative logic, "Such a view greatly alters the problem of evil. Even a being with perfect power cannot unilaterally bring about that which it is impossible for one being unilaterally to effect." To be a perfect agent means sharing the world with other agents, creatures whose actions make a difference in that world. For to be a being at all is to exercise power. As Plato put it, "Being is power." To be is to affect one's universe. "And it is impossible for one being unilaterally to effect the best possible state of affairs among other beings. In other words, one being cannot guarantee that the other beings will avoid all genuine evil. The possibility of genuine evil is necessary."[19] Griffin underscores that he is *not* saying that it is genuine evil that is necessary, but its *possibility*. (Let that distinction sink into our theodicy.) The creator has called forth not a world predestined to evil but a universe in which evil must be a possibility. To put that more invitingly: Creative freedom and with it the freedom to err is crucial to an actually good creation.

On this basis, then, Griffin can offer a distinctive form of omnipotence. He calls it "C omnipotence," C standing for "coherent" and "creationistic." We might add "cooperative." That differs dramatically from the conventional creationism of God's absolute power over a world "He" created ex nihilo. Griffin teaches a creativity attuned to the creation, indeed tuned ecologically to the *kosmos*, the "order" of the universe: Creation, from whichever beginnings, remains an interdependent flow of ecocreativity. Creation in the process model unfolds in a vibrational field with no absolute beginning or end.[20] C-omnipotence signifies the omnitude of power that a being in a world of beings—where being is power, not dominance—can have, can be, can exercise. I find the language of omnipotence automatically misleading, but in contexts where it is rhetorically important to affirm God's omnipotence, Griffin's definition lets us do so without contradicting the love.

In some contexts, we may have the chance to offer Tom Oord's amipotence, which of course in no way counters Griffin's argument for C-omnipotence. Amipotence can deploy its logic in those relatively amicable contexts where such vocabularic play is possible. Either way, we can retain a syllogism in which God's power and God's goodness do not contradict each other in the face of real evil. This is not a coherence of mere logic. It is a liberation from the power/love contradiction of theodicy—with its possibly *theocidal* effect. It has, it emits, a force of amicable attraction. The liberation is affective and therefore effective. It lets God live, for us and in us. By whatever names and namelessness.

Grieving and Rising

What then of Mark's and Matthew's Godforsakenness? Would Jesus have felt more God-trust at that gruesome moment if he'd had the benefit of process theology? I am not interested in committing such anachronism. Nor am I claiming that the affect of forsakenness can be once for all dispatched by the countering amicable affect. But the alternative theologic of a process theodicy does really undo the logic of divine controlling power, from the monopolizing omnipotence that bears no resemblance to Jesus's God or to that God's *basileia* to start with.

Godforsakenness may therefore mean in the gospels: The real evil in the world at certain moments intensifies suffering so fully that the possibility of the better world seems to vanish. Then divine power seems altogether obstructed, contradicted not by its own goodness but by the world's power. And when that contradiction cuts close, despair bleeds from the wounds of hope.

And yes, according to the Christian story, the despair is more than healed within a couple of days. But it matters that two gospels actually retained the crucified outburst in their narratives. Surely, it teaches us not to repress the grief, the pain, not to deny the sense of disappointment, even of betrayal. Letting ourselves feel it may be the condition of overcoming it. So we might let that Godforsakenness echo in our guts when we confront instances of systemic power's evil. Of imperial weapons of war ever ready for mass destruction, of hunger in a time of plenty, of garish economic disparities, of a neo-imperial economy melting the glaciers, warming the oceans, storming the shorelines, extinguishing the species, poisoning the earth, wasting the future.... The point is not to blame God. But to recognize and to grieve the horror.

So do not block that feeling of godforsakenness. Perhaps without it we do not rise up. Naming it may let you then remember that it is not a matter of a supreme power withholding itself for whatever just or just mysterious reasons. Perhaps the Godforsakenness means not that God has abandoned you or your world—but that the world has in that instance forsaken God. Who may therefore be suffering with us our forsakenness. Who therefore needs us to rise up ... in whatever medium or scale of materialization proves possible.

Even as our world faces new Good Fridays, we might—with no triumphalist illusions—live into the resurrection energy. Redemption as love-work remains an unpredictably and perilously entangled process. God cannot unilaterally save us from ourselves and our God-forsaking systems. Nor can we unilaterally do the saving. Grieving our grief, feeling our godforsakenness—and sensing afresh our god-relatedness—we may nonetheless begin again. And again.

The feeling of godforsakenness will not permanently disappear, I suspect, for any honest theist. But the griefwork can take place in trust, *pistis*, that what we call God doesn't reduce to pathetic impotence, fade into flat nonexistence, or coldly give up on us or on our world.

In this disclosure the old problem of theodicy, with the transmutation of omnipotence into a power of cosmic ecocreativity, works for us, not against us: If God is C-omnipotence, their power is loving, the power is love, the love is powerful. So, in memory of David Griffin, I begin to end with the last words of *God, Power, and Evil*:

> God does not promote any new level of intensity without being willing to suffer the possible consequences; because God constantly works to overcome the evil in the creation with good, and in human experience does this by simultaneously seeking to increase our enjoyment of life and to enlist our support in the effort to overcome evil by maximizing good.[21]

In the broad context of process thought, indeed of ecotheology in general, I see no reason not to let C-omnipotence collaboratively converge with amipotence. The divine willingness to suffer the consequences of every creature's process is inseparable from the divine love of it all. And that love, perhaps infinitely different from ours, does not signify any indifference to outcomes, nor any pleasure in the pain, like a nonconsensual sadomasochism, but rather a feeling with, a com-passion, that folds the suffering of the evil into a complex potentiality for good. If not—if we do not have faith that from the worst suffering of evil in our lives individual and collective lessons can be learned and better futures realized—how could we hope to resist and heal at all?

The unavoidable tensions between the suffering of genuine evil and the enjoyment of the good seem to have materialized in the uber-intense contrast of cross and resurrection. The joy of Easter was not then, nor is it ever, assured. in advance. A gift has nothing in common with a given; a promise is no guarantee. What in the meantime, no matter how mean it gets, must not be avoided, will be the moment—the impermanent moment—of godforsakenness.

7 / Weakness, Folly, Insistence, Glory

THE PHENOMENAL GOD OF JOHN D. CAPUTO

I want to start by pointing out my titular mistake.¹ I won't apologize for it, I'll use it. My original title compacted John Caputo's startlingly abundant series of God titles—*The Weakness of God, Folly of God, Insistence of God, Glory of God*. But that latter Caputo title does not exist. Indeed, Caputo might say that the glory has served as a blinding excuse for the *gory*—the sovereign force of Christian violence. It seems to have double-blinded me: I typed "Glory" instead of "Ghost" while mistaking "ghost" for "specters"—having recently read *Specters of God: Anatomy of the Apophatic Imagination*.² And the solar halo encircling the profile of Fra Angelico's angel on the cover does emit indubitable glory.

Yet ghosts, quite the opposite of glory, remain shadowy denizens of the darkness of our haunted houses or histories. Specters, even of God, do not effulge with revelation. They offer neither triumphs of certitude nor certainties of triumph. They spook more than they comfort. In shadowing the writing of John Caputo, they perform not explosions of splendid clarity but quite the contrary—the gestures of an "anxious apophatics."³ Since I myself don't manage to exorcise such ghosts, don't even try to, I find myself helped as well as haunted by Caputo's theopoetics. His God—the monosyllable, the image, the hint, the haunt—does quite phenomenally, indeed phenomenologically, *appear*: That word writes itself insistently in Caputo's oeuvre. Quite a phenomenon, especially for one not in any simple sense a theologian. Yet he is unmistakably, and unsimply, a theologian, a philosophical theologian, or more precisely, a theological philosopher. But theological philosophy marks no formal field, and so keeps Caputo's "God" subversively transdisciplinary.

In a munificence more shadowy than glorious, this theology is prone to dark out the glory of its theos. But amid its shades there takes place always at least the *theopoiesis*—"god-making," a constructivity mindful of itself and elegant in its autodeconstruction. That constructive sense has proven key to the improbable architecture of Caputo's "theopoetics of the perhaps." The Derridean *peut-être*, what might be, maybe or maybe not, has possibility itself dancing on the tightrope of the impossible, never trapped in some overbuilt theos. But with Caputo the possibility of God cannot be treated as an antique abstraction or a polite shrug. This possibility takes on an insistence that he has called "omnipotentiality." In his words, "We move beyond strong theology to weak; beyond theology to theopoetics; beyond omnipotence to the omnipotential; beyond essence and existence to insistence. ... And therein, in the face of the 'unprethinkable'—lies the apophatic."[4]

No mere a priori, that unspeakable unprethinkable, but a true abyss of meaning. He discerns it in Friedrich Schelling as "an anarchic unruly ground in the heart of being and of God, which blocks the progress of ontology by casting the shadow of unprethinkable being across its path."[5] Caputo nurtures such an anarchos in its apophasis, articulating its inarticulability. In this essay, I'd like to get from that abyss to some sort of *end*—a Caputan sort of end, endless or atelic or at least still unruly, its heart still beating. I will be wondering about how a certain oscillation between that abyss and a weakened, *almost* shared, panentheism, shows itself. This will tug us from Caputo's reading of Paul Tillich to Alfred North Whitehead's flagrantly cosmological sense of all-in-God and thereby to a theos overtly liberated from His all-power, even from his Hisness. And we venture from that reading of a God in process (with its primordial and consequent natures) to Caputo's oscillation between the insistence and the existence of God.

Ultimately, I must raise the question with Caputo about the cosmopoetics of a radical relationalism not only of God to world tout court but also to and in a world composed of the density of creaturely relations, only a fraction of which are human. Such connectivity raises the question—the ever more eerily haunting question—of the earth's material ecology. Do its manifold actual and impending endings draw us—unpostthinkably—toward the end that does insist itself upon Caputo's thought? I will be meditating on the apophatics we share, as it manifests a connectivity abyssal in its unruly insistence on all these verbalizations.

Abysmal Insistence

Specters of God takes us on a trip from an ontotheological to a hauntological imaginary. On its way the book performs a fresh retrieval of Schelling and his articulation of *dem dunklen Grund*. That dark ground sinks deep into earlier Christian history, back to Martin Luther's *deus absconditus* as well as to Meister Eckhart's mystical *Gottheit*. Caputo means to pry the radical Schelling of an anxious apophasis free from the Schelling of the "edifying apophatics."[6] So Caputo reads the abysmal mystery of the Godhead as disclosing a groundless ground "inscribed in being itself, including in the being of God." It opens something anti-hierarchical, anarchical, in every *arche*, something in which "everything is entangled with its opposite and becomes what it is only by overcoming what struggles against it."[7] And this something—anxiously—includes God, struggling with the not-God in that unruly *Grund*, where God cannot be quite said to be being God.

By way of his deep dive into Schelling Caputo opens a fresh portal into Tillich, whom he considers with good reason the major twentieth-century theologian. (Far be it from me to argue that Karl Barth should, as he usually does, get that honor.) *Specters* lets me admit that it was an early introduction to Tillich that hooked me, beyond some preliminary feminist and biblical mythopoieses, into theology as such. It was the radical core of his systematics that disarmed me, that famous proposition: "God does not exist. He is being-itself beyond essence and existence. Therefore to argue that God exists is to deny him."[8] Or as Caputo's *The Insistence of God* develops the idea elegantly: "I treat the name of God as the name of an inexistence, an insistence, a call that is visited upon us and demands our response."[9] His God does not exist but insists. Tillich's antecedent does not exist but is the ground of existence: being itself, not a being. So God is a symbol (in Tillich's groundbreaking definition of symbol as participating in that to which it points) of the God beyond God.

Admittedly, one unintended liberative effect of the Tillichian God beyond God on this 1970s feminist was its deflation—with no feminist intention—of the whole patriarchal imaginary of God the Father, King, Lord, Son, et al. That iconographic gallery of supernaturalized potencies comes predeconstructed within his vocabulary. Dipping back now with Caputo, I realize the debt to Tillich of feminist theology, well, of mine at least, but also of the ultraradical Mary Daly (who early attended his lectures at Harvard, before she abominated all male theologians). An example is her use of his *Courage to Be* for facing the *Angst* of being female.[10] For me another liberation flowed from Tillich's insistence that faith without doubt is not faith at all, but certainty.[11] As Caputo glosses that doubt, it unhinges the mythology and orthodoxy, the superstition and the supernaturalism, that obscure the work of "a deeper theology of the God beyond God."[12] Variations of an anxious apophasis indeed.

Along my peculiar trajectory, it was Whitehead and the process theology that followed (in an open reliance of theology upon philosophy, methodologically reminiscent more of Augustine or Aquinas than of anything Protestant)—which picked up where Tillich left off. Process thought tends to veer away from the unspeakable depths of a divine abyss into a poetically articulable divine interdependence with the world. The God-symbol in Whitehead hooked me into its critical alternative to both the changelessness and the omnipotence of God. What Whitehead called the primordial nature of God ("the Poet of the world") offers the creature no direct interventions but rather, to each and every critter in the cosmos at any given moment, a distinct possibility. These possibilities do not self-actualize but rely on enactment by the "actual occasion," the momentary event of the becoming creature, the cosmological unit of the universe. Divine input here bears no resemblance to classical omnipotence—rather it invites, calls, or—the technical term, it *"lures."* It does not control. Divine power is not that of coercion but of persuasion—*possible* persuasion by pure possibility. But the creature chooses from among myriad possibilities that constitute its whole history as its context, and in which that divine lure (largely subliminal) may play a minimal, or a significant, role. Process prayer does not beg God to intervene, fix, heal. It is a practice of attunement to the possible in the face of the possibly impossible. I have elsewhere considered in depth how the old omnipotence may be replaced by the *omnipotentiality* of what Whitehead called the primordial nature.[13]

And on the other side of the actual occasion, in the consequent nature, God receives, takes in, whatever has come to be in that moment. Here I want to signal the proximity of this consequent aspect to Caputo's book-titling tropes of the "folly" as well as "weakness" of God. In *The Folly of God*, he writes that "the weakness of God requires our strength to make God whole, and the folly of God is to let so much depend upon us."[14] There is here something akin to his later turn to Schelling's God: "the living, revealed God [who] longs for the companionship of the world."[15] The Whiteheadian version, though, travels down no German mystical paths. At the climactic moment of *Process and Reality*, God is named "the great companion, the fellow-sufferer who understands."[16] In the consequent nature, God internalizes the becoming world, integrating it within some cosmic collage of all that has been. In other words, God, taking in all that happens moment by moment, *is* in becoming. So there is here a way of saying God is not a being but a becoming, that God does not *exist* in any ontologically fixed sense. But most process theologians avoid much discourse of divine inexistence, not wanting to join the death-of-God team. Instead. we tend the radical relationality of the God-world entanglement.

More important for the present conversation, the century-old process deconstruction of omnipotence can read as an affirmation of divine weakness. This God insists on novel possibilities, but does not, *cannot*, force their actualization; and in prehending all that becomes, lives in a certain dependence on the creature—upon the cosmos, upon that inconceivably immense micro and macro assemblage of all critters at any given moment of the world's becoming. Yet process theology does not use the language of weakness, either, and not only because weakness won't preach. Weakness implies God has *less* of the power that would permit, if God had *more* of it, the desired interventions. Instead, the divine lure signifies a qualitatively different sort of power—that of potentiality. The divine invites actualizations not just for their own sake but for its own unfolding, its enjoyment, its suffering, its incomprehensibly compassionate collage of all that is. Indeed for its ever-complexifying self-realization. And I hardly need mention how this non-machismo early flashed at me: not as a divine femininity, but as a means to expose as idol the all-power that for so long sacralized masculine force. Not a chance to argue for *less* power but for an alternative potentia. And despite differences, I cannot help refreshing Whitehead's divine lure with Caputo's divine weakness, read as divine insistence.[17]

As I had long considered conversation between process and Continental thinking crucial, I was grateful that Caputo found my obsessive exegesis of the tehom of Genesis 1:2 a resource for his *Weakness of God (2006)*. My *Face of the Deep* had three years before argued against *creatio ex nihilo* for a *creatio ex profundis*—creation not from nothing but from the chaotic deep, the unruly *tehom*. Caputo recognized what I called tehomophobia at play in the "exaltation of the power of the father" with its sexism and homophobia.[18] And he knows that ancient deep to be underlying, or underflowing, the entire German mystical and Schellingian notion of the divine abyss. This present conversation permits me, however, to make explicit something else haunting my own work all along: Even as I found the process alternative to divine omnipotence indispensable, I have still needed to somehow smudge the picture of that quite distinctly and becomingly existent God with those primal waters—and later with a cloud of the impossible.[19] I had let the tehomic abyss mingle with the conceptual waters of Whitehead's "principle of the ultimate," which is markedly not called God, nor identified with any mystical dark ground. Rather it is named creativity, defined as "the many become one and are increased by one."[20] That "one" means each single, eventive creature in a moment, no cosmic totality.

Panentheistic Perhaps

So the flux of creative energy can be imagined as beginninglessly and endlessly mediated by the primordial and consequent dynamism of God, divinity only in relation to a world, some world, of becoming. That relation is often called *panentheism*: all in God. In its perspective the world gets enfolded in God (the consequent) even as God (the primordial) unfolds into the world. Yet world and God remain not separate but radically distinct, with worldlings all doing their own thing with primordial possibility. And it is not in the primordial vision of possibilities but only in that consequent nature that God can be called *actual*, may be said to *become*—and in that sense to "exist." This vocabulary works at a precarious angle to Caputo's, who convincingly ends up naming Tillich panentheistic. Tillich did not thus name his theology, or rather just once.[21] In fact, it is Charles Hartshorne, the primary student of Whitehead, who recovered for twentieth-century usage that term, which a theologian named Karl Krause had invented in 1828.[22] Why did Krause offer this neologism? Not irrelevantly here, he was trying to save Hegel but above all Schelling from charges of Spinozan pantheism.

Some process theologians avoid the term "panentheism," sensitive to its ready misreading as a container-like immanence of all things within God. So Caputo: "Panentheism says that God's existence is in ours and ours in God's. But in a theology of 'perhaps,' God does not exist; God insists, and it is our responsibility to bring about something that exists."[23] Process theology never asserts God's nonexistence, even in this nonreductionist mode; neither do I. But the deep affinity—yes, abysmally deep—is this: It remains our responsibility to bring something, and not just anything, into existence; to actualize in an indeterminate way the possibility called God's lure, or alternatively, God's insistence. And one might argue that then the creature's response—as its moment of becoming, indeed of becoming existent—may be, in a microcosmic sense, bringing God, the response-able God, into existence. Consequently. But conceptually speaking that consequent nature of God only becomes, comes to be, in freedom from any notion of a self-identically existent being, any static existence.

Perhaps in that becoming, we may after all discern an *ex-sistere* in the original sense: from *sistere*, to take a stand. And if existence means what comes in taking a stance, I dig it for God as well as for creatures. Or really for both together: God in that consequent nature is a consequence of the stance the critters take. And we *are* the stances we take, largely unconsciously, the decision we make amid possibility, existing for a flash, then folded into future moments. And into that timeful divine consequence. Sometimes, in other words, I gladly claim the concept of panentheism. For it concisely signals an alternative both to classical theism and to pantheism, an alternative other than atheism. It can suggest a dynamic braid of God in their two "natures" with the world, indeed with each creature, in an interweave of countless fibers.

I might, however, insist that this tenuously braided stance on God's existence is not alien to Caputo's key formulation: "The insistence of God is the inexistence of God, but the existence of God is liable to break out at any time, in great and world-historical events, like Paul on the road to Damascus, and in the smallest things, like the rose that blossoms unseen."[24] Beautiful. Certainly, insistence is not existence. An existence "liable to break out at any time," in macro or micro manifestations, does not imply any subsistent substance or existent thing. But it hardly rules out any sense of the "existence of God." That breakout existence seems rather to depend on the creature—Paul or a rose—to enact it. So I think rather than contradicting the above quasi-panentheism, Caputo in good deconstructive spirit supplements it, indeed heightens its eventiveness. And if so, it strengthens the process theological refusal of a substantial existence of God—or of anything, for that matter. The existent matter of the world is not substance, nor is God. So the formal cosmology of Whitehead gets not undone but lured closer to what we may gladly call with Caputo *cosmopoetics*.

Might we agree then that if *theos* as primordial—indeed theopoetic—possibility flows into the *pan*, each becoming member of the *pan* might actualize that divinity in its own concrescence just a bit, or not at all, or quite a bit? And that almost but not quite simultaneously, that *pan* flows into *theos*? We might read such a *panentheos* as spiraling event by event from the unprethinkable into an un*post*thinkable. Into, in other words, a future that teases, perhaps even mocks, all our edifying or end-timing projections. A future certainly not existing but, as the lure of possibility, calling us—hauntingly, insistently—to take a stance in the present.

And the dark ground? It signifies no thing and no place but the becomingness, the creativity of it all, thinkable only in its bottomless and also topless materializations. And perhaps in its darkness it signals really just another way of thinking the unthinkable. This bears on Caputo's deconstruction, whereby "the *ground of being* gives way to the inconceivable, unprogrammable *event*."[25] *Peut être*. But perhaps the reverse is also true: that the creativity, ungrounded, gives ground—not stable foundation but, abyssal *Ungrund*, roomy, womby, tomby, to that very event. Which would be an event, amid countless mutually entangled events, not created *ex nihilo* but self-creating *ex profundis*.

Cosmopoetic Connections

Yet there is nothing straightforward about keeping the web of interlinked events in lively relation to that abyss of creation, of creativity. In other words, the haunting *tehom* and its processual materializations need something very like what Caputo solicits in his reconstruction of Tillichian motifs: "Any possible systematic theology is redescribed as a tangled, entangled network of interwoven but open-ended connections."[26] Yes: Let entangled difference serve as the criterion of redescription. In what remains I will be tangling with nothing else. (*S'il y en a.*) So then we must ask: Might this insistence of God entail and even require an *intercreaturely insistence*? What about the way the world insists itself upon every member of itself, moment by moment, in a vast cascade of relations?

We have to do not just with the matter of human and divine relations, but with the whole materializing cosmos of creatures. In the Whiteheadian relationalism, the mutual immanence of actual occasions to each other imports a universe of relations. That influx of influence is felt from the perspective of any one creature, as those relations *insist* themselves upon that creature—in its becoming. The insistence never, not even at the microcosmic level, adds up to mere determination. And if with its modicum of indeterminacy the creature then *exists*, it is as a momentary stance insisting itself upon future occasions. It adds itself to the cosmic manifold, which will influence, insistently, each subsequent critter. So we could say the divine insistence upon the world is not the same as but is inseparable from the world's insistence upon each of its members—which fold into the becoming God and the becoming world simultaneously. And make up whatever existence flashes forth and again empties out.

The interconnectivity of God and world as enfolded in the endless entanglements of creatures finds a rare antecedent with the fifteenth-century Nicholas of Cusa. His *explicatio* of God in the world and *implicatio* of the world in God opens into an entire cosmic *complicatio*: "because each is in each and all in all, God is in all and all in God."[27] The relationality of God to world in some profound sense depends on the relation of creatures to each other: and not merely "to," as externally, inessentially, related, but *in* each other. In-sisting.

If I say the world comprises an ecology of entangled critters, insisting themselves upon each other, sometimes aggressively, sometimes poetically—

am I far from what Caputo offers as the "cosmopoetic reduction"?[28] For my own theological tangle of ecofeminism and process what was and remains key is the radical relationalism by which each actual occasion arises as a concrescence of its relations—but always with some difference of its own, some decision between possible actualizations. And that means also between varied possible materializations or repressions of God's lure. That decision (a technical term for Whitehead, distributed to all creatures) allows for variations, and at a certain point, for conscious choice, creative or evil or unconsidered. And that lateral field of interdependent becomings, human and vastly nonhuman, poses its own omnipotentiality for each subsequent event.

Yet as I read an earlier Caputo, he had (not unlike Derrida) lent little emphasis to that texture of entanglement, indeed to the whole material world of interrelations. So it is all the more significant to hear now his conceptual hospitality to the cosmic network of open-ended connections. And these entanglements surely keep the specters in play—not just as tropes of the haunting divine other but of every other. If the moment of materialization, of the actual occasion as concrete, is truly just a moment, do its whole past and its whole future not convey a spectral quality? Might these influences even as they insist on existing be read as ghosts?

As my *Cloud of the Impossible* had in explicating that connectivity gotten quite knotted into the physics of entanglement, down to the quantum level, it is a pleasure to find *Specters* reading physicist Karen Barad in support of an open-ended relationalism. She derives her ethics of responsibility from an ability to respond manifest even at the quantum level.[29] And she has knit from Niels Bohr's quantum indeterminacy a reading of the primary ontological unit as a "phenomenon." And phenomena, she writes, "are the ontological inseparability of agentially intra-acting components." Rather than merely interacting, "Distinct agencies do not precede but rather emerge through their intra-action."[30] Such quantum emergence bears the ghostly title of "spooky action at a distance." A term that began as Einstein's derision of this notion of instantaneous interaction at any distance became a technical term for a proven phenomenon.

There may now be discernible some spooky action at the distance between quantum theory and the specters that haunt Caputo. For example, physicist Paul Davies writes, "In the absence of an observation, the atom is a ghost."[31] Perhaps we are all ghosts outside of our actualizations as phenomena. Barad calls her philosophy of physics an ontology of relation, indeed an ethico-onto-epistemology. These primal relations, in their responsiveness, are not making conscious choices; yet, as she writes famously:

"A delicate tissue of ethicality runs through the marrow of being."[32] But among *us* animals, with the capacity to deliver stunning damage as well as enlivening creativity, ethics comes into consciousness in a new globality of crisis. In its delicacy that tissue of interdependence permits and suffers systemic abuse, indeed destruction now haunting the future in hardly precedented ways.

Planetary Specters

This brings us to my most urgent question. We—we the species—are now implicated in mass destruction at the planetary scale, in vastly different ways and levels of responsibility and victimization. We find ourselves, in Bruno Latour's language, "facing Gaia."[33] Gaia, not as the name of a goddess or unitary organism but of the vulnerable and now increasingly unruly membrane of terrestrial life, confronts us with the ever-spookier phenomena of ecological imbalance. So I would ask our theophilosopher of specters: Might "global boiling" be turning our history into a future of ghosts?[34] Might the human future be turning into a ghost of itself, of what it might have been? With species now vanishing thanks to global warming and oceanic toxification at a rate not seen in 10 million years, 1 million species are currently on the brink. A holocaustic specter of human and ecological destruction looms so close that I feel some selfish relief knowing I will not live into the second half of this century.

At the same time—and because of this specter—the meaning of creaturely intraconnectivity may be beginning to reveal itself with planetary *insistence*. At least to those who do not ignore the ghosts. And the creepy facts. As to the God-question: We are no doubt accustomed, perhaps since the '60s and Lynn White, to the critique of Christianity for its rendering the Genesis dominion glorification of the human and a warrant for exploitation.[35] A well-warranted critique. Ecologically alert Christians have for half a century worked to deconstruct that anthropocentric theology. We keep developing ecotheological accounts of Genesis and of the creator/creature relation that reverse the earth-damaging causal force of a technologically and economically secularized *imago dei*.

How might we attend to this oncoming trauma in terms of the open-ended connectivity of an entangled future? How in the Anthropocene might the insistence of the weak God call forth—if it can—an alternative to the gory glory of the *anthropos*? Is there here another reason to revisit the language of dark ground? Might we let it sink into the darkness of living earth, actual soil, the dirt of the Gaian membrane? Caputo reflects upon the abyss as *Ungrund* of all meaning and of any thinkable world.

Might that meditation also support a quite different but not contradictory emphasis—upon the dark *Grund* of earth itself?

We have few years left before that unruly ground materializes inescapably as a devastated and devastating *Ungrund*; and if I may be so rude: as a Man-made, not accidentally *white* man–made, uninhabitability. An anti-*oikos*. Not the End of the World as universe or even as planet; but quite possibly—the end of our habitat, our home-world, *oikos-kosmos* of the living earth. And with such an end opens up the *Ungrund* of all human meaning. Ah, unless of course we imagine some future of our species, or of our meaning, packed off in a spaceship to a terraformed Mars or beyond. Such escapism, while hardly less fictional than Christian supernaturalism, increasingly finds intelligent, even scientific, representation.[36]

Back on the home planet: Does the abysmal condition of our shared ground now reveal itself as apocalypse? If so, is that altogether regrettable? I have felt repeatedly pressed to retrieve *apokalypsis* as disclosure, not closure: an opening of possibilities precisely under catastrophic pressure.[37] Catastrophe is not inherently redemptive. But it *might* (I repeat) press open the impossible—that Derridean im/possible, now uninhibitedly grounded. *Peut être*—but only if its insistence is collectively, politically, and transnationally received. Which remains at best improbable.

Earth-ground—with its oceanic depth and atmospheric envelope—therefore calls now in an eerie apocalyptic *apophasis* of the nonhuman. Can the apophatic cloud of theology help us face what is unspeakable less in its awesomeness than in its horror? If so, does Caputo's "anatomy of the apophatic imagination" strengthen the chance of some longer-term future for our species, most of whose members after all do not bear responsibility for the capitalist causes of global warming? But how does such apocalypse facing us within our century relate to the question that has become so important to Caputo: the question of the ultimate End, perhaps due to the runaway acceleration of galaxies, a Heat Death, maybe a Big Rip, in, who knows . . . 80 billion years.

That End may seem to leave the question of our little planetary habitat behind in the dust. So I do worry that Caputo's focus on the final end of the cosmos, of the universe as a whole, might distract from the much more local, the desperately urgent, apocalypse, underway already. And we are already mostly distracted from it most of the time. Or maybe his apophatically end-time imagination can work differently: not to distract but to deepen. (Despite poststructuralist proscriptions of depth, taken as hierarchical verticalism.) This abyssal depth goes all the way down and therefore all the way out, way out to the spacetime where horizontal and vertical axes become indistinguishable. Maybe then it puts our manmade abyss into cosmic perspective. Instead of minimalizing the importance of our planetary distinctness, it may heighten it. Then we may gain a more capacious courage for cutting through the *Angst*. Not to space out but to face Gaia, spaciously. In the entangled material expanse of our ill-shared spatiality. Is there a way that occasional meditation on the end of the world—the universe—can from a certain tilt help prevent our pathetically premature Anthropocene end?

Caputo meditates (in the end) on the possibility of living the cosmic nihil beautifully, as a love story. Indeed, doesn't a love grow trivial, if it does not face and in some sense embrace death—even this death unfathomably beyond the death of humanity, long preceded, one hopes, by our species' death by some dignified old age? I wonder: Can the cosmopoetic insistence of love mobilize resistance to the abysmal *un*love story of human history—to the ecological nihilism of our civilization? Don't we need precisely such faith in the possibility of what in scientific terms is creeping daily closer to impossible? It may be that such terrestrial resistance must emerge as the primary form that the *theopraxis* of theology turned theopoetics will take. Not as the issue that trivializes all other issues but that interweaves them: in an earthbound solidarity of and with that difficult network of interwoven and open-ended relations.

Ecology as the issue of issues does quite literally *ground* all the others. Darkly, dirtily, cosmo- and most urgently Gaia-poetically. Caputo's cosmopoiesis oscillates always and, I think, I hope, ultimately Earth-groundingly, with the groundlessly, abyssally, grounding theopoieses. Facing death at a maximum scale, he does not give up on the name of God. That name remains "the most felicitous way I can imagine—and I am talking about an imaginary and confessing the limits of my imagination—to name the limits, which Derrida described as the possibility of the impossible, for with God all things are possible, including the impossible." And as Caputo adds, humbly and magnificently, "the possibility of the impossible is the definition of keeping the future open."[38]

So the best kind of apocalypse, the inglorious kind that dis/closes, that frees eschatology itself from both its supernatural and its secularized closures, may actually enliven our species' chances. Not that God will finally step in from on high (I repeat, I repeat), or that some ultratech solution will save us. Hope remains—spectral. Its God, phenomenal in love and death, pulses between weakness, folly, insistence . . . and a glory turned ghostly. But the possibility of the impossible does keep naming "the way," in Caputo's gracious eschatopoiesis: "to give things their future, to free them from the limits of the possible, to make all things new, constituting the theopoetic content of any 'new creation.'"[39]

We might hope not for freedom from the limits of the possible, but from the limits our species' deformed imagination has imposed upon possibility. A theopoiesis imagined as at once vision of new and unlikely possibilities and compassion for their material actualizations—it does not cease to haunt our history. It might be calling forth spirited solidarities even at this moment. In their phenomenal potentiality may they insist earthfully. No matter what.

8 / Poiesis of the Earth

"A BLACK AND LIVING THING"

>   is a black shambling bear
>   ruffling its wild back and tossing
>   mountains into the sea
>
>   is a black hawk circling
>   the burying ground circling the bones
>   picked clean and discarded
>
>   is a fish black blind in the belly of water
>   is a diamond blind in the black belly of coal
>
>   is a black and living thing
>   is a favorite child
>   of the universe
>   feel her rolling her hand
>   in its kinky hair
>   feel her brushing it clean
>
>   LUCILLE CLIFTON, "EARTH IS A LIVING THING"[1]

In an earth-grammar that pulses with succinct endlessness, Lucille Clifton (1936–2010), one of the leading American poets of recent decades, plies the path of a radical ecopoetics.[2] Early and prophetically, in poem after poem, she roots and twists her life as a Black woman into the life, the lives, of the planet. The "earth is a living thing," and it steps forth not just as organism but as animal. One may think of recent conversations about Gaia as a "superorganism"—not a goddess, not a person-like totality, but something like "a self-regulated system."³ But let us roll with Clifton's imagery of the earth, that "black shambling bear."

The bear's animation, its animal aliveness, conveys the sheer power of the wild. "Ruffling its wild back and tossing / mountains into the sea." Ferocious in its beauty, the image also tosses away any (invariably white) mama earth sentimentalism. Such a toss does not serve the ends of any environmentalism that neglects the feral power of the earth itself. The shamble of the great black bear carries the force of monstrous quakes, floods, shifts—the earth deterritorializing itself.⁴

Now, more than three decades after Clifton wrote the poem, we are more likely to imagine the earth—enraged at the toxic emissions and destructive ecologies of urban civilization, impatient with our abuse of its hospitality—tossing Manhattan than a mountain into the sea. But maybe such eco-impatience is a projection onto both the poem and the bear. Tinged with revenge, such an image might only intensify the feeling of alienation from our home—an alienation that has enabled every phase of the abuse. Perhaps the metaphor of the earth-animal's sheer power and volatility works better *without* projecting eco-vengeance onto it, without injecting that wildness with impatient rage. Still, that bear's mountain-toss does convey an energy kin to anger. As our sick civilization presumes upon earth's hospitality, violates and abuses it, as it fails to recognize the hosting earth for what it is—why would the planet *not* become scarier? Why would the extreme storms, fires, floods not be now so measurably amplifying?

Ruffling its back ever more wildly, the earth-bear may not be best read as vengeful—but perhaps as a host turning slowly hostile. The guests are showing more greed and indifference than appreciation for the abundant munificence of this nonhuman host. Who is nonetheless still hosting, but increasingly evokes Jacques Derrida's neologism *hostipitality*, hospitality fused with hostility. Yet Clifton's imagery insistently avoids anthropomorphic affect projection. And the poem itself does not swerve from its sheer delight in the wild varieties of earth's beauty. Nonetheless, a radically different tone, a tragic and critical perspective, cuts through her opus.

Clifton captures in poetry the emergent work of ecofeminism and anticipates the distinctive voice of ecowomanism. With the tradition of the enslaved ancestors that she proudly claims, as Abdel Mohsen Ibrahim Hashim demonstrates, she "calls for interconnection not only with nature, but also with her African American heritage."⁵ Thus in a poem published already in her 1972 collection *Good News about the Earth*, she writes:

> Being property once myself
> I have a feeling for it.
> That's why I can talk
> About environment,
> What wants to be a tree.⁶

Exposing the double commodification of earth and race, her vision resonates profoundly with the eco-extension of Black thought and activism, as in the liberation theology articulated definitively by James Cone at the turn of the century in "Whose Earth Is It Anyway?"—"the logic that led to slavery and segregation in the Americas, colonization and Apartheid in Africa, and the rule of white supremacy throughout the world is the same one that leads to the exploitation of animals and the ravaging of nature."⁷ Clifton's warnings roll through the key decades of both centuries with prophetic insistence. In an untitled poem published in 2004 we hear:

> the air
> you have polluted
> you will breathe
> the waters
> you have poisoned
> you will drink . . .⁸

And indeed, human economic practices are now twisting the hospitality of the earth toward hostility. Or, in her words, again with a more understated and no less consequential affect:

> the patience
> of the universe
> is not without
> an end.⁹

Perhaps then it becomes all the more important to better mind—at the same time—the earth's patient cycles, to read the nonhuman vibrancy that encompasses our living and our dying. "And the earth . . .

> is a black hawk circling
> the burying ground circling the bones
> picked clean and discarded.¹⁰

Another antisentimental image of the planet. In the practice of many Indigenous peoples and in Tibetan Buddhism, in the ritual called "sky burials," the human body after the ritual mourning gets left to the birds—particularly hawks and vultures—as nourishment. What ecological rigor is practiced in this recycling, with the picking clean of the dead body, even the skeleton, discarded but without any waste. In this nutritious cycling of death and life, the earth hosts the corpse. And in eco-reciprocity, the human returns the hospitality, the body offered as food. Not much has been theologically made of this vastly pre-Christian sacramentality of the body as host: take, eat, this is my body. Clifton tunes less to the hospitality of the dead human than to the ecology of the earth-hawk, wasting nothing. The cycle of life poses the primal alternative to the one-way voracity that pollutes and poisons, that does not feed but feeds upon the Earth.

> It is a black hawk circling: and the earth
> is a fish black blind in the belly of water
> is a diamond blind in the black belly of coal.[11]

Blackness as earth crosses from mammal to bird to fish. And it opens into the roomy, womby expanses of sea and earth. In the elemental darkness surrounding the diamond left in the hospitable ground, lines between organic and inorganic continue to dissolve. Here in this poem free of any but the bones of humanity, the diamond is no more exploited than the coal. Or the fish. These earthlings live at home in the earth that they are. Here the reader may or may not think of the environmental damage of mining, particularly coal mining. Unpoetic fact: of all the fossil fuels, coal emits the most carbon per unit. Clifton's poem came out in 1993. Without imposing intentionality, we note that her poem came out just as—in the early '90s—through improved computer modeling and analysis of the ice ages, the consensus formed around a significantly older hypothesis: human-caused fossil fuel emissions were bringing discernible global warming. Is Clifton here warning? Or perhaps—attending. Tending.

And now suddenly materializes, as the final stanza, the most tender imaginable picture of our planet. The earth . . .

> is a black and living thing
> is a favorite child
> of the universe
> feel her rolling her hand
> in its kinky hair
> feel her brushing it clean.[12]

The preciousness of the earth, so galactically rare, possibly unique, in its hospitality to biological life, is here imagined as a favored child, beloved of the universe. A universe playing with her child's hair. This ritual of affectionate brushing, with hair so textured, thick, is not unfamiliar to African American culture. Through the image of the living earth—as child, not mother—Clifton returns to planetarity the vitality of sensuous feeling, of pleasurable touch. And of cleansing.

It is only in that last stanza that for this poem blackness manifests its racial signification. How then can the reader miss the reverberation between Black life and the live matter of the planet? Gently, succinctly, Clifton delivers a fresh metaphor of the relationality of the cosmos itself. The universe—a universe barely knowable in the expanse of its dark energy, dark matter—embraces the earth in intimate care. And there is nothing casual for Clifton about the convergence of the cosmic with the racial blackness. On the intersection of racism with the economics of exploitation and environmental destruction, her vision was from the start prophetically, devastatingly, unfailing:

> only to keep
> his little fear
> he kills his cities
> and his trees
> even his children. Oh
> people
> white ways are the way of death
> come into the black
> and live.[13]

Come into the black and live.[14] Whether I, and enough others of my pallor, soon enough, will come into that black, and with all other earthlings *live*—remains questionable. But we might hear, feel, heed the call. We may discern what deadening ways remain our own, systemically, spiritually, planetarily. And in order to face, and continue to face, the deadliness, critique needs the supplement of poetry. A poetry that is also an activation, a becoming, a creating— a "making," in the first sense of *poiesis*.

So we may keep returning to Clifton's image of earth's delight in its universe-mother-home. This earth is pictured not as polluted, dirtied, but as being brushed clean by the universe. Her poem does not suggest cleansing it of humans. If we could live in the imagination of our earth, a planet so hospitably held by the cosmos, we might appreciate the asymmetrical but reciprocal relations of care. We might more urgently protect the earth that in asymmetrical immensity hosts us so intimately. Even as the universe hosts the earth. But how can we earthlings host our earth-host?

Perhaps only playfully, like a favored child, with no resentment of our utter dependence? But this would mean for our species to become-like-a-child-again—this species that has lost all childlike innocence or simplicity; this species with a few doing most of the exploitation, jointly wasting the matter of the earth *mater* and the mattering of most of its people. And that majority of people, particularly of color and female, will only suffer more and more from the depredation of the planet.

Nothing about this early nineties poem fades now from resonance: The earth remains wild black bear and delightful black daughter. Yet as the extractions and the extinctions roll on, the damage of our species to that child keeps worsening. Now we find ourselves in a decade of countdown to irreversible climate catastrophe. Of raging deterritorializations that will, without radical *re*territorializations that bind our systemic priorities back to earth, toss more and more terrestrials into the abyss. We are left with no reason for our pale optimisms. But perhaps we may sense a shadowy hope, a hope darker of affect, skin and universe: to become earth child again.

Such dark becoming-child-again cannot mean erasure of all that has been done and learned. For worse and for better. This childlikeness does not childishly eliminate responsibility. It might though energize the ability to respond. It might empower the disempowered. It might—hopefully—let us face the unbearable damage. Face the bear's mounting rage. Responsibility—when it is an ability and not just a demand—enacts the reciprocity of responding and being responded to, of hosting and being hosted, of touching and being touched, of making and unmaking—and yet again, as creatures, creating.

The last word, the swerve from the past present to the yet possible, from power to poiesis, from optimistic pallor to the darkness of hope, can only be Clifton's (2004):

what has been
can be unmade

it is perhaps
a final chance.[15]

Part III: Love-tangles of Theology

What has been so energetically privatized and commodified as what we call—hardly even hoping to free it from cliché—love? Given, however, the force fields of power discussed so far and therefore the need for an effectual alternative, not to power but to its modality of dominance, an equal but alien motivating force may be indispensable. How else energize any struggle for democracy and for the life of the Earth? Ethics itself needs a sustaining motivation, something besides virtue and the right. Something that *feels* right. Even inviting. Something that channels affect into league with ethics and thereby serves as a lure.

What besides love has such potential to tangle us into relations exceeding self-interest—only because it can interest that self? For it always already begins to tease open, to materialize, the self's most mysterious desire. Its desire for what exceeds it. For the more-than-itself. Arising even under the most degraded and the most deluded circumstances, what matters more? Well, basic physical needs? Sure. The *more* that is needed often takes elementally material form. But what will motivate an adequate response when the needs of others exceed one's own? "Love" offers itself as answer to that question because the range of ethical motives itself needs motivating. Always and again.

Love: an ancient trope, endlessly passé, for that motivation of motivations. Its mattering lies in its making some thing, some one, else matter. An else, an other, always exceeding the self. And so it can never quite rein itself in. In base betrayal or high fidelity, it keeps self-exceeding. Desire for that other someone, something, overflows. Into everything. No matter what consciousness of that "everything" is in play. Such other-and-all-mattering has of course already enfolded in this book the signifiers of an ultimate mattering—the trope even more desperately degraded than love: God. It lives only when love escapes captivity and commodification. God the life of love, love the life of God. And occasionally, life the love of God. But one can, sometimes one must, reflect on love without naming any God. Sometimes that name strangles the life out of our love. Yet sometimes it entangles us in the amorous excess. But what it names works both ways unnamed as well.

Theo-logos does let the divine show itself in language, maybe even materialize *as* logos. Which is to say it means to dis/close God. And this without necessarily claiming any absolute or exclusive revelation through a one and only incarnation of True Love. To the contrary the love-command surely renders interfaith communication imperative. "Birds with Wings Outspread" therefore considers a passage from the Qu'ran. In our (species') now manifest planetarity, serious and open exchange of diverse wisdoms can no longer be innocently avoided. This does not blur their traditions into oneness. It does invite them each into their own unknown, into their own self-exceeding.

If there was something singular about the main historic signifier of embodied love, that two-millennium-old one, certainly it rendered love far from the merely private or personal. Love turned cosmic. And demanding. No matter what: The entanglements that constitute and exceed us won't stay hidden. They may be systematically or violently repressed, but they press back for recognition. Being recognized, the entanglements that make up the material relations of anything in the universe to anything else take on a fresh animacy. The intimacies of love are not canceled but ecologically edged with its infinity. That love can take divine names, it can go nameless. Its names matter only as actions. If amorous energies entangle us in a universe made of material enactments—well, how else would we matter?

9 / Amorous Entanglements

THE MATTER OF INTERCARNATION

If the Incarnation signifies for Christian theology the single event in which transcendence and immanence fused in a body, has its singularity tragically backfired?[1] The doctrine of the Incarnation soon presented itself as the exception that proves the rule: the ruling of the world by a supernatural sovereignty. In its—no, His—ontotheological over-and-above, he kindly condescends to intervene here and there, even as he summons his subjects to join him eschatologically in an ultimate transcendence of earthly matters. Of earth matter. Bound for heaven, no longer earthbound, Christians were to leave the economies and policies of the planet to the Lord (Son or Father), which is to say, to his sovereign representatives.

I have not thereby summarized the history of Christianity. I have offered a caricature of the betrayal of a messianic moment, that moment signified in the becoming-flesh, Jewish flesh, of a radical possibility. The betrayal was gradual, fitful, partial, taking place through the centuries, now millennia, beyond his death. It signifies a surrender to Caesar massive in its institutions religious and secular, insidious in its parasitism on the flesh and blood of its messiah, its *christos*. The baptized betrayal operates by means of the standard rendition of the Christ as transcendent exception. Yet to abandon the symbol of the Incarnation to its betrayal is to deprive the civilization indelibly and multiply shaped by Christianity of the symbol's originative, indeed original, meaning—that of an event performing not a supreme exception but a unique *in*ception. It insists on the enfleshment of the spirit, not on an exit from earthly materiality but on the embodiment of fresh possibility.

I am therefore tempted to transmute "the Incarnation" into the *intercarnation*. This would pit a relational materialization of immanence against the exit strategy of transcendence.[2] A spirited interactivity of bodies then decenters the singularity of one transcendent spirit becoming flesh. But such a binarism can hardly avoid performing its own exceptionalism. Perhaps then this: Let the intercarnation serve not as a rhetorical replacement but as a theological nickname for the ancient incarnation. As syntagma and as symbiosis, it recognizes itself as no exception to the history of Christianity, a history dense and furious with its own autocritiques and innovations. It may, however, recognize itself as hermeneutical inception. Intercarnation therefore lives mindfully and strategically from the Christian narratives of the particular incarnation. The particular, the different, unique—even the transcendent—need not signify the exceptional. We will discern a kinship between the interactivity of this intercarnation—in its God-relation—with what is sometimes called panentheism. Inasmuch as the latter performs a version of christology (and knows that it does), this intercarnate process remains faithfully contextual. That means it recognizes vast differences and delicate threads of continuity between the biblical context and the present one. Its messianic impulse calls therefore for enfleshment amid the material life and systems of the present context of the Earth.

In other words: An intercarnating theology cannot refuse responsibility for the capitalist/climate apocalypse that a christological exceptionalism has done much to fund. That version of incarnation has invested itself in a dynamic modern set of exceptionalisms: national, racial, sexual, capitalized, and all folding into the ever-renewed *human* exceptionalism that now poses the primary problem for the human future. This essay explores the political theology of this full spectrum of exceptionalism and seeks material, even so-called new materialist, alternatives. But rather than read exceptionalism as coterminous theologically with transcendence, I consider the tense and potentially creative relation of materialism's sheer immanence with panentheism's traces of a troubled transcendence.

Beyond and beneath every exceptionalist one-off, the intercarnation signals not mere opposition but up-close juxtaposition to the narrative of the single incarnation. For that One has always carried a potentiality immanent to Christianity and exceeding—transcending—the Christian sovereign exclusivisms: the possibility of a radical redistribution of divinity. God can therein be read as radically nonexclusive, inclusive of all that is: pan-en-theos. And therein gets redistributed all of the entangled materiality of the "heaven and earth" old and new.

Such a cosmos of entanglement endlessly precedes the life of Jesus and at the same time exceeds its Christian embodiments. The very "in" of the incarnation then signals an interactivity with all flesh, all materiality. The captures and incorporations of incarnation—*Christology, Inc.*—have always required imperial conversion. So I want to argue that the liberation of incarnation to its interdependence with all bodies requires something very like a political theology of the earth.³

The exception, *excipere*, that which "takes out," swerves in such a political theology into the inception. Then God can appear as all-in *(pan-en)*: a comedown from traditional transcendence! But this divinity is not coming down or in to an immanence whose radicality depends on the moment of a post-christian or post-theist takeout—a kind of transcendence of transcendence. Secularism can perform its own exceptionalist purism. Any intercarnational inception will appear far more impure in its movements between history and potentiality.

For in this time of accelerating climate-warming and earth-waste, there is no time to waste the endlessly echoing biblical outcry against the powers of oppression. "Tell old Pharaoh, Let my people go." The ancient possibility of a creation-honoring justice, of a revolutionary love, still trickles around the planet from Judeo-Christo-Muslim sources of prophecy. Might we recycle those hints more efficaciously? *Might we* actually *do* the "new creation," its justice, its renewal of the face of the earth? Initiate the messianic age? A hint of it, a beginning, a—perhaps last—chance? Of course, we do not know what to do, how to do it, and whether it will matter. It might make a little difference; it might seem futile amid the pharaonic globalisms. And yet our alternative interrelations, our local struggles and systemic attention, also reverberate across the planet—in material effect and in growing awareness. Might it be our cosmically overloaded terrestrial entanglement that turns the perilous interlinkages of our history, our context, our mutual immanence into places of planetary hope?

Hope, again, still? As I write (and harrowing elections come and go), we face the mounting improbability of stopping the planetary overheat. The transnational sovereignty of neoliberal capitalism holds the drivers of extinction in place. The crises of human injustice—race, class, immigration—distract even progressive politics from those few degrees of global warming. The improbable threatens to harden into the impossible. We seem to keep finding ourselves, selves of any or no religion, circulating in the ambience of the biblical Apocalypse turned apocapitalist. As time continues to run out, we (that facile pronoun, yes) may just keep excusing ourselves, taking ourselves out, *excipere*—either by way of Christian right denialism or of honest progressive nihilism. And so by default taking out the human future. Or? Is it possible—still, yet—to break through the determinism of most apocalypticism in a spreading *apokalypsis*, a dis/closive inception of our intercarnate planetary life?

Either way, we face the dense entanglements of a history from which there is no escape. The past lives in our moment-to-moment present. There is no exit from the entanglement of our becoming—in the immanence of that history to each of us, in our immanence to one another, as we permeate each other's futures. And in that future's *imminence*, which opens the perspective of the "to come." In its Derridean "messianicity" that coming comes indubitably invested in a certain transcendence: not in the optimism of escape or the miracle of intervention, but in a hope without guarantee; in the possibility of that other, unconditional condition or spectral *arrivant*, yet to come.[4] If that other would come from an eschatological exterior, it tempts us to view it as the pure alterity of an absolute difference, divine or—otherwise. Absolute otherness perches at the opposite pole, along the poststructuralist spectrum, to absolute immanence. The temptation to a transcendence that is pure otherness might be Abrahamic or it might be deconstructive. Indeed, the latter might read as an autodeconstruction of any presumption of pure transcendence. We might then reread *transcendire*, "going beyond," not as going up and out but more exactly as going *through* and only so *beyond*. And so, to come.

Inasmuch, however, as transcendence comes unbound—in the name of whichever ultimate—from the flesh of the earth, from intercarnational immanence, we might resist its temptation. For in its very transcending, its moving beyond, this "coming" iterates Walter Benjamin's messianic moment as "*ungeheueren Abbreviatur*": "monstrous abbreviation," the uncanny contraction of an immense, a perilously persistent, history.[5] It evokes a moment not outside history but of history's deep *within*. That inside opens to a beyond that does not take place (if it takes *place* at all) outside of its relations but only within new ones—relations to that material history, in its planetary diaspora, even its cosmos. In that contraction the moment performs a recapitulation of its world. And like the Deleuzian repetition with a difference, it exceeds what has been not by escaping it but by enfolding it—repeating it. But no repetition is identical to that which it repeats. The variation of difference, of course, endlessly differs as it unfolds.

From the impure perspective of that self-exceeding inside, one is no longer capable of the absolute *either* of pure immanence *or* pure transcendence. For the radicality of the "to come" springs from the *radi, the root,* of becoming. "Radicle" signifies the source of the plant's root. So the radical is not the pure but the root materialization of becoming, from which beginning repeatedly and differently takes place. The beginning shoots up from a root not as a vertical singularity but from a root system, or a rhizome, horizontally spreading, deep or shallow, in the ground.

In other words, if the messianic "to come," with its peculiarly attractive radicality of transcendence, is taken as separation from the mottled material practices of earthly becoming, it will continue to betray its own chances. Then it might as well stick with the one-off Christology, Inc. And the force field of earthly disregard initiated in otherworldly terms can thereby continue to waste the planet, and to do so with the sovereignty of its secularizations. It could indeed have the last word: the logos of the end of the world. Yet the theological option would have been—might still be?—to bring its christologos into resonance with all things earthly. Into an intentional relation to the *logos*, the *principium*, as it already everywhere unfolds. In all, *pan*. Its panentheism does not control but may intensify the creativity of our becomings. After all, John 1:2 does not read that all things "were created" through the logos, but *ta panta egeneto*: through the logos "all became..."

In contrast to an exceptionalist Incarnation and Second Coming, the "to come" might be read as the messianic call to, and calling of, our immanent becoming. That coming then marks its transcendence no longer as a supersessionist descent or a supernatural future, or as abstractions and extractions from the earth. In its "going beyond" it crosses historical, not supernatural, boundaries. Such transcending would signify precisely the transformative potentiality of immanence: the capacity of entangled bodily becomings to exceed what precedes them. In a language of political theology: They become sites not of the sovereign exception but of the possible inception.

An earth becoming that shoots vegetally up would not be ontologically alien to the *messianic coming* that in Walter Benjamin "flashes up." Then immanence becomes hospitable to a transcendence that ceases to evacuate materiality. It is no accident that a leading thinker of the new materialism, Karen Barad, opens the flashing Benjaminian novum into a current constellation of science, politics, and surprisingly, Jewish mysticism. Benjamin himself, tapping the sixteenth-century Isaac Luria's notion of the creation, fragmentation, and ultimate repair of the world (*tikkun olam*), read his Kabbalah through Marx. The work of repair requires an immanent praxis shot through with and made possible by the flashing up of the infinite from within the finite.

Here is the dramatic swerve Barad contributes: "*The messianic—the flashing up of the infinite, an infinity of other times within this time—is written into the very structure of matter-time-being itself.*" Conducting its political charge into contemporary crises of race, immigration, and climate, Barad wires this messianicity into her own game-shifting reading of quantum entanglement. Quantum "entanglements are not intertwinings of separate entities, but rather irreducible relations of responsibility. There is no fixed dividing line between 'self' and 'other,' 'past' and 'present' and 'future,' 'here' and 'now,' 'cause' and 'effect.'" Barad makes crystal clear that no reduction of difference to a single or a universal One arises from the nonseparability of the quantum ones. Entanglements are not a name for the interconnectedness of all being as one, but rather specific material relations of the ongoing differentiating of the world. Entanglements are relations of obligation—being bound to the other—enfolded traces of othering. Othering, the constitution of an "Other," entails an indebtedness to the "Other," who is irreducibly and materially bound to, threaded through, the "self"—a diffraction/dispersion of identity.[6] Here Donna Haraway's notion of diffraction supports Barad's dance with Derridean difference. "'Otherness' is an entangled relation of difference (*différance*). Ethicality entails noncoincidence with oneself."[7] Speaking of noncoincidence, my *Cloud of the Impossible* hosts a dense discussion of quantum entanglement, involving Barad and several other physicists who might count as new materialists (at least from Niels Bohr on) in their push beyond the mechanical immanence of the old materialism. Here let me just note that the quantum nonlocality hints at a spatiotemporality of such unfathomably—and instantaneously—interlaced becomings as to demand theological contemplation. What flashes up with messianic incipience exposes a mystical bottomlessness, Jewish and more.

In the tension of the becoming and the "to come," I am creeping around the question of panentheism: the all-in-god. Does it carry the radicality of immanence, or rather the authority of Abrahamic transcendence? As for the latter, "the sibling rivals of the family of Abraham" (A. O. Miller) intensify that authority in competition among themselves—and so at certain moments do seek to transcend their version of transcendence by mutual exclusion.[8] Panentheism, with its immanence of mutual inclusion, emerges in the cracks of that authority. It does speak for a living rhizome among the minority discourses, often but frequently not Christian, directly or indirectly related to Whiteheadian thought.[9] As a word, panentheism, marked by its "*en*," conveys its immanence explicitly. It therefore differs definitively from pantheism, which communicates an identity of substance more than a relation of nonseparability. Immanence requires a reality, divine in this case, which *all* are within, not one with which they are identical.

So, one could say that panentheism is more radically immanent than pantheism—if less purely nontranscendent. But it is precisely the pressure to separate itself from pantheism that can strip panentheism of its radicality. That separation may be a crucial rhetorical move vis-à-vis the institutions of monotheism. However, as we learn from Mary-Jane Rubenstein's splendid *Pantheologies*, the *"horror pantheismus"* has sustained a long theological habit of demonizing a barely extant constituency: whatever we are, we are *not that*, that pantheism, that confusion of God with world, worse, with Pan, the goat, that monstrous stinky hybrid of divinanimality. And that heresy—as Spinoza's accusers and excommunicators shuddered—claims "'that God has a body'—namely, the body of the world itself."[10] Pane*n*theism cannot mark itself off from that latter version of the heresy. Such different thinkers as Charles Hartshorne, Sallie McFague, and Ivone Gebara have, in that sequence, yoked their avowed panentheisms to the metaphor of *the universe as the body of God*. And McFague and Gebara do so as ecofeminist theologians, committed to decolonizing every kind of body. Yet that does not mean that for them the bodies of the universe add up to or become identical with divinity. In these varied voices the cosmic body of God is quite precisely distinguished from any simple unity of divinity and world. Such a reduction, by collapsing the zone of immanence—its *in*—into identity would disallow any relationship *between*. Identification precludes interaction. And these panentheisms all value relation over identity, substance, sameness, or unity.

So unless one's materialism dictates a simple identism of mind and body—not the case with Whiteheadian, ecofeminist, or new materialist bodies—God's having a body does not reduce divinity to a finite or bounded entity. Matter itself has morphed into a force field of materializations, of events of embodiment admitting of no final boundary of space or time. The vibratory indiscernibility of matter and energy in twentieth-century physics began in Whitehead to disclose not just its philosophical but its theological implications, effecting a universe of vibratory interrelation in which what is called God serves not as first cause, otherworldly exit or final terminus. As "the Divine Eros" of it teases forth new becomings and takes them in. This "initial Eros" signifies the inception as both novel beginning then divinely interiorized.[11] The mutual immanence of God and world thus reflects, indeed *exemplifies*—is not an *exception* to—the interconnectivity that characterizes all actualities as relations between multiple becomings, and only so as materializations.

"Every actual occasion exhibits itself as a process: it is a becomingness. In so disclosing itself, it places itself as one among a multiplicity of other occasions, without which it could not be itself."[12] Whitehead's actual occasion thus converts the enduring substance—*res cogitans* or *extensa*—of separable individuals into something radically other: the relationally constituted moments of becoming. This "becomingness" instigates a profound shift (not a transcendence!) of ontology. Relation is no longer external. It is a matter, indeed a materialization, of "mutual immanence" or of "internal relations" constituting emergent subjects (superjects), rather than a metaphysics of attributes possessed by substances. For Whitehead, every subject—quantum, queen, queer—experiences and responds spontaneously to the world in which it is entangled. Each process of becoming counts as an affective materialization of its cosmos. One might say each is an *abbreviatur* of its world. In other words, relation no longer signifies an interaction between beings that exist prior to the relation itself.

The resonance with Karen Barad's innovative language of "intra-active becomings" is striking. She has composed—drawing on a different, later, and largely Continental philosophy—a full-fledged "relational ontology" as the basis for her "posthumanist account of material bodies." These bodies do not appear as classical agents, merely *inter*acting with their objects from the outside. "Rather, phenomena are the ontological inseparability/entanglement of intra-acting 'agencies.'"[13] The cogent, indeed urgent, applicability of her "agential intra-action" to matters of climate weirding is close at hand. Her ethics of responsibility is built from the cosmological bottom up, by way of ability to respond, into human relations to the nonhuman. In concluding *Meeting the Universe Halfway* she asserts that "we are always already responsible to the others with whom or which we are entangled, not through conscious intent but through the various ontological entanglements that materiality entails."[14]

In other words, immanence would signify an agential mutuality of intra-action—not that of mere *inter*action between preexistent entities. For the actual entity takes place in the moment, the spacetime, of the becoming. This is different from immanence understood as an identity of all, or as a totality, or even as a single encompassing 'within' of the world. Its relational spatiality is itself being constituted moment by moment, here and there, everywhere. Only abstractions of itself can form a vessel-like immanence that would "contain" all becomings. So there would be actually nothing, or nothing actual, beyond this immanence. In this sense an immanence of mutual entanglement is more radical—more elementally constitutive—than an immanence of unitary inclusion, or of total identity, which would always already transcend its constituents. The Whiteheadian theology no more resembles such a unitary immanence than it does the opposite of a dualist transcendence.

Nonetheless, the panentheist deity does not lack transcendence. Hence, in Whitehead's chiasmic conclusion: "It is as true to say that God transcends the World, as that the World transcends God." Conversely: "It is as true to say that the World is immanent in God, as that God is immanent in the world."[15] And I hope it is clear that this is precisely not the takeout transcendence of metaphysical alterity but the transcending that is an exceeding, a going beyond, not as supersession—for the past is carried forward within it—but as the movement of "novel becomings." The divine as Eros provokes the transcendence, and then suffers and enjoys it, immanently relating to each becoming and to all together—in their mutual immanence. In any event of becoming, the creature transcends its past world as it will itself be transcended—in the next moment—by its future, and at the same time by a divine excess that flows in inverse relation to the immanence. A variety of process theological texts have made the case for the greater fidelity of this panentheos to the biblical legacy to be found in the dualistic versions of classical theism. And be it said that the process panentheism has for over half a century pursued its thought in rigorous service to the ecology of the earth. The process proclivity to activism finds amplification in the important engagement of Whitehead by strictly secular theorists associated with the new materialism, such as Jane Bennett and Donna Haraway, and more systematically, the political philosopher William Connolly.[16] They do not argue against the theistic language, which can quite readily be avoided.

There is, however, an argument against the panentheistic deity that comes from neither the new materialism nor classical theism or pantheism. I am thinking of the deconstructive discourse of the "to come" evoked earlier, in the Derridean sense of alterity, as supplemented by John Caputo in what he offers as a "theology of perhaps." "Panentheism says that God's existence is in ours and ours in God's. But in a theology of 'perhaps,' God does not exist; God insists, and it is our responsibility to bring about something that exists."[17] So long into the epoch of the "death of God," Caputo unleashes a nuanced provocation. Suspending the ontologically flat question of the "existence of God," his "insistence of God" takes on a truly suspenseful indeterminacy, inviting in the interactivity of its becoming. One might indeed be prone to read the all-in-God as everything existing within the givenness of divine existence. But Caputo may here have missed the key process or panentheist dynamism of becoming, in which there is no flat and given existence, not of any actual entities, creaturely or divine. There is only the process of intertwined actualization in a moment—and therefore no escape from our responsibility to realize, to actualize, divine possibility.[18] Caputo then goes on to make exactly the sort of argument against classical theodicy that panentheism has already made, (rightly) noting that the "hoary theological 'problem of evil' thus has nothing to do with all the choices that a sovereign omnipotent and omniscient God could have made but failed to make."[19] He makes this crucial case, however, as though it falls in line with his critique of panentheism, without acknowledging the nearly century-long Whiteheadian deconstruction of precisely that sovereign omnipotence.

On the same page Caputo announces that "the insistence of God is the chance that God can happen anywhere.... The existence of God is liable to break out at any time."[20] That outbreaking evokes a messianic eventiveness kin to Benjamin's and Barad's "flashing up." But his proposition fails to comply with his own announcement of God's sheer nonexistence. Rather, he is here suggesting an existence characterized by startling eventiveness, by an unpredictable, uncontrollable happening—but as, still, "the existence of God" breaking out. I am just pleading not for mere consistency but for this recognition: The "existence" of any bodies, in Whitehead as well, actually *exists* to debunk any straight ontological givenness or ontotheological existence. It is all about God and every other actuality, *happening*. The discourse is not of existence but of becomings, of actualizations. And this happening holds true also of God, whose "consequent nature" happens only in response to the world's happenings. Indeed, Whitehead performed nearly a century ago the deconstruction of any substantialist, self-identical presence, of any flat existence—of God or creature, of the mode of existence that Caputo (even if he wrongly projects it onto panentheism) rightly rejects.

Yet the process, like the ecofeminist, panentheism would do well to contemplate the following Caputan proposition: "The name of God is the name of an insistent call . . . that is visited upon the world, and whether God comes to exist depends upon whether we resist or assist this insistence."[21] No classical ultimate or first principle there. Consider that in Whitehead's *Process and Reality* the "ultimate is termed 'creativity'; and God is its primordial, non-temporal accident."[22] So startlingly—this God is not "the creator" but the first creature of creativity. In Whitehead, however, the dependence is not just upon specifically human constructions (as Caputo presumes).

God emerges in relation, in the immanence of mutual participation in and with all that becomes. So even if our species destroys itself, God would keep finding, by other names and with other critters throughout the universe, interesting modes of existence. And the aspect of God that precedes and exceeds the cosmos of bodies (the primordial as distinct from the consequent nature) does not in Whitehead "exist" as already actual but rather is composed of and proffers pure possibility. The chance of novelty at any given moment, amid the infinity of other times within this time, flashes up.

If panentheism remains in this way in tensive connection with the messianicity of deconstruction, it comes oddly close, from another angle, to the forthrightly godless immanence of Deleuze. The mutual immanence of panentheism does materialize something like the "plane of immanence" that Deleuze lays out as thinking itself. "Concepts are like multiple waves, rising and falling, but the plane of immanence is the single wave that rolls them up and unrolls them."[23] It would in this not accidentally mimic the enfolding *complicans* of all things in the divine infinite of Nicholas of Cusa; and its *explicans*, its unfolding, of all things "in and as the multiple." "God is in all things in such a way that all things are in God . . . as if by mediation of the universe. It follows that all are in all and each is in each."[24] The fifteenth-century Cusa, accused of pantheism in his day, is my prime pre-Whiteheadian ancestor for panentheistic immanence.[25] His enfolding/unfolding influence lies in the background of *The Fold*, in which Deleuze meditates on Leibniz—and in some depth on Whitehead. The thinking of the plane of immanence does not restrict itself to any thought, mind, or indeed epistemic register: It is "movement that can be carried to infinity."[26] Indeed, its moving immanence seems to signify, or to enliven, the intra-active dynamic of becoming: "One does not think without becoming something else, something that does not think—an animal, a molecule, a particle—and that comes back to thought, and revives it. The plane of immanence is like a section of chaos and acts like a sieve."[27]

Deleuze insists, furthermore, that "wherever there is transcendence, vertical Being, imperial State in the sky or on earth, there is religion; and there is Philosophy whenever there is immanence." However argumentative, philosophy happens among friends and, even in ancient Athens, as a "ground from which idols have been cleared."[28] This grounding immanence seems to perform its own transcending of all sovereign transcendence—in a moving beyond, a becoming exceeding any *fin*, an infinite movement in and through the molecules of matter and the geophilosophy of the Earth.

In the newer materialisms the Deleuzian influence remains fierce. Many forms of it operate in and out of the study of religion, but with little friendship with theology, as evidenced in the ecologically energized work of Brian Massumi or Timothy Morton. Yet the agonism is fruitful, inasmuch as it veers from antagonism, and with the help of such thinkers as William Connolly and Karen Barad, allows certain relations with theology to manifest on the plane of immanence.[29] For must that chaosmic plane not now show itself as *insistently* hospitable to the mutual entanglements of multiple religions and irreligions engaged in planetary projects of ecopolitical sanity? The mutual immanence, and so the (very immanent) self-transcendence it makes possible, demands crossings between multiple—Indigenous, interreligious, and also secularized—methods of religious practice.[30] Future vibrancies of the Earth in and through its human populations still remain—whatever anthropocene proportions of planetary life and elemental integrity will not be healed—possible.

And yet do we abandon what we recognize cannot be healed? Reflecting on why the call for new materialism has become urgent, Mel Chen lands "well beyond rejecting either secularism or spirituality," instead wishing "for an ethics of care and sensitivity that extends far from humans' (or the Human's) own borders." It is, she reveals, "in queer of color and disability/crip circles, neither of which has enjoyed much immunity from the destructive consequences of contemporary biopolitics, that I have often found the blossomings of this ethics . . . queerings of objects and affects accompanied by political revision, reworldings that challenge the order of things."[31] Her "interarticulate" reflection on her own unhealable dis/ability—indeed, usually what is termed disability is precisely not subject to remediation, to renormalization—has opened her to an attentive and fluid interdependence with the inanimate as the site of "mattering."

One can read Chen in proximity to the disability theology of Sharon Betcher and her pneumatological "prosthesis." With her brilliant call for "intercorporeal generosity," she unfolds an immanent ethics of the "obligation of Social Flesh." Under the sign of "the ruin of God," she writes: "By bringing persons close to flesh, one is reminded of the basic passage of a world of becoming, and we thus can begin to break through the Western effort to standardize the body, to value and offer status only to bodies so tightly normalized."[32] As the codes of the normalization of ability, of sexuality, of coloniality break down, great accompanying breakdowns become apparent. "As with earlier death of God or radical theologies, God here—in this disability theology—becomes ruined, emptied, that nothing-something, so that we are face-to-face with each other—with the sensual flush of sentience and its precarious vulnerability, its injurability."[33]

Increasingly Betcher shows how the metaphor and the practice of "disability" prepare us to deal with the growing urban and ecological damage of the earth itself.[34] In other words mindfulness of her crip/tography may help us to prepare for the difficult adaptations required on a feverish planet, with its mounting multiplication of disabled ecosystems. Such adaptations unfold within the flesh of a radical immanence, transcendence itself not elided but disabled, and perhaps rendered therefore capable of movement "beyond" the delusions of both a thinly outdated supernaturalism and an ever-updated normalcy.[35] What better criterion of intercarnation—as the very becoming of Social Flesh—than intercorporeal generosity? And what clearer incarnation of love? Minding our diverse disabilities, sharing our multiple capacities, this multibodied mutuality might even pull unlikely possibilities out of the ruins

Together with all the other ruins—all the dis/abled, denormalized, bodies of Earth, human and other—*theos logos* yields a precarious picture of the imminent future. Might it also yield a greater solidarity, if we can work our mutual immanence mindfully? The ancient eschatological future of the new heaven and earth emerged only amid unbearable injury. If its "to come" once carried the royal memory of Davidic anointment, its crucifixion has never stopped. Its sovereignty has gone to ruin. But perhaps its "weak messianism" (Benjamin) flashes up in new ways. (Even Deleuze and Guattari invoked the "new earth and a new people.")[36] When our plane of immanence unfolds toward such a future, a particular past comes enfolded. So then we must keep thinking with the Hebrew *hashamayim*, the heavens, not of a supernatural beyond or metaphysical transcendence, not a separate plane, but beginning with the first meaning, "sky," a watery atmosphere reaching out into the mysterious, darkly luminous endlessness viewed from the earth.

This new atmosphere and earth may be requiring in its shifting, subtle materiality a new atmosphere of us humans, on our discursive plane of immanence—an atmosphere of impure immanence in radical ecodemocratic alliance. On this plane ever new crisis will remain imminent, requiring a thinking that energizes rather than depletes the planetary future, that situates the future in an earth and atmosphere severely wounded, multiply dis/abled, partly ruined—and nonetheless not incapable of promising, animating, embodiments. Like the "multispecies becoming-with" of Donna Haraway, for which she proposes "Terrapolis" as "an open, worldly, indeterminate and polytemporal" place or plane. It plies not just any new materialism. "Terrapolis is rich in world, inoculated against posthumanism but rich in compost, inoculated against human exceptionalism but rich in humus, ripe for multispecies story-telling."[37]

As the multiply embedded exceptions fall away, incapable of such multispecies narrative, do surprising inceptions of responsible entanglement begin to take flesh among us? Even us humans? In its exceeding of old transcendences, in its immanence of new becomings, a panentheism of indeterminate creativity and embodied generosity may not cease—to come. Its terran intercarnation need not supercede the two-millennium-old event of the incarnation. Rather, freeing that event from the exceptionalism that contradicts its own messianic becoming, the flesh of the intercarnation entangles bodies ancient and emergent in its own amorous radicality.

10 / "Birds with Wings Outspread"

ISLAM, CHRISTIANITY, AND THE EARTH

How rare and refreshing it is to re-embed the encounter of world religions in the context of the living, material world.[1] That *world*—of manifold environments on our single planet—is being invited to come out of the background and into the focus of religious sensibility. As a Protestant systematic theologian, Jürgen Moltmann, has formulated the depth of the challenge: "The so-called great world religions will only prove themselves to be 'world religions,' when they become *Earth religions* and understand humanity as an integrated part of the planet Earth."[2]

Even after decades of ecological movement within these world religions, the challenge remains daunting. Particularly in their Abrahamic modes, these traditions have been nervous about their own earthiness, fearing it could lead to idolatrous nature-worship, pantheist naturalism, modern reductionism, materialism, atheism. But thank God (by whatever name you call upon Her, Him, or It) I do not, in the context of this conversation on nature, environment, and the world religions, have to make a case for the deep earthiness of our faiths. We can think from the shared presumption that the *world* of a world religion no longer refers simply to its universal outreach or truth claim. Its planetary reach now, as it always could and should have, signifies at the same time the ecological responsibility of our faith practices, theologies, and institutions. Religious pluralism now translates into ecological pluralism.

The participants in a conversation on religion's material context do not need convincing that the Earth—as the context of us all, as the world that we humans coinhabit alongside all those nonhuman others with which we are intimately interrelated—is characterized by rapidly mounting crises.

Even before various political pivots at once against democracy and environmentalism, we knew we were in trouble. As the ice melts and the seas rise, as the forests burn, the droughts intensify, the atmosphere and oceans are poisoned, and extinctions multiply as the food supply decreases, and we (*anthropoi*) continue exponentially to increase along with socioeconomic injustices and displacements—every religious resource we can muster will be needed. Even before the new wave of aspirationally fascist anti-immigrant politics hit much of the Christian West, we realized that migration, poverty, race, and xenophobia (which still disproportionately signals Islamophobia) can no longer be understood in abstraction from the effects of climate change.[3] So then how in particular might Christian theology work multireligiously, testing its eco-pluralism especially in this case in relation to Islam?

There are really just three points I want to make in this essay. I offer them in the hope that they help us communicate across our religions about this planetary crisis. Indeed, by talking together it is *hope* that we hope—the tautology unavoidable—to get and to give: hope for a planetary future that is worthy of the earthly, earthy, hopes of each of our traditions.

My first point here will be that the developing climate emergency should not be treated as a state of *exception* but as a now inescapable *emergence*. The legal notion of the state of emergency is driven by a politics, indeed a political theology, centered in an emergency power defined as the power of the exception.[4] Yet what if in fact multiple, distinct, historical exceptionalisms—the racial exceptionalism of white Anglo-Saxonism, the nationalist exceptionalism of United States power, the economic exceptionalism of global capitalism—propel the current emergency? These exceptions end up proving their *rule*. Here I focus on a very old, theological, and *un*exceptional interplay between an anthropocentric and a Christian exceptionalism.

The second point follows from the first: An alternative political theology is needed. And it requires an alternative to the sovereign power of the exception. But it would need to be an alternative capable of rising to the occasion of coming (and increasingly unexceptional) ecological catastrophe. The key to this alternative is characterized by what I have often called *entangled difference*. Here difference is to be read not as separation but as inseparable relation. If we are constituted in and by relations—good ones, toxic ones, unknown ones—then our very differences shape the interlinkages that make us up. This is true of individual, economic, ethnic, and, of course, species diversity. And in this conversation we attend particularly to this truth as manifested in religious diversity, whether we respect difference or practice a numbing indifference. In our interfaith reflection on nature, we may begin to consider that just as all creatures develop interdependently, so too, *naturally*, do our religions. This is the ecology of the creation: We are all in it together. This insistence may—if strengthened by our political theologies—help us face planetary catastrophes, to prevent them, if possible, and to adapt, if not.

So then catastrophe itself can here and now become a catalyst for transformation. That allows me to state my third point all too simply: If we ask what can turn catastrophe into a catalyst, the answer begins with hope. Without hope, no action, no planetary emergence from mere emergency, no political theology of entangled difference: so—no reason for hope. That tautology comes encoded in our sacred texts—particularly in the prophetic, messianically energized eschatological traditions. Hope, of course, is itself a deeply and problematically religious idea, one that is all too easily—especially, I confess up front, in Christianity—abstracted, pacified, supernaturalized and diverted from our shared earth futures. Conveniently, these distortions open the door to all manner of trivializing and colonizing secular optimisms. Indeed, hoping against hope.

Exception or Emergence

Let us consider the first thesis: that this unprecedented emergency should not be treated as a state of exception but as a now inescapable emergence. Exactly what will emerge is unpredictable. It will involve ecosocial catastrophe, no doubt, but how extreme catastrophe will be depends on global human response. Is the right image of the human response so far that of a car speeding down a mountain toward a cliff with still possibly just enough time to brake? Or rather, as many environmentalists now say, are we already off the cliff?

Climate change will intensify all manner of already existing conflicts and inequalities. It does not so much cause them as it inflates them. The example of Syria and the rise of ISIS was telling. In the context of five years of unprecedented drought and Assad's repressive response, the refugee crisis became dire. A broad anti-immigrant Islamophobia has been driving the electoral successes of right-wing parties in Europe. The problem is transnational. In the United States we are hardly done with the trumping of democracy and its inherent anti-immigrant and climate-denialist party politics. But there are also global signs of a fusion between a certain right-wing environmentalism, focused on overpopulation, with anti-immigrant zeal. One of the worst examples of this "green-cloaked nativism" was the terrorist massacre of forty-nine people in two mosques in Christchurch, New Zealand, with the perpetrator describing himself "as an eco-fascist unhappy about the birthrate of immigrants."[5]

The dangerously overlapping crises of ecology and immigration may be jointly considered in terms of political theology, in its rendition of the major concepts of modern politics as secularizations of theology. Sovereignty—defined, of course, in terms of the exception—is accordingly modeled on divine omnipotence. Political theology gets largely defined by the German legal theorist Carl Schmitt's work from the 1920s on. It centers in this proposition: "Sovereign is he who decides on the exception."[6] The exception reads as kin to the miracle—a novum that interrupts business as usual, with power both to make the rules and to break them. A medieval model of divine sovereignty thus translates into Western political exceptionalism. As its sovereignty derives from Christian supremacism, its force depends on the reverberation of the single Incarnation—the ultimate human exception.

If it is a Christian exceptionalism that has sanctified modern secular models of imperial sovereignty, we could track its effects on the circulation of Anglo-Saxon racial exceptionalism, of US exceptionalism, its American dream, and its manifest destiny, and of the neoliberal global capitalist pantheon of the exceptionally wealthy.[7] But for the sake of the present interreligious focus, note particularly how this exceptionalism unfolds in a thousand-year arc of crusades. It begins with Pope Urban II in 1096, with an aggression meant to bring European powers to a new unity: "Let those who have been fighting against their brothers and relatives now fight in a proper way against the barbarians" (Turks and Arabs).[8] With this prototype of Schmitt's politics of friend versus foe, Muslims could then be endlessly framed as the perfect enemy. Fast-forward almost exactly one millennium to Bush I's declaration of a "new crusade," soon echoed by Bush II in his war on "Islamofascism."[9] The latter powered up a coalition Islamophobically united in the interests of big oil and the sovereignty of neoliberal capital.

As Giorgio Agamben had earlier argued, the state of exception—he was minding international laws concerning prisoners—insidiously became the rule. He recalls the camps, the *lager*, of the Second World War, and he gestures simultaneously toward the proliferation of new camps: the massive refugee camps recently inflecting the political landscape of Europe.[10] But neither Agamben nor other interpreters of political theology were yet attending to the *ecological* context of such mass immigrations and subsequent dehumanizations.

Nonetheless, once one perceives the connection of various waves of Islamophobia—waves both religious and secular—to a founding Christian exceptionalism, one might wonder: Does climate change not remain peripheral to such political theology? Or might one begin to recognize that what is enabling climate catastrophe is at root another effect of the same old

Christian exceptionalism? But this time it is taking the explicit form of our *species* exceptionalism: the notion of the human as not just markedly different from other creatures, not just uniquely talented, but as the supreme exception—Man, as the denaturalized creature who transcends the material interdependencies of the Earth. And now of outer space as well.[11] The exceptional status of Jesus as the Christ folds out of and back into cutting edges of this human supremacism.

Ecology of Religions

A second thesis: Creaturely interdependence constitutes the content of the alternative to the politically theological exceptionalism—and so to the anthropic exceptionalism that claims holy legitimacy. Isn't that anthropocentrism after all based on the very first chapter of what for Jews and Christians is sacred text? For decades, Christian ecotheology has been returning to that narrative of the creation of the human in the image of God. Some come to question the sacrality of Genesis 1.26–28, as it grants "dominion" to humanity to fill up and subdue (*kabash* in Hebrew) the earth. Its citation has endlessly justified the modern Western domination project. But if the text is read in context, other ecotheologians argue, dominion can only mean environmental "responsibility." After all, what God declares "very good" is not the exceptional human but rather "everything that God had made" (Gen 1:31): the whole Genesis collective, what Lynn White in 1966 dubbed "the democracy of all God's creatures."[12]

If "to except" means at root "to take out," the *imago dei* does not then mark us as the *exception* to the creaturely collective. Rather, we arise as its communicative *exemplification*. Our distinctiveness is here indubitable: We are created in *imago dei* to partake of God's creativity, called to exercise our creativity with stewardly care. Thus the papal eco-encyclical amplifies it: "to till and to keep the earth" (Gen 2.15), not to exploit and to waste it. And so certainly the Christian countertradition that hears "the cry of the poor, the cry of the earth" has evolved an alternative to the economic, political, anthropocentric exceptionalism of Western civilization.[13] Pope Francis was explicitly calling all humans, no matter what religion, for the sake of *all* inhabitants of our "common home."

Quite consistently, the theological traditions that emphasize the gift of creaturely diversity do tend also to recognize the gift of *religious* diversity. Interfaith relations and ecological relations both express a deep—an ontological—relationalism, as is clear in the half-century contributions of process theology, for example, and of ecofeminism. I chose to study with a Christian process theologian, John Cobb, first of all because he taught that it is not just secular liberalism calling Christians to begin to learn from other religions. It is Christ (as the logos of "creative transformation") calling—not just to conversation, let alone to conversion, but to a mutual transformation of religions. Cobb's comparative focus was on Buddhism. In the background, shadowed by the Holocaust, lay already a depth of Christian-Jewish dialogue. More recently, with a particularly strong movement between Christianity and Hinduism, the "comparative theology after religion" of John Thatamanil teaches a "comprehensive qualitative orientation" that in its capacious relationalism embraces the multiplicity of theological traditions.[14]

As for process theology, it was no coincidence that Cobb's comparative work came accompanied by the ecotheology of which he was already a prophetic progenitor (*Is It Too Late?* in 1972). Whiteheadian cosmology lent itself both to a radical relationalism of creatures, let alone religions. We pluralist Christians have, however, not come far in recognizing how much we may yet learn from our sibling religion Islam, precisely to help us overcome the Christian anthropocentrism. The Islamic Declaration on Global Climate Change (2015) offers an apt and timely entry point: "If we each offer the best of our respective traditions, we may yet see a way through our difficulties."[15] Consider this citation it offers from the Qur'an: "No living creature is there moving on the earth, no bird flying on its two wings, but they are communities like you" (6.38). That captivating evocation of the importance of animal communities resonates with the biblical Genesis, whose every creature is "good." But the Qur'an adds something of crucial importance: Birds, bees, bears—these are not just creatures, but communities of them, as are humans. This endows nonhumans with a developed register of relational complexity and, therefore, of social dignity.

This citation follows: "Surely the creation of the heavens and the earth is something greater than the creation of humankind, but most of humankind do not know this" (40:57). I know of no sacred text of Christianity that directly and pointedly names the whole cosmic context as greater than the human, and also largely unknown to be such. And subsequent Christian creation theology has tended to treat the creation of "the heavens and the earth" as something like the background for the creation of us exceptional ones—or as our magnificent container. Hence, indeed, that the heavens (sky, outer space, and extrasensory abode) and earth are actually counting as *greater* in the relativities of the creation than us imago-bearers—this has gone, indeed, unrecognized. Yet such a Qur'anic sweep of cosmological grandeur does not diminish human uniqueness. But the text in a flash undermines human exceptionalism.

The Qur'an forges a new sense of *tawhid*, a unity of peace that is not sameness but honors difference. This is what, in *Ecology and Islam,* Abdul Aziz Said and Nathan Funk call "peace in Islam," rendered then as "ecology of the spirit."[16] Ibrahim Ozdemir, speaking for multiple Muslim environmentalists, lifts up the following gorgeous passage:

> Don't you see that it is God Whose praises all beings in the heavens and on earth do celebrate, and the birds with wings outspread? Each one knows its own mode of prayer and praise. (And God knows well all that they do) (24:41–42).[17]

May I respond: Don't we see how this text says something terribly fresh? It echoes old Hebrew psalms of trees clapping their hands, of all the earth worshipping the Lord. "Let everything that has breath praise the Lord" (Psalm 150:6). But the Islamic text makes the pointed claim not only that all beings praise but that they *pray.* In context (don't you see?) the prophet's emphatic acknowledgment undermines our sense—our standard Christian dominion-sense—of being the exception before God. And as there can be no *image* of Allah that is not idolatrous, there is no *imago dei* of the human. So the prophet's poetic iconoclasm frees prayer itself from anthropocentric talk-talk-talk into a mode—or rather a great earthly multitude of modes—of communication with God. A God who "knows well all that they do" and evidently cares. Might we want to relearn such cosmic attunement from the birds now, as we spread our wings to face the consequences of our species' predatory and increasingly self-destructive narcissism?

Put abstractly, the alternative to sovereign exceptionalism can be couched as entangled difference. Our differences do not get diminished. Rather, they get situated—sometimes exaggerated, sometimes opposed, sometimes downplayed—within our webs of interdependence. This relationality echoes that of quantum entanglement, the physics that attests to the instantaneous "intra-activity" (Karen Barad) of all things, at the most minimal material level of the electron, across any measurable distance whatsoever.[18] Recognizing that all relations are relations of difference—that however much we differentiate, decide, and separate, we can never quite extricate, that indeed at the most basic material level we remain ontologically nonseparable from our universe of relations—keeps us thinking cosmologically. Perhaps even praying. And the creation turns us always back to our own spatiotemporality, to our planet and its ecology of badly frayed but inescapable relations.

Entangled difference applies as much to interfaith exchange as it does to intercreaturely ecology. Do I become less Christian if I learn more from Islam? No. My Christianity just gets more complicated—folded together with the faiths of others. It was folded together with Judaism and with

Hellenism from the start. Every new dialogue enables a mutual enfolding. Not a homogenization. In Christianity this pluralist potentiality is brought to light by the early Renaissance Nicholas of Cusa, who (almost alone among Europeans up to his time) studied the Qu'ran and who called for a religious peace based on awareness of divine mystery. His epistolary text, *On the Peace of the Faith*, claims urgently that we cannot "know God" in such a way as to exclude the truths of other wisdom traditions.[19] In *Cloud of the Impossible*—Cusa's metaphor for the unknowability surrounding the divine—I borrow from him a mystical language of enfolding and unfolding: the divine *complicatio* and *explicatio*. All is enfolded in the divine, read as an infinity beyond knowing, from which all—including necessarily all religions—unfold. No one, and also, pointedly, no one religion, cognitively masters God. The divine infinity is everywhere, and therefore unfolds in different ways, according to different perspectives, exemplified in diverse religions. I find Cusa's argument from 1453—forged then in the face of the catastrophe of the Ottoman defeat of Constantinople and the intense Islamophobia it provoked—still remarkably timely. It lends ancestral help in constructing an interreligiously Christian theology.

So, Jesus? He can be read as the embodiment of a love that seeks to materialize in all ways, in all creatures, in all prayers. The gospel then helps us who are Christians to challenge the notion of the single, ontologically exceptional Incarnation. Christ, we might say, reads not as the supreme Exception but—following the medieval Abelard—as the great Exemplar. What of John 14:6, the bane of religious pluralism? "I am the way, and the truth and the life." This verse gets routinely mispronounced as, *I am THE way, THE truth*. In context, however, the text has nothing to do with other religions (not even Judaism, which is anyway not yet understood either as a "religion" or as an "other"). He was reassuring his disciples, who were expressing fear of losing their way if he, as he is hinting, suddenly dies on them, that they will not lose their way. For they know him, and therefore they know this way. He had entangled them in his life—a life that exemplifies the path they want to stay on. As example, it opens the path to them. Such exemplarity is thus more faithful to the text than any Christian exclusivism

If Christ is for his followers the way, he exemplifies for us a path of radical hospitality and respect for the stranger, a path that branches much later into interfaith exchange and to the repair of the earth. That is the work of resistance to the approaching "barbarism" threatened by democratic and climate collapse: the persistent, shifting labor of just love.[20] It is perhaps not far from the way of an ecological *tawhid*. Which is not to say it is the *same* way. The point is not to impose homogeneity upon diversity of religions, let alone species, but to entangle our differences mindfully. In the urgent *tawhid* of solidarity.

If we can systemically interweave our religious diversity with our remaining ecological diversity—that is, if we can fold our very human religious diversity into attention to the nonhuman heaven and earth—our species may just have a chance of a viable future. An ecology of religions then enlivens the ecology of the planet. Of course it is a chance needing to be yanked from the jaws of emergency. So then let us insist on a new collective emergence. It would be the way of a political theology of the Earth.[21]

"Sweet and Verdant"—an Abrahamic Ecology

Third thesis. or at least hypothesis, which responds to the question: How do we shift climate catastrophe into catalyst? Hope, I re-repeated above. Not optimism, not denial, not despair. Without hope, *nada*—*nihil*, nihilism. We will surrender to the seductions of consumerism, the intensities of more immediate crises, or the paralyses of despair. Even such attempts at interreligious exchange as the present one will seem futile. But what does hope hope *for*?

Hope as a normative value, as first of all a mode of perception, has its origin in biblical texts.[22] It names divine intention "to give you a future and a hope" (Jeremiah 29:11). It comes from the prophetic tradition of the novum: "I am about to do a new thing, now it springs forth, do you not perceive it?" (Isaiah 43:19). So the novum must also not be confused with the exception, which will only reinforce the hopeless rule of the same old sovereignties. This hope is for a transformation of the heavens (*hashamayim*—the atmosphere) and the earth, for a radical renewal of everything, of the whole genesis collective.

The great textual danger those of us who find voice within and between the Abrahamisms must address may come down to this: the pull toward a passive reliance on omnipotent power that, with an occasional miraculous intervention and providential planning, keeps it all under control. So when we trash the Earth, it must be God's mysterious will. Then we hope for a supernatural takeout—lifting us up to heaven—rather than for the renewed atmosphere and earth. Such exceptionalist hope is the very hope we must hope against. For as Moltmann put it, exactly half a century after *The Theology of Hope*, "We have no need to leave this world behind in order to look for God in a world to come. We only need to enter this world with its beauties and terrors, for God is already there. God waits for us through everything that God has created, and speaks to us through all of the creatures."[23]

The ancient prophetic writings of hope all took place in the face of historical crisis. Of them the book of Revelation may be rhetorically the most extreme.[24] John's hallucinogenic vision outs the total destructiveness of a power-hungry world empire, offering in great detail the economics of its global trade: the "cargo of gold, silver, jewels, and pearls, fine linen . . . olive oil, choice flour . . . horses and chariots, slaves . . ." (Rev 18:12). The apocalyptic trauma however does not end, as rumor would have it, with the end of the world. "The end of the world" is not a biblical production but a later discursive reduction. The book actually ends with a renewed, highly and graciously urbanized, New Jerusalem of a planet: "Let everyone who is thirsty *come*. Let everyone who wishes take the water of life as a gift" (22:17). In our epoch of expanding drought and toxification, this aquatic grace carries new meaning. And it reverberates in a different eco-spiritual register—not of a standard "world religion" but an Indigenous one—with the chants of Standing Rock Sioux demonstrators: "*mni wiconi, water is life.*"[25] They were not quoting John of Patmos. They share with him a common source . . . sometimes called life.

Tragically, the biblical text itself turns *Gift* into poison (its German sense) when it feeds fatalism, antagonism, and human helplessness. The profound shrinkages and insecurities of the world religions then add an edge of desperation. Perhaps ecosocial catastrophe can become catalyst only if we read our apocalypses through the prophetic exemplifications of justice, mercy, of unity(*tawhid*). Then, even amid the terrors of the Earth, we may know ourselves—known. Called. The prophetic tradition works beyond theism, as in, for instance, the text of Naomi Klein, *This Changes Everything: Capitalism vs. the Climate*. Like Pope Francis a year later, Klein revealed for an immense public, and in a spirit of disarming hope, the interplay of environmental and economic degradation:

> [I began to understand how] climate change—if treated as a true planetary emergency akin to those rising flood waters—could become a galvanizing force for humanity, leaving us all not just safer from extreme weather, but with societies that are safer and fairer in all kinds of other ways as well. . . . It is a vision in which we collectively use the crisis to leap somewhere that seems, frankly, better than where we are right now.[26]

The relation Klein envisions between ecological and economic struggles remains even now—if in no way reassuring—promising. And what is that galvanizing force of which she speaks but the hopeful catalyst that can shift emergency into creative urgency? "Now or never," as she insists more recently.

An oddly analogous relation to that between ecology and economy obtains between global warming and religious difference. It is a relation that has the toxic potential to mix antagonisms and fuel the fires of planetary apocalypse. Alternatively, in an interconnectivity become mindful, we can galvanize our interreligious and our intercreaturely solidarities. This broad coalitional possibility will necessarily involve political resistance to predatory capitalism. So then a catastrophic triple jeopardy becomes a triple hope. This is the way that a political theology of the earth would tilt economic, religious, and ecological crisis toward new beginnings. Crisis becomes the site not of mere emergency but of improbable emergence. If crisis exposes our delusions of independence and control as self-deception, new modes of earthly collaboration might become actually possible, and possibly actual: through cooperation among and beyond religions, broadened into earthly conviviality among and beyond humans.

Too hopeful?

Perhaps. But the following words ring true. The Islamic Declaration on Global Climate Change concludes with a Hadīth related by Abu Sa'īd Al-Khudrī:

> We bear in mind the words of our Prophet (peace and blessings be upon him): The world is sweet and verdant, and verily Allah has made you stewards in it, and He sees how you acquit yourselves.[27]

And as Saffet Catovic, one of the co-authors of the Declaration, put it in aptly down-to-earth language: "With this climate change issue, especially these last two years, religious leaders around the world are not praying against each other, they're praying with one another for a common cause. Because the realization has set in that we're gonna have nothing left."[28] In awareness of the odds, and nonetheless or therefore in the hope of creative creaturely solidarity between our faiths, for the sake of our common home, I pray with you today. With wings outspread.

11 / Animality, Animacy, *Anima Mundi*

TOWARD AN AGE OF ENLIVENMENT

When we ask what does, what will, continue to matter, no matter what, and if our question arises in view of planetary degradation, and if we don't give up the question for its reckless overgeneralization—at least we know what the answer is *not*: matter abstracted into lifelessness.[1] Inert matter. While the deadening will, of course, keep funding its own commodification, dead stuff fails to enliven ecological interest, let alone action on its behalf. So in the circuit of thought and practice, won't the materiality that actually animates our interest be best served, best serve itself, if we regularly, rhythmically, take note of its own animacy? Without fear of being accused of animism?[2] Animacy all the way down, around, up.[3] The animacy of matter itself, its movement all around us as animal, and—at an odd theological angle—even as the anima of the world.

It is primarily as animals in relation to all those other animals marked as nonhuman that we become attentive to the animacy of our shared existence. And the boundless life of plants grows continuously into view. But the primary carriers of climate change are the emissions, temperatures, atmospheres, oceans—all marked as *in*animate. So I wonder if alongside presumed natural inanimacies the quite lifeless abstraction of those few degrees of temperature, of all climate statistics, works to numb and deanimate public demand for mattering actions. That would be a tragic and hidden side effect.

Might it be that our planetary future—if we are to enjoy such—depends on a rereading of our animality, indeed on the enlivenment of human animality as not only an instance of multispecies life but as an expression of the Earth's elemental vibrancy? And more broadly, as broadly as breadth goes, of the animacy of matter itself?

The present reflection will first consider the animal in its transdisciplinarity, by which animality in its materializations of race, gender, sex, and religion is observed in the standard animacy hierarchy running from the inanimate on Up to Us. Second, as boundaries between animate human, animal, plant, and inanimate creatures soften into a broader ecology, the question arises of the animacy of materiality itself—what Jane Bennett so influentially invokes as "vibrant matter."[4] Then in a third section, this question spirals (beyond her firm atheism) into a meditation on the metaphor of the *anima mundi*, the soul of the world—a world thereby coded as the animal body of God. And if we elude smoothing the animacies into some reified neoanimacy, might we hearten the chance of a fully animate future for all of us animals, even the chance of a chastened Age of Enlivenment— the possibility that solemnly diminishes as the planetary temperature rises?

Animalizing

I was grateful recently to co-teach a seminar on Religion and the Animal.[5] My ecotheology had earlier been somewhat overgeneralized vis-à-vis nonhuman creatures. Its attention to climate change has been lacking (rather typically of the genre) their specific liveliness, indeed their embodied animacies—whether they are the charismatic mammals of the land, the fluid and flighty denizens of sea and air, the buzzing creatures of the so-called Insect Armageddon.[6] *That* name, meant altogether entomologically, inadvertently hints at a new relation of the animal to theology. But we need not return now to the Apocalypse itself. Its metaphoric resonance with attention to how extinctions lead to many ends of many worlds remains inescapable.

David L. Clough's two-volume systematic theology unfolds a magisterial contribution to the theology of the (nonhuman) animal.[7] In communion with both Karl Barth and Paul Tillich, Clough insists that the doctrinal theology of his study is "primarily driven by an ethical question: what should we do in our relationships with other creatures?"[8] With unprecedented compass, he develops a rigorously Christian understanding of animals by way of the doctrines of creation, reconciliation, and redemption. *Imago dei* becomes a call "to take responsibility for other creatures," cannily decrypted as the very opposite of its familiar deployment to justify a dominion of misuse and indifference. He works out the future in quite traditional eschatological terms—the terms of a post-death animacy repudiated almost automatically by most ecotheology—and thereby solicits strong biblical and theological support for the inclusion of nonhuman animals in an ultimate bodily resurrection. Clough's interdisciplinarity involves examples from biology or empirical study (such as Jane Goodall) that illumine his doctrinal argument, which builds on surprisingly affirmative references to the theological importance of nonhuman animals in sources such as Augustine, Aquinas, and Luther. He reminds us that John Wesley, for example, in interpreting the "groaning of creation" of Romans 8, claims that "the whole animated creation waiteth for that final manifestation" and "shall be delivered."[9] And as a thinker methodologically close to the indubitably anthropocentric Karl Barth, Clough demonstrates how "Barth is disconcerted by the lack of fit between the anthropocentrism he has just set out and the accounts of creation present in Psalm 104 and the closing chapters of Job."[10] For purposes of altering the relations of Christian publics to the nonhuman, Clough's doctrinally and biologically engaged approach to the challenge of animal futures makes an invaluable offering.

The present theological endeavor takes a tinier but broader approach. The human/nonhuman animal relation demands that we think also along vectors not just interdisciplinary—but *trans*disciplinary, such as designated by gender and race studies. Varieties of inter-*human* oppression habitually presume and deepen what the scholar of sex, gender, and ecology Mel Chen calls the "animacy hierarchy."[11] For our seminar it was key to spiral back to a pathbreaking work for the connection of feminism and animal studies, *The Sexual Politics of Meat: A Feminist-Vegetarian Critical Theory*.[12] It was as a *religion* scholar that Carol Adams performed this unprecedented 1990 exposé of the degradation and exploitation of animals operative in the animalization of women—women then rendered as the projected passive "meat" for male consumption. The woman and the animal serve as "absent referents" in a civilization of systemic violence toward both. Contrary to most earlier feminism, she did not seek to deanimalize women but rather to emancipate both human and nonhuman animalities. Ecofeminist theologians, disproportionately Roman Catholic (from Rosemary Radford Ruether's crucial "ecofeminist theology of earth-healing" to Elizabeth Johnson's response to Darwin's evolutionary challenge to Christianity) would move with more explicit theological arguments to empower this feminist solidarity with animality.[13] This solidarity of fellow animals.

In another register of animalization, the civilizational association of nonwhite races, most flagrantly those of African descent, with the beasts has enabled Western modernity. With particular historical force it has fed the affects of US white supremacism, justifying the institution of slavery on the model of the captivity and exploitation of animals and persisting in this century as a political force for the dominion of and by the white

Christian right. So with "they're like animals" still circulating—usually but not always unspoken—in the US, most antiracist work must deal with the animal primarily by exposing its degrading projection upon Black humans.

For, of course, race, like gender, sexuality, and other identity snarls, must not now be collapsed into just one "issue" among others. It is all the more impressive, therefore, to witness an emergent, highly nuanced transdiscipline of antiracist animal theory. Zakiyyah Iman Jackson demonstrates that "anti-blackness is actually central to the very construction of the 'animal' that recent scholarship wants to interrogate and move beyond."[14] To do that, however, those fields must question their own frameworks. She shows how key African American, African, and Caribbean works of literary and visual art generate conceptions of being and materiality that creatively disrupt a presumed human-animal distinction—the binary that persistently reproduces the racial logics and orders of Western thought. And with the self-described "Queer Black Troublemaker and Black Feminist Love Evangelist and an aspirational cousin to all sentient beings," Alexis Pauline Gumbs, the resonances of animality and Blackness poetically cross the planetary waters, teaching by analysis and example how to "listen across species, across extinction, across harm."[15]

This register of racializing animalization is also developing within religious studies, as Carol Wayne White unfolds her argument that the projection of a vile animality onto African Americans cannot be culturally healed without involving racial, animal, and gender eco-ethics—as spiritually inflected.[16] Thus she analyzes the work of Ernst Haeckel (1834–1919), the zoologist who coined the term "ecology" and counts as an indisputable father of the movement. At the same time his theory of polygenesis, with his notions of evolutionary hierarchy locating people of African descent closest to apes and dogs, came embedded in a wider theory of German racial purity.[17]

As whiteness continues to warp our species' rendition of Earth's cross-species animality, it would seem that the denial of our own animality requires human scapegoats, often gendered or racialized as other, upon whom to project the repressed human animality. Our *humanimality*. Theologically speaking, its systemic repression works in tandem with the oblivion to what some of us have called *divinanimality*—the very animacy of the creation, as our last section will suggest.[18] But with or without theology: To do justice to the complexities of the *human* social world demands understandings of the animal and *therefore* of the human that deconstruct the operative animacy hierarchy. In the meantime the denial of our animality works hand in hand with global capitalism to drive the sixth mass extinction event, . . . the first in 65.5 million years.[19] About a million species are on track for extinction in the coming decades. Perhaps one third of the birds, a quarter of the fish, a half of the mammals . . . Oh those stats. And we animals who are driving the extinctions? Does the fantasy of technosupremacism, if not posthuman virtuality, relieve us of our animal precarity?

Animate Materiality

If the human world—whatever escapes to metaverse, outer space, or supernatural heaven it imagines—has its animacy only as part of the planetary ecology, our habitable future (*s'il y en a*) will depend on a systemically awakened humanimality. But our relations to other animals come inseparable from the entire ecology. Therefore, we live entangled not just with the slower liveliness of plants but with myriad creatures that do not normally count as animate—like the CO_2 molecules that drive both plant life and global warming. So I am wondering how to keep our sense of animacy—now tuned to and by our own animality—circulating through all the *nonanimal* animacy of the Earth.

One example of such guidance is offered by biologist Merlin Sheldrake's irresistibly readable *Entangled Life*. Note its subtitle's relevance to the matter of the human future: *How Fungi Make Our Worlds, Change Our Minds & Shape Our Futures*. Fungi, we learn, are a form of the microbes that cover every inch of the planet. They are considered neither animals nor plants. Each square inch of topsoil contains several *yards* of fungal filaments (take in that "abstraction"). Fungi also inhabit, mostly harmlessly, every bit of our own bodies. Plants depend on fungi to provide them with nutrients from the soil, such as phosphorus or nitrogen, in exchange for energy-giving sugars and lipids produced in photosynthesis—the process by which plants use sunlight to convert carbon dioxide into energy-rich organic compounds. In other words, "Plants are socially networked by fungi. This is what I meant by the 'wood wide web.'"[20] The relationship between plants and fungi gave rise to the biosphere as we know it and supports life on land to this day. Sheldrake narrates his mounting astonishment as a young biologist as he realized that life is "full of intimate collaborations," of close relationships between supposedly unrelated organisms. They "prompt us to think in new ways about what it means for organisms to 'solve problems,' 'communicate,' 'make decisions,' 'learn' and 'remember.'"[21]

Sheldrake does not evade the planetary implications: "Some of the vexed hierarchies that underpin modern thought start to soften. As they soften, our ruinous attitudes toward the more-than-human world may start to change."[22] He came to realize that "to talk of individuals [as separate substances] made no sense anymore. Biology—the study of living organisms—had transformed into ecology—the study of the relationships between living organisms."[23] In other words, if we are to undermine the dualism not just of human-animal or animal-plant but of living-nonliving, then reading the relational ontology of these fungal microrganisms, not animal but animate, helps to earthily animate ecology from below. Animating our sense of animacy serves the wood-wide and world-wide web.

Let us now pull back from this fungal focus to view that ecology as habitat Earth—as living room, as a space for living that is in some sense itself alive. The Earth itself takes on a fresh and energizing animacy, beyond modern notions of nature and of matter. The scholar of religion Clayton Crockett writes in *Energy and Change* that "Gaia is a fitting name, but not a proper name of Earth. Gaia is a secular name or figure for what we are used to calling Nature."[24] But Nature has been the deanimated Other of the culture/nature dichotomy of modernity. Crockett's eco-energetics materializes as an earth-binding "cosmotheology." He shows how in league with Isabelle Stengers's Whiteheadian cosmopolitics, Bruno Latour reads Gaia as "composed of agents that are neither *deanimated* nor *overanimated*."[25]

Theories that overanimate stem from an oversimplification of planetary life as that of a single organism, and count for Latour as a scientifically irresponsible kind of holism. Ontologically, Latour emphasizes, Gaia is not a unitary whole, not a closed system: "It is made up of agents that are not *prematurely unified* in a single active totality."[26] In other words, his Gaia names neither an entity nor a being divisible into parts, but a complex process of terrestrial genesis and generation. And of potential, perhaps even political, regeneration. With Isabelle Stengers he avows commitment to—in her words—"resisting the coming barbarism."[27] These variously animated earth-agents constitute the matter of the Earth, including the detotalized, nonseparable elements of matter—or of, as Latour prefers, *materiality*—itself. So then in this form of materialism that is still quite new, relative to modernity, the animacy hierarchy tumbles all the way down. Differences between creatures, between species, do not reduce but rather strengthen the reading of all materiality as animate. And in the interest of such a reading, let us regularly remind ourselves that arguments for matter's animacy posed highly developed alternatives to the modern status quo all along. For instance, Bennett's *Vibrant Matter* converges on the following line of thought from 1787: Johann Gottfried von Herder, in his enlivening critique of Kant, would put an end to all the objectionable expressions of how God, according to this or that system, may work on and through dead matter. Matter is not dead but lives. For in it and conforming to its outer and inner organs, a thousand living, manifold forces are at work. The more we learn about matter, he shows, the more forces we discover in it, so that the empty conception of a dead extension completely disappears.[28]

Tragically, for whatever will follow modernity, it was instead just such scientifically rich recognition of the liveliness of matter that—almost—disappeared.

Bennett's transformative theory of vital matter offers a fresh "thing power": the notion of all bodies as "actants," none merely acted upon. Her writing of an "animal-vegetable-mineral-sonority cluster" investigates the agency of bodies as clustered within "assemblages." Assemblages name "groupings of diverse elements, of vibrant materials of all sorts . . . living, throbbing confederations that are able to function despite the persistent presence of energies that confound them from within."[29] She finds in these interdependent actants what Latour calls a "slight surprise of action," where appear not mere actor-subjects or acted upon objects but events. So the agency of assemblages human and otherwise operates always with an edge of indeterminacy and in "a world of vital, crosscutting forces."[30]

Bennett draws out the implications of a physics or metaphysics of such vibrant materiality for political theory. "The political goal of a vital materialism is not the perfect equality of actants, but a polity with more channels of communication between members"—members human and nonhuman. Such a polity is readily related to Latour's "parliament of things."[31] Bennett's political ecology of things concludes with

> a kind of Nicene Creed for would-be vital materialists: "I believe in one matter-energy, the maker of things seen and unseen. I believe that this pluriverse is traversed by heterogeneities that are continually doing things. . . . I believe that encounters with lively matter can chasten my fantasies of human mastery, highlight the common materiality of all that is, expose a wider distribution of agency, and reshape the self and its interests."[32]

Amen to her creed's challenge to the standard creed's Almighty patriarchy of mastery. But the challenge must go further. It must demand not that Christian theology disappear (as she might reasonably prefer) but that it work to liberate rather than to supersede or block the matter-energy of the Creation. And, indeed, I would add, of the Incarnation.

God Matter(s)

To sneak a further hint of divinity into the force field of the new creed, Alfred North Whitehead, as a recognized source of the new materialism, offers an opening.[33] Not unlike Herder, it was because new physical revelations of the vibrancy of matter—specifically its breaking into quantum vibrations—called to this leading mathematician that he shifted fully to the work of philosophical cosmology. It is not that all so-called actual entities, or occasions, the ontological spacetime units of Whitehead's universe, are in the biological sense alive: not "overanimated." But they are certainly not underanimated, let alone inanimate.[34] Each actual occasion comes entangled in its relations; it *feels* ("prehends") its entire world acting upon itself, and in becoming itself, acts upon its world. Such feeling is usually unconscious but never without some awareness—and that slight surprise of the indeterminate. So one can say that each actual occasion is indeed animate, though not technically organic. "Life cannot be a defining characteristic. It is the name for originality, and not for tradition. . . . Life is a bid for freedom. . . . It lurks in the interstices of each living cell."[35]

In his later work Whitehead directly troubles any boundary between "organic" and "inorganic." In the 1938 *Modes of Thought* one chapter is titled "Nature Alive."[36] This pan-animacy emerges directly from the cosmology of interdependent becoming characteristic of every quantum of matter-energy. In other words, the vertical animacy hierarchy collapses here. Or more precisely, it dissolves into the oceanic relationality of becoming—without leveling the vastly divergent layers of complexity and intensity within and between actual entities. Again differentiation is not reduced but required by this relationality. Creatures all come constitutively entangled in their differences from each other. The creation unfolds in countless throbs of entangled difference, endless repetition tinged with surprise.

But for our discussion of animate futures, what does theology have to say, beyond squirming to get loose of the old Master of all matter? Particularly, what does the Whiteheadian glimpse of deity contribute? The lively movement of Whiteheadian process theology—largely shunned by conservative divinity schools—indeed, by a broad spectrum of Christian orthodoxy—persists in its God-inflected cosmology.[37] Without wandering far into Whitehead's vocabulary of primordial and the consequent natures of God (which I do in Chapter 7) we may suggest that God works in the world as lure, or initial aim, to future becomings—indeed, to more animate futures. Each lure's content is a possibility, possibility that lands, like the proverbial sower's seed, differently in each actual occasion of becoming. Actualization aims at intensification. "God's purpose in the creative advance is the evocation of intensities."[38] We might consider animacy a metonym for that intensity of experience—not for a particular level or category of life but for the vibrancy of creatures. In every event. Of their mattering. So the divine lure works in this cosmotheology not by imposition of design but inspiration of creativity—or else it can't work. It guides not by powers of control but by seeds of persuasion. Which often fail to take root.

And in Whitehead this animacy of the universe also contributes to the intensification of God's own experience. There is an interanimation between creator and creature that belies the standard unilateral divine action. It whispers its affinity with ancient metaphors of *ruach* vibrating (*meherephet*) over the face the waters, of creative collaboration of creatures with creator, who calls the sea and earth themselves to bring forth (Gen 1). So the "it is good" reads, then, not as divine self-congratulation, but as delight in the creativity. A genesis in which this God takes part—becomingly.[39]

Hence, the tragic force of the title of the German process theologian Julia Enxing's book, which updates Genesis: *And God Saw That It Was Bad*.[40] One version of Whiteheadian thought draws, as does Enxing, on Charles Hartshorne, who reads the world as God's very body. But to imagine the world as God's body is not to equate God with the world. Process theology can be called panentheism, not pantheism.[41] And if God then signifies the soul of the world—it is also not by way of an infinitely magnified soul-body dualism. Rather, this divine animacy lives inseparably, if it lives, from the life, the animacy, of the world. "In this sense," as Matt Segall elegantly frames his *Physics of the World-Soul*, "although the community of finite organic occasions makes up the unity of the Cosmic Animal, the latter [for Whitehead] 'is not a static organism'; rather '[it] is an incompletion in process of production.'"[42]

Animal Mundi

So do we have with the recent discussions around animacy a refreshment of the ancient *anima mundi*? Not an image I (or theologians in general) have done much with. Yet this conversation draws it forth irresistibly. I have, however, been intrigued with how in the fifteenth century Nicholas of Cusa offers the image of the cosmos as an animal. He is drawing Plato far from any stereotype of dualism: This is the Plato according to whose "likely account" in the *Timaeus* the cosmos comes into being as a "living creature."[43] For Cusa, this creature, this animal-cosmos, resembles a living organism or body animated not just, he clarified, by a secondary anima immersed in it but by "God as its soul."[44] So this divine anima of the world is *God* unfolding—*explicans*—in a universe-animal that can meaningfully be called the body of God, a cosmos where each creature is said to enfold—*implicans*—the universe, and therefore God. "Because all things are in all things, God is in all and all is in God." Cusa is reading soul not as a substance inherently independent of body but as the animacy of individual animals and other creatures; and at the same time as their aliveness in the animacy of the divine itself.

In this cosmo-theology the omni-animate deity cannot be flattened into pantheism. The creatures never add up to their creator, who enfolds them in an infinity that always exceeds comprehension—and any totality. For such panentheism the God in whom all *is* comes at once radically differentiated and inseparable from any and all creatures. Cusa translates the medieval "cloud of unknowing" into the "cloud of the impossible"—a fresh apophatic strategy of intellectual humility that provokes brilliantly novel, indeed scientifically prescient, insight. (His discernment that the Earth is not the center of the universe precedes Copernicus by a century, for example.) So his world-soul is not merely and opaquely unknown. Rather it animates startlingly fresh, proto-scientific knowledge even as it escapes cognitive mastery.

Perhaps in order to elude the substantialist separability of "soul" from its matter, *anima mundi* is better translated as "animacy of the world": God then signifies the very animacy of the world animal. Some theists may worry that, despite Cusa's clear sense of the apophatic infinity, such divine animacy reduces God to mere immanence. It surely does intensify intuitions of the immanent divinity as Spirit, not just as a third Person, let alone as a lower manifestation of God, but as Godself. Yet in this mysticism God cannot unfold into the dynamic multiplicity of the world animal without the dark reverberation of the groundless infinity, the transcendent excess, of the divine unknowability. But transcendence, insistently, does not mean separation. That infinite creativity, like Paul Tillich's divine abyss, does not admit of division from anything else—and certainly not from the anima mundi as the animacy of (not the same as) the *animal* mundi.

Practically speaking—tugging the mysticism of the anima mundi into the fragile life of the present planet—a divinity will not fix things for us. Christians, in particular, need to let each other know this. This divinity is both too apophatically transcendent and too constitutively immanent, to be called in as our emergency repairman. Or depended on even for the final fix. The repair of the world, *tikkun olam,* is, as it always was, in large measure up to us. To us in the fullest sense—in cocreativity with the creation and knowingly or not, with its creator. But in our time, with climate change advancing beyond repair, we are likely to despair of our species' will, let alone capacity, to meet this greatest of challenges.

Does any alternative to the deanimating spiral of despair, numbness, and indifference now not require a reanimating vision—which will take spiritual, philosophical, aesthetic forms? But then, of course, the public and political enactment of the vision needs incarnation: It needs to be enfleshed.[45] It aims at material embodiment. Personal, interpersonal, communal, and systemic. Which is to say it needs nothing short of the energetic transformation of the political economy of our present global assemblage.

Last Dance

Impossible? Or perhaps we can feel—right there where the darkness turns unknowable, mysterious—the animating force of an incarnation (an incarnativity?) that invites, that needs, that enables, our participation.

If so, we recall, despite its doctrinal encumbrances and escapes, that incarnation means first of all, and for each of us, enfleshment in and as animal body. I am trying to hold close the realization that the animals that you and I *are* remain collectively vibrant only as we recognize our kinship first of all to the nonhuman ones. Across all our wild and entangled differences. Only so can the animal that the world *is* live more fully in and as us. Those nonhuman animals mediate the animacy of the nonhuman universe—fungi, flora, and fauna, and finally every quantum of energy of which the world is assembled—to us as also ours. Our own not to own but to join. And to incarnate.

Then theologically speaking, the animal mundi may dance more vibrantly with the anima mundi, the cosmos with its own spirit. And our species' animality, our humanimality, then may be glimpsed circulating through our own divinanimality. Despite our "best" efforts, however, we—we the species—may finally betray that life of the Earth. Terminally for us, if not for the planet. But then we also betray the anima of the universe, the very spirit of life. Original sin thereby grinds down drearily into final sin. But the apocalyptic window has not shut yet. It still dis/closes . . .

The animating creativity of an alternative calls out to us, singly and together: to repair our relations to the other animals, including the other humans, to all the animate life that assembles us as a cosmos, a living world. And the more *other* those humans, as well as those other creatures, the more animating the work. From the tormented bodies of our own species come forth still unknown gifts of courage in the face of what we do not know , how to face. And as we repair relations to groaning Gaia, to the entire genesis collective, to that universal, perhaps multiversal world animal—only so do we heal our relation to its anima. Which was, will have been, at work, in this repair all along. Never doing it for us, only and always enlivening its possibility.

12 / Dear Young Theologian

It feels like the right time—the right stretch, saeculum, or time of many times—to write this letter.[1] Theology, when it does not abstract itself from context, comes into its own in times of crisis. It carries resources for any scale and variety of apocalypse. Through the throb of decades, I remain grateful to work with a discourse that, without sacrificing ancient depth and evolving breadth, insists on addressing the realities of shifting crisis, local and global. As I write, a global pandemic lingers,[2] a European war and a Middle Eastern one persist, the longer-term planetary challenges of democratic fragility, white supremacism, immigration, and destitution insist. As you read (sadly, I know this) the encompassing calamity of a compromised climate creeps and surges, ever more visible and still dangerously hidden.

In the face of such challenges, theology, unlike the academic disciplines muted by sense of irrelevance to the crisis, does not stay silent. Contextual, political, and ecological forms of theology meet these shifting menaces with a discourse of responsible meaning and action. But before we can assess any theology's responsiveness to collective crisis, do we perhaps need to pause, pivot, and respond to the crisis of theology itself? Of its viability as a discourse and a practice? Its fragility, existential and institutional, personal and planetary?

Oh, that.

I prefer to get on with the creative work, with its meditative and its timely demands, rather than assess the long-term viability of Christianity, religion, God-talk—theology itself. I have dedicated a life to theology, it has meant a live practice, a discourse that pulses in waves of social change (for me, initially antiwar protests and the women's movement) and currents of transdisciplinarity. Not just discourse between, *inter*, disciplines but pushing *trans*formatively beyond the academy.³ A discourse that makes waves of its own, sweeping up from a mysterious depth. Not its death. Some unknowability that tinges all that we know. In its shadows I have been endlessly surprised by the fresh gifts of ancient metaphors. The vibrancy of theology—pastoral, philosophical, or prophetic—has over and over taken me off guard. In its resistance to stale orthodoxies and aggressive certitudes, it tugs me into its polydox potentiality as well as its mystical darkness.⁴ I want all that for my students and rediscover it with them. I wish it for you.

This vibrancy has presumed a world, even a community, in which theology has work and home. Once on this journey, I was fortunate to keep finding versions of church and of academy where theology is understood to be a necessary, living, and progressive voice. So there has been institutional support offering ever-fresh permutations of an ancient history of context-based scholarship. Beyond theological schools and seminaries, the critical engagement of theology in many secular institutions committed to the study of religion(s) also bears rich fruit. Yet religion departments, nervous about confessional bias, uncritical belief, or offense to academic secularism, cannot usually provide a home for theologians. As a live process and not just an object of analysis, theology has continued to depend on institutions widely, indeed wildly, varying but rooted in some denominational tradition, and involved in the education of clergy.

There is, as I write (and as you read), no way to be confident in the future of such theologically hospitable contexts. One cannot altogether ignore statistical trends. Decade after decade, the stately processional of established religions marches on toward demise. The well-endowed elite of theological schools may persist indefinitely, as may their rich and reactionary opposites. Others struggle on, with varying degrees of creativity and viability. This scene hardly provides assurance of a livelihood for any young(ish) theologian reading this letter. The murky prospect of professional insecurity must be noted. I have for many years reminded myself to address it with prospective PhD students in theology. Not to advise against the study of theology, no, not at all. The point is to undertake it with mindfulness of the professional improvisation such uncertainty may entail; to cultivate flexibility in formal self-descriptions (you may be a theologian, a philosopher, a scholar of religion, or some combination, depending upon context);⁵ and to keep vocational options diversified. Forms of research, teaching, and practice can extensively vary and intersect practically. Practices of ministry—hugely diverse—may or may not be involved. Fortunately, such variation expresses not just a pragmatic professional ploy but the animated dimensionality of theology at its transdisciplinary best. And in the presumptive honesty and humility of its calling.

So then I also want to say: Theology has often endured institutional vulnerability, as in the face of persecutions, first under the Roman Empire, and subsequently under conditions of interreligious antagonism. And even more, the centuries of modernization, requiring few direct proscriptions, have steadily marginalized religion as such. Autobiographically, I have only known Christianity as fragile—which indeed made my involvement possible. As someone from a childhood of family dysfunction and instability, I had to learn to thrive in certain temporary margins, to grow from the ever-shifting unknown. The kind of theology I found, accommodating of a certain chaos, invited self and world transformation, not institutional security. Of course, it also wanted relatively stable support for radical change, which the developing margin of liberal-progressive Christianities has offered. Vastly much transformation has happened, and swiftly, rising on the tides of the great movements against racism, sexism, heterosexism, war, classism, ecological suicide, movements enacting—however unconsciously—the transformative spirit of the prophets, of the gospels. The Spirit of creation itself. This dissident creativity has in many cases strengthened the attractive power not just of theology, but of the schools and congregations enlivened by such multifaceted metamorphosis.[6] Not necessarily, however, of their endowments, denominations and numbers.

The statistics of institutional religious vulnerability, not unlike those of climate change, have not on the whole relented. (Still the case, no?) They cannot predict definite outcomes, but they do portend defining dangers. The language for the deep stakes of this threat to theology itself is hardly new. The rhetoric finds its longest and strongest expression in the tradition of the death of God. For, of course, what else can the faltering and fading of so many institutions and discourses of *theos-logos* mean? It is the *theos* of these institutions, the God whose churches are failing, who fails with them. The prophet of the death of God, Friedrich Nietzsche, was not celebrating but recognizing this death. Declaring that it is "we who killed him," he was anticipating the dire consequences of such metaphysical violence.[7]

Nietzsche's contemporary and friend for a time, Richard Wagner, narrated this death in the final opera of the *Ring of the Nibelungen: The Twilight of the Gods*. He cloaked the demise of divinity in the ancient Norse myth of Ragnarök. The music irresistibly celebrates with Brünnhilde the death of the divine and the human patriarchs who betrayed her. The twilight of *those* gods, *those* guys, becomes the end of history. She sets on fire not just their corpses but their world. As the ring is returned to the mermaids dancing in the watery depths, a new world becomes possible. It is tempting to read the death of God in the light, the dramatic twilight, of such a nineteenth-century fantasy.

A death of *His* institutionalized apparatus, *His* all-control, the power projections of two millennia of Western Civ upon Him. The death of *His* world, not *the* world. One need not, and I do not, read any such vision as the death of all possible facets or faces of divinity. And so of any plausible logos of theos. The mytho-philosophical death of God may have been, may still be, the *sine qua non* of some improbable rebirth or resurrection.[8]

Still. Truth be told, you young theologian: For all its modernist iconoclasm, the death of God always felt *old* to me. Its theological prophet Thomas Altizer was a member of a church I attended on my own in junior high. I bumped into the *Time* magazine cover "Is God Dead?" at my local drugstore in September 1966. *Radical Theology and the Death of God* was piled high in the bookstore window.[9] Only when two decades later I began teaching at Drew's Theological School, did I learn that Altizer had participated in academic conferences there in the '60s, in conversations among many hermeneutical experiments in theological honesty. Again—this death that briefly defined "radical" theology, and sometimes still does, has long felt not uninteresting but old, like a flashy but faded white male drama. I did not and do not celebrate the death of "His" legacy and institutions, only of their deadened and deadening patrimonies. I could not have done any theology outside of the liveliness of a concrete alternative, both to that Western history and to its defining death.

And the sense of an alternative—an improbable and really possible alternative—does not fade. Even amid the secularizing dregs of the Enlightenment lurks still the possibility of an Age of *Enlivenment*. If in some unpredictable version it were to happen, it would not be, I suspect, predicated upon the atheism signaled by God's death, even as undersigned by much radical theology. Nor will it come down to a reprise of any older theism. It might, however, owe something to the wide varieties of radical theology, which greatly exceed any death-of-God dogma.

There are many clues to such a possibility. None of them is quite adequate, and most refract some hint of ancient and yet still coming epiphany. The possibility shimmers in all the colors and sexes and species of a liberating theology—even of a cosmology soaked in the sacred waters of all that is, that was, that is becoming. That All whispers an unspeakability of "God"—an ancient *apophasis,* letting you know that you do not know, a speaking as you cannot. Its darkness shines upon so many historic Ways, intersecting and diverging, sometimes brusquely, ways also to open theology experimentally into its future. For me the half-century pathway of process theology was crucial, sometimes called panentheism: all-in-God. That One *in* whom "we live and breathe and have our being" (Acts 17:28). One that enfolds the multiplicity of the all and unfolds it otherwise, and so can never be simply and self-samely One. In its pneumatological breathing it enlivens all creatures, peoples, ways . . . If we will only catch that breath.

Sometimes one may recognize its Nazarene materialization, its enactment of revolutionary love.[10] And that ancient embodiment helps to land truths from every other spiritual tradition, Abrahamic, or Asian, or Indigenous, or emergent, not blurring into unity but into fresh intercarnation of that All.[11] Hints may come from ancient orthodoxies, for which "God became human so that the human can become God." Or from an old, forbidden pantheism, sensing divinity utterly everywhere, or from a fresher pantheology, insisting not that all *is* God but that nothing divine can be separated from its creative manifold; or from anatheism and its "God after God," in infinity and in the infinitesimal; or from a God spectral but insisting; or from the varieties of panentheism, all things flowing into and out of a theos ever becoming[12] And then also come the fresh flashes of race, sex, gender, class, and ecological liberation embodiments, ever intersecting and pressing.

These all lack the dogmatism of straight theism or atheism. And, by the way, they all lend a Way to honor, not repress, your sometimes deep-down doubt. Your uncertainty about the very Existence. These too many clues do at the same time keep you (and me) mindful of the intuitions, breaths, glimpses, you get of the meaning of it All. Not a totality or finality of significance, but perhaps: some hint of meaning-fullness meeting us on occasion here, now, on the ground—and all the while escaping our grasp.

Meaning does not reduce to knowing. Nor does theology mean knowing God. That *logos* signifies a meaning never captured by knowledge and therefore inspiring ever new understandings—as long as it is not *mis*understood as certainty, a meaning that does not put an end to your quest, does not silence your big questions. Even in its Christic form, that logos will not harden into final Answers. Its plenitude wants testing, realizing, loving, actualizing, and altering. And so you might permit theological constructions—recognized as experimental, evolving—to ripen in you. Requiring your nurturing, your pruning. Your making.

For if theology is to live it will be as a constructive art. "Constructive theology" (a twentieth-century evolution of the eighteenth-century term "systematic theology") does not make God up. It does not fabricate a deity out of nothing, *ex nihilo*—nor out of fear of nihilism. But it takes responsibility for the human, contextual, effect-and-affect-rich work of theological language. It knows itself as the effect of imagination and practice, of aesthetics and ethics, of tradition and of novelty. It may even imagine that something very like what we (still sometimes) call God takes some unknowable part in the construction. And if its logos does not yield certitude, it may lend confidence—*con/fides*, a fidelity with, in relation.

But in the meantime, even enlivened by a relational confidence, many of the vulnerable institutions that host such conversations keep becoming more fragile. And without them, who will facilitate needed new works of iconoclasm and of creative iconoplasm? Who will teach the skills of theological history, homiletics, and debate, the practices that enable reformation of our religious bodies and transformation of our world bodies? These bodies, collectives theological and planetary, are ailing. They are in varying degrees of crisis.

Eerily—but perhaps not surprisingly—theology and the planet are ailing together: the worlds of religion and the bigger worlds they inhabit: social, political, ecological worlds. The sufferings are not merely parallel but entangled: Any honest theology knows itself interconnected with those bigger worlds and accountable for them. So does some advantage, some dark grace, emerge in this *con-fides* of togetherness? Can the fragility of our God-talk help us address—with the courage of an honesty born of grief, of losses already suffered and losses still to come—the fragility of our larger worlds? Even the vulnerability of our shared planet?

We do not know the future of theology or of Earth. Yet we may be confident that at least some form of theology, even if it would seem unrecognizable to us as such, will be. Perhaps it is becoming already, there in the margins of our uncertainty, our struggle, our hope. We can guarantee no future for a particular form of ecclesia, of religious gathering or teaching. We *can* work to assure that in whatever materialization, the best of theology, the most just, the most loving, the most All-embracing will persist in forms that we may not be able to predict. And this work counts, because it lets our present breathe into an open future. To live mindfully in the present, to wrestle with its challenges, lets us affect possible futures and effect better ones. No matter their improbabilities.

So it is with the planet, now, when we do not know what futures are possible for our species. Just as there will be some sort of spirituality, of religion, of theology, there will be some sort of Earth-world. But the great ghost of human extinction sits on the horizon. Or (not much better) the specter looms of a small percentage of humans, primarily of the class and race whose economy brought on climate change in the first place, surviving in some bubble at the expense of all the rest. I won't indulge here in apocalyptic prognostications—except to (re)(re)remind us that *apokalypsis* does *not* mean The End of the World. It means "unveiling," therefore "revealing"—both of our civilization's pattern of destruction, trending suicidal, and of the possibility of transformation by confronting the pattern. Uncertain disclosure, not know-it-all closure.

A certain Christian misreading of apocalypse abounds in late modernity. It sets up a movement of all time from a point of creation from nothing, through a Christ climax, on to The End, omnipotently predetermined to reduce "this world" to nothing. That linearity takes overtly fundamentalist, softer liberal and sublimated secular forms. So as a theologian, I have found little work more important than deconstructing that destructive timeline—and reconstructing the time of creation as an open and creative process.[13] The theos of such a logos, such a Word, calls us to make the best possible choices under our so very varying circumstances. Us one-by-one and always also together. To choose the better possibility in, say, the case of climate change, will not mean returning to some prior norm or normalcy. Yet we humans can—with a big enough "together"—still choose to alter the relentless course of ecosocial destruction. We might still get on course for a world of revitalized and reconfigured local communities, vibrant with solidarity across and within the life of the Earth. And theologically we must keep repeating: Humans cannot make that choice if we hold out for an omnipotent solution either by supernatural intervention or supersecular technofix.

Your life and work, dear young(ish) theologian, will matter: not in *spite* of the crisis of theology and of its material world, and not *because* of it, but *in* and *through* it. What if the creative logos of that theos is right now trying to materialize in you—your work, your voice, your way? The proverbial sower sprinkles tiny seeds, randomly it may seem, but so very many of them. They may fall on rocky ground, into thorny chaos, or onto a path with no soil. Our ways may keep us distracted from new possibilities, confused, numb, or hopeless as to their potential. Our certainties may prove groundless. Our uncertainty may read like an evasion of the truth of doom. Yet the very unknowing can open into earthier ground. Might a seed of possibility be germinating there? And now another? And . . . ?

No matter what,
Catherine

Acknowledgments

The twelve chapters of *No Matter What: Crisis and the Spirit of Planetary Possibility* arose from a variety of engagements and meditations, all situated in recent history. They express an urgency characterizing this period: "this" period, this holographic present, broadly conceived. These essays all take part in the work of what still, if precariously, lives by the name of theology. Nonetheless, if their no-matter-whatness signifies a sense of ultimate concern, such concern does not necessarily or easily reveal its object as "God"—that now barely possible name. Yet a theological thread does hold these diverse reflections together. Planetary ecology and situated politics materialize toxic religious backgrounds as well as prophetically spirited possibilities. It matters, therefore, that theology work with fresh effectiveness against its own entrenched deformations. In that spirit, these essays share the complex original meaning of the Latin *concerno*, at once to distinguish and to relate, to decide and to mingle, to "sift" differences together. And that means here and now to acknowledge the improbabilities of the better possibilities that are at stake.

To sift these essays into a single text is already to perform such differential relation. And that could happen only with the splendid support of my editor John Garza. Of course, to acknowledge the gifts of his indispensable collaboration is also to thank Fordham Press for this publication. It comes within a long string of books, most of which take the form of fourteen (and counting) volumes of the Transdisciplinary Theological Colloquia series based on conferences at my home institution. Indeed, whatever I attempt theologically comes inseparably related to the marvelously diverse faculty, leadership, and students of Drew's Theological School. I am particularly grateful for the involvement of Drew doctoral students. I especially thank my research assistants over the period of this volume's emergence: Dan Siedell for his efficacious and collaborative curation, Carolina Glauster for rigorous support at the edge of possibility, and then J. D. Mechelke, for swift management of the vagabond demands of a late round of editing.

The essays of this volume beg the acknowledgment of endlessly more interlocutors, casual or formal, long ago or recent, than can be typed here. But I must name a few whose initiative remains sine qua non to specific essays in this collection. Deep gratitude pulses across the planet to Zairong Xiang for his solicitation of the second essay, and to Kseniia Trofymchuk for the courageous Ukrainian zoom conference that yielded the third. Part Two has significant dependence upon ever-friends Clayton Crockett and Tom Oord. For the last Part, let me acknowledge Muhammad Shafiq for his vital interfaith work; Julia Enxing for the rich Dresden conversation behind Chapter 11; and for the final bit and its epistolary frame, Henco van der Westhuizen.

As to truly last rounds, the actual run to the finishing line, thanks go to Teresa Jesionowski for her superb editorial refinements.

Amid and beyond it all, I take not for granted but for keeps the musically loving support of Jason Starr.

Notes

Introduction. No Matter What:
Crisis and the Spirit of Planetary Possibility

1. Second wave feminist theologians intensifying awareness of the body and its broader ecology include Rosemary Radford Ruether, Judith Plaskow, and Elizabeth Johnson. See also my first book, *From a Broken Web: Separation, Sexism, and Self* (Boston: Beacon Press, 1986).

2. Catherine Keller, *Face of the Deep: A Theology of Becoming* (New York: Routledge, 2003).

3. Now however many billions of exoplanets we know of, we are failing to know the Earth, at least in the biblical sense, as "Adam knew Eve." It does not seem that our current astronomy, decentering the earth as one among many planets in our galaxy and a gazillion in our universe, has done the life of the planet much of a favor.

4. See Keller, *Face of the Deep*, 7.

5. Jürgen Moltmann, *The Spirit of Life: A Universal Affirmation* (Minneapolis: Fortress Press, 2001), 161.

6. The "inception" pitted against the "sovereignty of the exception" (Carl Schmitt), particularly against white exceptionalism. See "Political: Sovereign Exception or Collective Inception," chap. 1 in Catherine Keller, *Political Theology of the Earth: Our Planetary Emergency and the Struggle for a New Public* (New York: Columbia University Press, 2018).

7. "Musky," here referring to the billionaire, who as Mary-Jane Rubenstein puts it, "infamously wants to 'save' humanity from its bondage to Earth." Mary-Jane Rubenstein, *Astrotopia: The Dangerous Religion of the Corporate Space Race* (Chicago: University of Chicago Press, 2022), ix.

8. Rubenstein, *Astrotopia*, 181.

9. Sylvia Wynter, "The Ceremony Found: Towards the Autopoetic Turn/Overturn, its Autonomy of Human Agency and Extraterritoriality of (Self-)Cognition," chap. 8 in

Black Knowledges/Black Struggles: Essays in Critical Epistemology (Liverpool: Liverpool University Press, 2015), 244.

10. Timothy Snyder, "Ivan Ilyin, Putin's Philosopher of Russian Fascism," *New York Review of Books*, March 16, 2018.

11. Alfred North Whitehead, *Process and Reality: An Essay in Cosmology*, corrected edition, eds. David Ray Griffin and Donald W. Sherburne (1929; New York: Free Press, 1978), 343.

12. Amy Sullivan, "America's New Religion: Fox Evangelicals," *New York Times*, December 15, 2018.

13. Thomas Jay Oord, *The Death of Omnipotence and the Birth of Amipotence* (Grasmere, ID: SacraSage Press, 2023).

14. John D. Caputo, *Specters of God: An Anatomy of the Apophatic Imagination* (Bloomington: Indiana University Press, 2022).

15. Lucille Clifton, *Good News about the Earth* (New York: Random House, 1972), no. 11.

16. Lucille Clifton, *Mercy* (Rochester: BOA, 2004), 74.

17. The expression of and reflection on grief, a close and necessary companion to a non-privatized love, is crucial for life in climate crisis. See Britt Wray, *Generation Dread: Finding Purpose in an Age of Climate Crisis* (Toronto: Alfred A. Knopf Canada, 2022). See also the work of two of my former doctoral students, Marion Grau in Oslo, Norway, and Jacob J. Erickson in Dublin, Ireland. See Grau on performances of grief: "Extinction Rebellion and the Ritualization of Climate Grief: Performing Species Loss and Putting Climate Justice on the Agenda," *Counterpoint: Navigating Knowledge*, October 20, 2021. And Erickson on grief and magical thinking: "A Climate Grief, Observed: Transforming Our Ecologies and Theologies of Magical Thinking," *Berkley Forum*, Berkley Center for Religion, Peace, and World Affairs at Georgetown University, April 16, 2020. Erickson is at work on a book manuscript, "*Climate Grief and the Theopoetics of Planetary Feeling*," that will offer a robust reflection on this lamentably pressing topic.

1. Creeps of the Apocalypse: Climate, Capital, Democracy

1. An earlier version of this essay appears in *Assembling Futures: Ecology, Economy, and Democracy*, ed. Jennifer Quigley and Catherine Keller (New York: Fordham University Press, 2024). That anthology is based on the 2022 Transdisciplinary Theological Colloquium, a conference series running at Drew University since 2001.

2. William Connolly, *Aspirational Fascism: The Struggle for Multifaceted Democracy under Trumpism* (Minneapolis: University of Minnesota Press, 2017).

3. A Rebuttal: Ronald Bailey, "Capitalism Is the Key to Fixing Climate Change," Reason: Free Minds and Free Markets, September 9, 2019, https://reason.com/2019/09/20/capitalism-is-the-key-to-fixing-climate-change.

4. Kathryn Tanner, *Christianity and the New Spirit of Capitalism* (New Haven, CT: Yale University Press, 2019).

5. Another register of "trans" unfolded at the student-led Transdisciplinary Theological Colloquium at Drew in 2018: "Trans: Human/Divine Bodies Beyond Boundaries," http://2018.drewttc.com/.

6. For an in-depth exploration of "apocalypse" as dis-closure, see my *Facing Apocalypse: Climate, Democracy, and Other Last Chances* (Maryknoll, NY: Orbis Books, 2021).

7. Tanner, *Capitalism*, 28.

8. Mike Pompeo, who adds: "Indeed, we have quietly entered a dangerous competition with Russia for Arctic resources." Jennifer Hansler, "Pompeo: Melting Sea Ice Presents 'New Opportunities for Trade,'" CNN, May 7, 2019, https://www.cnn.com/2019/05/06/politics/pompeo-sea-ice-arctic-council/index.html.

9. Joerg Rieger, *Theology in the Capitalocene: Ecology, Identity, Class, and Solidarity* (Minneapolis: Fortress, 2022), 40ff. See also my response, "Theology in the Capitalocene: An Interventions Forum," September 14, 2022, in Vanderbilt Divinity School's Newsletter of the Wendland-Cook Program in Social Justice, https://www.religionandjustice.org/interventions-forum-theology-capitalocene.

10. Marion Grau, *Of Divine Economy: Refinancing Redemption* (New York: T&T Clark, 2004), 226.

11. Tanner, *Capitalism*, 1–7.

12. Tanner, *Capitalism*, 7.

13. David Wallace-Wells, *The Uninhabitable Earth: Life After Warming* (New York: Tim Duggan Books, 2019).

14. Bruno Latour, *Down to Earth: Politics in the New Climatic Regime* (Medford, MA: Polity Press, 2018), 19.

15. Jesse Barron, "How Big Business Is Hedging against the Apocalypse," *New York Times Magazine*, April 11, 2019.

16. The IPCC (Intergovernmental Panel on Climate Change) gives us about a decade from now. See my reflection (with Agamben's) on Paul's "time that remains," in Catherine Keller, *Political Theology of the Earth: Our Planetary Emergency and the Struggle for a New Public* (New York: Columbia University Press, 2018), 51–55.

17. Caspar A. Hallmann et al., "More Than 75 Percent Decline Over 27 Years in Total Flying Insect Biomass in Protected Areas," *PLoS ONE* 12, no. 10 (2017): e0185809. Cf. Paula Kover, "Insect 'Armageddon': Five Crucial Questions Answered," *The Conversation*, October 25, 2017.

18. The most famous single sentence of "political theology" as such is indubitably: "Sovereign is he who decides on the exception." Carl Schmitt, *Political Theology: Four Chapters on the Concept of Sovereignty*, trans. George Schwab (1922; Chicago: University of Chicago Press, 2005), 5.

19. J. Kameron Carter, "Black Malpractice," *Social Text* 37, no. 2 (2019): 67–107. Italics mine.

20. W. E. B. Du Bois, "The Souls of White Folk" (1919), in *Darkwater: Voices from within the Veil* (Amherst, NY: Humanity Books, 2002), 56.

21. Ernst Bloch, *The Principle of Hope*, vol. 1, trans. Neville Plaice and Stephen Plaice (1954; Cambridge, MA: MIT Press, 1995). See also discussion of Bloch in Catherine Keller, *Apocalypse Now and Then: A Feminist Guide to the End of the World* (Boston: Beacon Press, 1996).

22. Tanner, *Capitalism*, 28.

23. For a scintillating examination of the Babylon figure's relation to the ancient and ongoing sexual imaginary, see Stephen D. Moore, *Untold Tales from the Book of Revelation: Sex and Gender, Empire and Ecology* (Atlanta: SBL Press, 2014); Jennifer A. Glancy and Stephen D. Moore, "How Typical a Roman Prostitute Is Revelation's 'Great Whore'?" *Journal of Biblical Literature* 130, no. 3 (Fall 2011): 551–569.

24. Keller, *Facing Apocalypse*, 111–114.

25. Wolfgang Streeck, *How Will Capitalism End? Essays on a Failing System* (Brooklyn: Verso Books, 2016), 24.

26. Streeck, *How Will Capitalism End?* 16. Streeck writes, "By attending to the need for democratic political legitimacy and social peace, trying to live up to citizen expectations of readily increasing economic prosperity and social stability, [government policies] found themselves at risk of damaging economic performance." At the same time, efforts to prioritize economic growth tended "to trigger political dissatisfaction and undermine support for the government of the day and the capitalist market economy in general" (16).

27. Streeck, *How Will Capitalism End?* 20. "That marriage was made not in heaven but in the urgency of establishing a new order after the catastrophe of two world wars (make deals not war) and in the face of the communist competition."

28. Paul McGuire and Troy Anderson, *Trumpocalypse: The End-times President, A Battle against the Globalist Elite, and the Countdown to Armageddon* (New York: FaithWords, 2018), 97ff. "They sold America down the river long ago—as did their EU counterparts—with numerous trade treaties that promote globalism."

29. William E. Connolly, *Climate Machines, Fascist Drives and Truth* (Durham, NC: Duke University Press, 2019) 54.

30. Tanner, *Capitalism*, 156.

31. Tanner, *Capitalism*, 157.

32. Tanner, *Capitalism*, 201.

33. Kathryn Lofton, *Consuming Religion* (Chicago: University of Chicago Press, 2017), 93. Italics mine.

34. Tanner, *Capitalism*, 219. Tanner adds, "Along the very line of the ethics of self-transformation that is the relay or transfer point of its various dimensions, the hinge or axis around which the whole turns, that aspect upon which this entire old world has riveted itself."

35. Carter, "Black Malpractice," 95.

36. Carter, "Black Malpractice," 95.

37. Connolly, *Climate Machines*, 52–53.

38. The relevant essay was recently published on its own: Jamie Allinson, China Miéville, Richard Seymour, and Rosie Warren, *The Tragedy of the Worker: Towards the Proletarocene*, The Salvage Collective (Brooklyn: Verso Books, 2021).

39. China Miéville, "Silence in Debris: Towards an Apophatic Marxism," *Salvage* 6 (November 2018): 115–144. Miéville is a renowned novelist, Marxist historian and found/co-editor of this journal.

40. China Miéville, "Death Cults of East Anglia," in "Toward the Proletarocene," *Salvage* 7 (October 2019).

41. Miéville, "Death Cults of East Anglia."

42. Miéville, "Death Cults of East Anglia."

43. See my "Political: Sovereign Exception or Collective Inception," chap. 1 in *Political Theology of the Earth*.

44. See my *Face of the Deep: A Theology of Becoming* (New York: Routledge, 2003).

45. Marcia Pally, *Commonwealth and Covenant: Economics, Politics, and Theologies of Relationality* (Grand Rapids, MI: Wm. B. Eerdmans, 2016), 351.

2. The "We" of Catastrophe, the Throb of Cosmogony: Eco-Thinking with Sylvia Wynter

1. This essay was previously published as "The 'We' of Cosmogony, the Throb of Catastrophe: Eco-Thinking with Sylvia Wynter," in *Ceremony (Burial of an Undead*

World), ed. Anselm Franke, Elisa Giuliano, Denyse Ryner, Claire Tancons, and Zairong Xiang (Leipzig: Spector Books, 2022).

2. Sylvia Wynter, "On How We Mistook the Map for the Territory, and Re-Imprisoned Ourselves in Our Unbearable Wrongness of Being, of *Désêtre*: Black Studies Toward the Human Project," chap. 4 in *Not Only the Master's Tools: African-American Studies in Theory and Practice,* ed. Lewis R. Gordon and Jane Anna Gordon (2006; New York: Routledge, 2016), 124.

3. Sylvia Wynter, "The Ceremony Found: Towards the Autopoetic Turn/Overturn, Its Autonomy of Human Agency and Extra- territoriality of (Self-)Cognition," in *Black Knowledge/Black Struggles: Essays in Critical Epistemology*, ed. Jason R. Ambroise and Sabine Broeck (Liverpool: Liverpool University Press, 2015), 245.

4. Sylvia Wynter and Katherine McKittrick, "The Unparalleled Catastrophe for Our Species?" chap. 2 in *Sylvia Wynter: On Being Human as Praxis*, ed. Katherine McKittrick (Durham, NC: Duke University Press, 2015).

5. Wynter and McKittrick, "Unparalleled Catastrophe," 73.

6. Wynter and McKittrick, "Unparalleled Catastrophe," 68.

7. Wynter and McKittrick, "Unparalleled Catastrophe." Cf., 30–35.

8. Wynter, "The Ceremony Found," 244.

9. Wynter and McKittrick, "Unparalleled Catastrophe," 73.

10. Wynter, "The Ceremony Found," 245.

11. Wynter and McKittrick, "Unparalleled Catastrophe," 73.

12. Wynter, "The Ceremony Found," 244.

13. I play out the false alternatives of optimism/pessimism in double contrast to a shadowed hope, in Catherine Keller, *Facing Apocalypse: Climate, Democracy and Other Last Chances* (Maryknoll, NY: Orbis Books, 2021), 16–17.

14. Anselm Franke, Elisa Giuliano, Denise Ryner, Claire Tancons, and Zairong Xiang, "Ceremony: Burial of an Undead World," in *Ceremony*, 7–11.

15. Wynter, "The Ceremony Found," 244. She retains the capitalization of Word.

16. Wynter, "The Ceremony Found," 245.

17. Sylvia Wynter, "The Ceremony Must Be Found: After Humanism," *boundary 2* 12, no. 3 (Spring–Autumn 1984): 42.

18. Wynter and McKittrick, "Unparalleled Catastrophe," 73.

19. Wynter here cites "South Africa's martyred Steven Biko." Wynter and McKittrick, "Unparalleled Catastrophe," 73.

20. In *Face of the Deep: A Theology of Becoming* (New York: Routledge, 2003), I develop a full-bodied alternative to the *creatio ex nihilo*, a *creatio ex profundis*.

21. Wynter, "The Ceremony Must Be Found," 42 ff.

22. Wynter, "The Ceremony Found," 242.

23. Alfred North Whitehead, *Process and Reality: An Essay in Cosmology*, corrected edition, ed. David Ray Griffin and Donald W. Sherburne (1929; New York: Free Press, 1978). Whitehead and Bertrand Russell had written *Principia Mathematica*, 1910–13.

24. See, for example, Monica A. Coleman, *Making a Way Out of No Way: A Womanist Theology* (Minneapolis: Fortress Press, 2008); Carol Wayne White, *Black Lives and Sacred Humanity: Toward an African American Religious Naturalism* (New York: Fordham University Press, 2016); Karen Baker-Fletcher, *Dancing with God: The Trinity from a Womanist Perspective* (St. Louis: Chalice Press, 2006). See also the work of one of Baker-Fletcher's students, John Ivan Gill, *Underground Rap as Religion: A Theopoetic Examination of a Process Aesthetic Religion* (New York: Routledge, 2020).

25. John B. Cobb Jr., *Is It Too Late? A Theology of Ecology*, 50th anniversary edition (1971; Minneapolis: Fortress Press, 2021). Of course, Latin American liberation theologians were already exposing the role of economics in US neocolonialism/neo-imperialism.

26. John B. Cobb Jr. and Herman Daly, *For the Common Good: Redirecting the Economy Toward Community, the Environment, and a Sustainable Future* (Boston: Beacon Press, 1989).

27. Herman Daly, "This Pioneering Economist Says Our Obsession with Growth Must End," *New York Times Magazine*, July 17, 2022.

28. See, for example, the Cobb Institute (cobb.institute), the Institute for Ecological Civilization (ecociv.org), Pando Populus (pandopopulus.com), Living Earth Movement (livingearthmovement.eco), and The Center for Process Studies (ctr4process.org).

29. The "divine lure," or "initial aim," is process theological language for the noncoercive will of God, offering possibilities not imposing outcomes, moment by moment. For initiating accounts of process theology see John B. Cobb Jr. and David Ray Griffin, *Process Theology: An Introductory Exposition* (Louisville: Westminster John Knox Press, 1976); Catherine Keller, *On the Mystery: Discerning Divinity in Process* (Minneapolis: Fortress Press, 2008).

30. Gill, *Underground Rap*, 116, 167, 169.

31. J. Kameron Carter, *The Anarchy of Black Religion: A Mystic Song* (Durham, NC: Duke University Press, 2023), 137.

3. Political Theologies at War: A Virtual Talk with Students in Ukraine

1. The present essay was originally titled "The Other as Subject: Political Theologies of Autocracy and Democracy" and presented at a virtual conference with Ukrainian theology students on July 22, 2022. It was then published with the same title in *Theological Reflections: Eastern European Journal of Theology* 20, no. 2 (2022): 79–90, https://doi.org/10.29357/2789-1577.2022.20.2.6. (As I attend to final proofs, June 2024, the war continues unabated.) For the broader background of this essay's point of view, see Catherine Keller, *Political Theology of the Earth: Our Planetary Emergency and the Struggle for a New Public* (New York: Columbia University Press, 2019).

2. Carl Schmitt, *Political Theology: Four Chapters on the Concept of Sovereignty*, trans. George Schwab (1922; Chicago: University of Chicago Press, 2002), 5.

3. President Paul von Hindenburg signed the Emergency Decree for the Protection of the People and the State (or the "Reichstag Fire Decree") on February 28, 1933. Justified as a defense against Communist violence, the decree suspended the democratic aspects of the Weimar Republic and declared a state of emergency. Hindenburg's appointed Chancellor of the Reich, Adolf Hitler, was able, just over three weeks after the passage of the Reichstag Fire Decree, to tighten his grip on Germany by the passage of the Enabling Act. This act gave Hitler's cabinet the power to decree laws without their being passed by the Reichstag—thus giving Hitler dictatorial powers. https://encyclopedia.ushmm.org/content/en/article/reichstag-fire-decree.

4. Carl Schmitt, *The Concept of the Political*, expanded edition, trans. George Schwab (1932; Chicago: University of Chicago Press, 2007), 26.

5. For instance, on the prominent role of a form of Hindu fundamentalism in current Indian nationalism, see Milan Vaishnav, "Religious Nationalism and India's Future," in *The BJP in Power: Indian Democracy and Religious Nationalism*, Carnegie Endowment for International Peace (April 4, 2019), https://carnegieendowment.org

/research/2019/04/the-bjp-in-power-indian-democracy-and-religious-nationalism#religious-nationalism-and-indias-future. The US example is discussed in many of the current essays, particularly Chapter 5.

6. And beyond those hearings, the indictment of May 31, 2024.

7. "President Vladimir Putin justified the annexation of Crimea by evoking the concept of a 'Russian World' (*Russkiy Mir*). He spoke of Russians as living in a 'divided nation' and highlighted the 'aspiration of the Russian world, of historic Russia, for the restoration of unity.' He also stressed the existence of a 'broad Russian civilization,' which has to be protected from external forces (particularly from the West) and which he defines as the sphere of Russian interests. According to the DGAP's Ukraine expert Wilfried Jilge, Putin's intensive evocation of the idea of *Russkiy Mir* in 2014 was by no means a momentary manifestation during the Russia-Ukraine crisis. The concept was devised by intellectuals, academics, and journalists close to the Kremlin around 1995–2000 and publicly introduced into political discourse by Putin in 2001." German Council on Foreign Relation, "Russkiy Mir: 'Russian World,'" May 3, 2016, https://dgap.org/en/events/russkiy-mir-russian-world.

8. Timothy Snyder, "Ivan Ilyin, Putin's Philosopher of Russian Fascism," *New York Review*, March 16, 2018. I also lean on David G. Lewis, *Russia's New Authoritarianism: Putin and the Politics of Order* (Edinburgh: Edinburgh University Press, 2020).

9. Snyder, "Ivan Ilyin."

10. Snyder, "Ivan Ilyin."

11. David G. Lewis, *Russia's New Authoritarianism: Putin and the Politics of Order* (Edinburgh: Edinburgh University Press, 2020), 3 ff.

12. Snyder, "Ivan Ilyin."

13. Mark Hosenball, "US Senate Committee Concludes Russia Used Manafort, WikiLeaks to Boost Trump in 2016," *Reuters*, August 18, 2020, https://www.reuters.com/article/idUSKCN25E1UZ/.

14. Quoted in Snyder, "Ivan Ilyin."

15. Snyder, "Ivan Ilyin."

16. Amy Mackinnon, "LGBTQ Russians Were Putin's First Target in His War on the West," *Foreign Policy*, October 7, 2022, https://foreignpolicy.com/2022/10/07/lgbtq-russia-ukraine-war-west/.

17. "Putin's Macho Image," Reuters, December 5, 2011, https://www.reuters.com/news/picture/putins-macho-image-idUSRTR2UVJN/.

18. Richard Foltz, "Homophobia as a Wartime Marketing Tool: Some Russians Fear the West Will Make Them Gay," *The Conversation*, October 25, 2022, https://theconversation.com/homophobia-as-a-wartime-marketing-tool-some-russians-fear-the-west-will-make-them-gay-192826.

19. Quoted in "In Sermon, Russian Church Leader Kirill Links Ukraine War with Gay Pride Parade," ed. Amit Chaturvedi, *NDTV World*, March 9, 2022, https://www.ndtv.com/world-news/in-sermon-russian-church-leader-kirill-links-ukraine-war-with-gay-pride-parade-2812228.

20. https://dgap.org/en/events/russkiy-mir-russian-world.

21. See the public statement, "A Declaration on the 'Russian World' (*Russkii mir*) Teaching" at the online platform, *Public Orthodoxy* on The Sunday of Orthodoxy, March 13, 2022, https://publicorthodoxy.org/2022/03/13/a-declaration-on-the-russian-world-russkii-mir-teaching/.

22. Snyder, "Ivan Ilyin."

23. Quoted in Snyder, "Ivan Ilyin."
24. Persian Manicheanism, dualistic framing of the universe in terms of absolute principles of good and evil, though long considered a Christian heresy, also reads as a religion of its own.
25. Quoted in Snyder, "Ivan Ilyin."
26. Alfred North Whitehead, *Process and Reality: An Essay in Cosmology*, corrected edition, ed. David Ray Griffin and Donald W. Sherburne (1927; New York: Free Press, 1978). For additional introductions to process thought within the present volume, see especially Chapters 2, 6, 7, 9 and 11.
27. Thomas Jay Oord, *God Can't: How to Believe in God and Love after Tragedy, Abuse, or Other Evils* (Gramsmere: SacraSage, 2019). See Chapter 6 in this volume.
28. Whitehead, *Process and Reality*, 343.
29. Lewis, *Russia's New Authoritarianism*. See his detailed analysis of the Schmitt/Putin link in chapter 1, "Authoritarianism, Ideology and Order," and chapter 2, "Carl Schmitt and Russian Conservatism," where he analyzes the normalization of Schmitt's concept of the sovereign exception.
30. Quoted in Lewis, *Russia's New Authoritarianism*, 204.
31. Quoted in Lewis, *Russia's New Authoritarianism*, 202.
32. Lewis, *Russia's New Authoritarianism*, 204. See chapter 9 of that book, where Lewis analyzes Schmitt's notion of the *katechon*, the restrainer, as derived from Paul's Second Letter to the Thessalonians and as applicable to the Russian messianism at work in Putin's exceptionalism.
33. For the classic process theological exposition of theodicy, see David Ray Griffin, *God, Power, and Evil: A Process Theodicy* (Louisville: Westminster John Knox Press, 2004). And Oord, *God Can't*.
34. Arturo Escobar, *Pluriversal Politics: The Real and the Possible* (Durham, NC: Duke University Press, 2020), xix. Ontological or pluralistic politics draw on the concept of radical relationality: "All entities that make up the world are so deeply interrelated that they have no intrinsic, separate existence by themselves" (xiii).
35. Lyudmyla Khersonska, "I Planted a Camellia in the Yard," trans. Katherine E. Young, in *Words for War: New Poems from Ukraine, ed.* Oksana Maksymchuk and Max Rosochinsky (Boston: Academic Studies Press, 2017). You can see both original and translation here (seemingly a website created and maintained by publishers): https://www.wordsforwar.com/i-planted-a-camellia-in-the-yard.

4. Apocalypse After All? Climate, Politics, and Faith in the Possible

1. This chapter is based on my lecture at the University of Zurich in 2019. Much of the argument and exegesis derives from my Facing Apocalypse: Climate, Democracy and Other Last Chances (Maryknoll, NY: Orbis Books, 2021).
2. Amanda Hess, "Apocalypse When? Global Warming's Endless Scroll," *New York Times*, February 3, 2022.
3. Pope Francis, *Laudato Si': On Care for Our Common Home*, Encyclical Letter of the Holy Father (Huntington, IN: Our Sunday Visitor, 2015), §161 (p. 107).
4. Catherine Keller, *Apocalypse Now and Then: A Feminist Guide to the End of the World* (Boston: Beacon Press, 1996); Catherine Keller, *Facing Apocalypse: Climate, Democracy, and Other Last Chances* (Maryknoll, NY: Orbis Books, 2021).
5. Caspar A. Hallmann et al., "More Than 75 Percent Decline over 27 Years in Total Flying Insect Biomass in Protected Areas," *PLoS ONE* 12, no. 10 (2017): e0185809. Cf.

Paula Kover, "Insect 'Armageddon': Five Crucial Questions Answered," *The Conversation*, October 25, 2017.

6. "Newsletter: A Climate Apocalypse Now," *Los Angeles Times*, September 14, 2020, https://www.latimes.com/world-nation/newsletter/2020-09-14/climate-change-wildfires-california-oregon-washington-todays-headlines.

7. Richard McGahey, "Fearing a Commercial Real Estate 'Apocalypse,'" *Forbes*, September 26, 2022; Kung Chan, "The 6 Horsemen of the Apocalypse for China," *The Diplomat*, January 14, 2023, https://thediplomat.com/2023/01/the-6-horsemen-of-the-apocalypse-for-china/; Coleman Spilde, "California Greets 2023 with Apocalpyse Weather," *Daily Beast*, January 1, 2023, https://www.thedailybeast.com/california-greets-2023-with-apocalypse-weather-as-major-storms-continue.

8. Dina Khapaeva, "Putin and the Apocalypse," *Project Syndicate*, January 24, 2019, https://www.project-syndicate.org/commentary/nuclear-war-putin-orthodox-approval-by-dina-khapaeva-2019-01.

9. "Israel-Palestine Crisis Has 'Reached an Unprecedented Level of Dehumanisation': Independent Rights Expert," *UN News*, United Nations, October 29, 2023, https://news.un.org/en/story/2023/10/1142952.

10. Keller, *Now and Then*.

11. Hal Lindsey, *The Late Great Planet Earth* (New York: Bantam, 1973), 142, 158.

12. Damian Carrington, "Global Warming of Oceans Equivalent to an Atomic Bomb per Second," *The Guardian*, January 7, 2019, https://www.theguardian.com/environment/2019/jan/07/global-warming-of-oceans-equivalent-to-an-atomic-bomb-per-second?CMP=share_btn_link.

13. Déborah Danowski and Eduardo Viveiros de Castro, *The Ends of the World*, trans. Rodrigo Nunes (Malden, MA: Polity, 2016).

14. Rita Brock, "An Epidemic of Moral Injury," *Christian Century*, September 8, 2021, https://www.christiancentury.org/article/how-my-mind-has-changed/epidemic-moral-injury.

15. Paul McGuire and Troy Anderson, *Trumpocalypse: The End-times President, a Battle against the Globalist Elite, and the Countdown to Armageddon* (New York: FaithWords, 2018).

16. Jacqui Patterson, "Your Take: Climate Change Is a Civil Rights Issue," *The Root*, April 23, 2010, https://www.theroot.com/your-take-climate-change-is-a-civil-rights-issue-1790879295.

17. Melanie L. Harris, *Ecowomanism: African American Women and Earth-Honoring Faiths* (Maryknoll, NY: Orbis, 2017); Jeremy Williams, *Climate Change Is Racist: Race, Privilege and the Struggle for Climate Justice* (London: Icon Books, 2021); Kathryn Yusoff, *A Billion Black Anthropocenes or None* (Minneapolis: University of Minnesota Press, 2018).

18. See Amy-Jill Levine, ed., *A Feminist Companion to the Apocalypse of John* (New York: T&T Clark International, 2009). See also Stephen D. Moore, *Untold Tales from the Book of Revelation: Sex and Gender, Empire and Ecology* (Atlanta: SBL Press, 2014).

19. Even in resisting the timelessness of the straight Jungian view of archetypes, nonetheless clearly an element of Carl G. Jung's insight into the crystallization of certain primordial patterns in a collective unconscious works in its critique of egoic individualism and its attention to psychocultural depth-resonances, with the current examination of the ancient prototypes of the Apocalypse. See my *From a Broken Web: Separation, Sexism, and Self* (Boston: Beacon Press, 1986).

20. Robert Rapier, "2022 Saw The Second Highest Oil Production in US History," *Forbes*, January 6, 2023.

21. See, for example, Jürgen Moltmann, *Theology of Hope: On the Ground and the Implications of a Christian Eschatology* (1964; Minneapolis: Fortress Press, 1993), 22 ff.

22. David Wallace-Wells, "Beyond Catastrophe: A New Climate Reality Is Coming into View," *New York Times Magazine*, October 26, 2022.

23. Sally McFague, *Super, Natural Christians: How We Should Love Nature* (Minneapolis: Fortress Press, 1997).

24. For more on the process theological "divine lure" see Chapter 6 in this volume.

25. Rebecca Solnit, *Hope in the Dark: Untold Histories, Wild Possibilities* (Chicago: Haymarket Books, 2016).

26. In *New York Times*, January 14, 1962.

27. Emily Dickinson, "Hope Is the Thing with Feathers," in *The Poems of Emily Dickinson*, ed. R. W. Franklin (Cambridge, MA: Harvard University Press, 1999).

5. Nationalism and a New Religion: Foxangelicals and the Agonism of an Alternative

1. This essay was published in prior form as "Foxangelicals, Political Theology, and Friends," in *Doing Theology in the Age of Trump*, ed. Clayton Crockett and Jeffrey W. Robbins (Eugene, OR: Cascade Books, 2018), 89–100.

2. John D. Caputo, *What Would Jesus Deconstruct? The Good News for Postmodern and the Church* (Grand Rapids, MI: Baker Academic, 2007).

3. Amy Sullivan, "America's New Religion: Fox Evangelicals," *New York Times*, December 15, 2017.

4. Carl Schmitt, *Political Theology: Four Chapters on the Concept of Sovereignty*, trans. George Schwab (1922; Chicago: University of Chicago Press, 2002), 5.

5. Carl Schmitt, *The Concept of the Political*, expanded edition, trans. George Schwab (1932; Chicago: University of Chicago Press, 2007), 26.

6. Schmitt, *Concept of the Political*, 29.

7. Schmitt, *Concept of the Political*, 29.

8. Schmitt, *Concept of the Political*, 27.

9. Hannah Arendt, "The Seeds of a Fascist International," in *Essays in Understanding: 1930–1954*, ed. Jerome Kohn (New York: Harcourt Brace, 1994), 140–150.

10. Tom DeLay, *Against: What Does the White Evangelical Want?* (Eugene, OR: Cascade, 2019), 145.

11. DeLay, *Against*, 144.

12. DeLay, *Against*, 22.

13. William E. Connolly, *Aspirational Fascism: The Struggle for a Multifaceted Democracy under Trumpism* (Minneapolis: University of Minnesota Press, 2017).

14. William E. Connolly, *Capitalism and Christianity, American Style* (Durham, NC: Duke University Press, 2008).

15. Connolly, *Capitalism and Christianity*, 22. Connolly builds here on "Marx's insight into assemblages between private life, embedded spirituality, and the state." So Connolly marks the "point at which Weber and Marx meet. For the mature Marx never did isolate a set of tight contradictions of capitalism; and . . . the ethos of Protestant Christianity incorporated into early state-capitalism was strongly disposed to blame poverty upon the character of the poor. Marx intimates in 'The King of Prussia' how

capitalism, the state, and Christianity are intercoded to a significant degree, with a change in any finding some expression in the interior of the others" (21–22).

16. Connolly, *Capitalism and Christianity*, 48.

17. Marcia Pally, *White Evangelicals and Right-Wing Populism: How Did We Get Here?* (New York: Routledge, 2022).

18. Pally, *White Evangelicals*, 131.

19. Sullivan, "America's New Religion."

20. Bob Smietna, "Many Who Call Themselves Evangelicals Don't Actually Hold Evangelical Beliefs," Lifeway Research, December 6, 2017, https://research.lifeway.com/2017/12/06/many-evangelicals-dont-hold-evangelical-beliefs/. Lifeway Research is part of Lifeway Christian Resources, an entity of the Southern Baptist Convention. Theirs is not a neutral view on what is meant by "evangelical beliefs," and so all the more telling.

21. Sullivan, "America's New Religion."

22. William E. Connolly, *A World of Becoming* (Durham, NC: Duke University Press, 2010), 66.

23. See Hadas Gold, "Megyn Kelly: Jesus and Santa were White," *Politico*, December 12, 2013.

24. *The Armor of Light*, directed by Abigail E. Disney and Kathleen Hughes (Purple Mickey Productions, 2015), 1:26.

25. John B. Cobb Jr., *Christ in a Pluralistic Age* (Eugene, OR: Wipf and Stock, 1998); John B. Cobb Jr., *Spiritual Bankruptcy: A Prophetic Call to Action* (Nashville: Abingdon Press, 2010).

26. For a gripping exposition of this liberal/progressive Christian history in its particularly US form, see Gary Dorrien, *The Spirit of American Liberal Theology: A History* (Louisville, KY: Westminster John Knox Press, 2023), a capacious compression of his three-volume work, *The Making of American Liberal Theology* (Louisville, KY: Westminster John Knox Press , 2001, 2003, 2006).

27. Connolly, *Aspirational Fascism*, 15.

28. Chantal Mouffe also names a third way beyond liberal consensualism and mere antagonism, as a "democratic agonism." *The Return of the Political* (Brooklyn: Verso Books, 2005), 6.

29. William E. Connolly, *Facing the Planetary: Entangled Humanism and the Politics of Swarming* (Durham, NC: Duke University Press, 2017), 79.

30. Herman E. Daly and John B. Cobb Jr., *For the Common Good: Redirecting the Economy toward Community, the Environment, and a Sustainable Future*, 2nd ed. (Boston: Beacon Press, 1994). They take up the notion of the "common good" in careful mindfulness of its potential for misconstrual as a totalizing, unifying, or somehow homogenizing signal.

31. Stefano Harney and Fred Moton, *The Undercommons: Fugitive Planning and Black Study* (New York: Minor Compositions, 2013).

32. Rebecca Solnit, *Hope in the Dark: Untold Histories, Wild Possibilities* (Chicago: Haymarket Books, 2016

33. China Miéville, "Silence in the Debris: Towards an Apophatic Marxism," *Salvage* 6 (November 2018). The great novelist and political theorist here meditates on the need for an undogmatic, sometimes silent, Marxism, if solidarity is to develop.

34. Connolly, *World of Becoming*, 113.

35. Catherine Keller, *Political Theology of the Earth: Our Planetary Emergency and the Struggle for a New Public* (New York: Columbia University Press, 2018).

36. See Catherine Keller, *On the Mystery: Discerning Divinity in Process* (Minneapolis: Fortress Press, 2008).

37. Ernst Bloch, *The Principle of Hope*, vols. 1–3, trans. Neville Plaice, Stephen Plaice, and Paul Knight (Cambridge, MA: MIT Press, 1986).

38. That Blochian narrative underlies my *Apocalypse Now and Then: A Feminist Guide to the End of the World* (Boston: Beacon Press, 1996), helping it to resist its own temptation to a reductive reading of John's Revelation to the religion of vengeance it indubitably resources.

39. Keller, *Earth*. 54ff.

40. George Fox, *The Works of George Fox*, vol. 7 (Philadelphia: Marcus T. C. Gould, 1831), epistle 227.

41. Lauren Berlant, *Cruel Optimism* (Durham, NC: Duke University Press, 2011).

42. Catherine Keller, *Face of the Deep: A Theology of Becoming* (New York: Routledge, 2002). Here I meditate on the repression of the actual Hebrew meaning of Genesis 1:2, in which God's creation presupposes an oceanic formlessness. Creation from chaos was then replaced by *creatio ex nihilo*, in a civilizational demonization of chaos. *Face of the Deep* proposes instead a "*creatio ex profundis*."

6. Power, Theodicy and the Amipotent God

1. This paper was originally delivered at a conference organized by Thomas Oord, "Power and the God of Love," in Napa, California, in November 2022. It is now forthcoming as "Power, Apocalypse and the God of Love," in *From Force to Persuasion: Process-Relational Perspectives on Power and the God of Love*, ed Andrew M. Davis, Cascade's Perspectives in Process Studies Series (2024). I was glad to be able to dedicate the talk, and therefore now the essay, to process theologian David Ray Griffin. who has done work brilliantly relevant to—no matter what! David died in November 2022.

2. David Ray Griffin, *God, Power, and Evil: A Process Theodicy* (1976; Louisville, KY: Westminster John Knox Press, 2004).

3. Catherine Keller, *Facing Apocalypse: Climate, Democracy and Other Last Chances* (Maryknoll, NY: Orbis Books, 2021). This book updated for the current millennium my *Apocalypse Now and Then: A Feminist Guide to the End of the World* (Boston: Beacon Press, 1996). See also Chapters 1 and 4 in this volume.

4. Fred Guterl, "Climate Armageddon: How the World's Weather Could Quickly Run Amok [Excerpt]," *Scientific American*, May 25, 2021. Cf. *Scholarly Community Encyclopedia*, s.v., "Climate Apocalypse," https://encyclopedia.pub/entry/29680; David Spratt and Ian Dunlop, "Existential Climate-Related Security Risk: A Scenario Approach," Breakthrough—National Centre for Climate Restoration, May, 2019; Peter Ditlevsen and Susanne Ditlevsen, "Warning of a Forthcoming Collapse of the Atlantic Meridional Overturning Circulation," *Nature Communications* 14 (July 25, 2023): article no. 4254, https://www.nature.com/articles/s41467-023-39810-w.

5. See Keller, *Facing Apocalypse*, chaps. 1 and 5.

6. Jürgen Moltmann, *The Crucified God: The Cross of Christ as the Foundation and Criticism of Christian Theology*, trans. R. A. Wilson and John Bowden, pref. trans. Margaret Kohl (1973; Minneapolis: Fortress Press, 1993), 276. I feel compelled to note that this greatest of living European theologians has died at ninety-eight years of age, on June 3, 2024, during my final proofreading of the current manuscript.

7. Jürgen Moltmann, *The Living God and the Fullness of Life*, trans. Margaret Kohl (Louisville: Westminster John Knox Press, 2015), 44.

8. Moltmann, *The Living God*, 45.
9. Moltmann, *The Living God*, 44–45.
10. Søren Kierkegaard, "Eine literarische Anzeige," in *Gesammelte Werke*, 17. (Cited in Moltmann, *The Living God*, 45).
11. Thomas Jay Oord, *God Can't: How to Believe in God and Love after Tragedy, Abuse, or Other Evils* (Grasmere: SacraSage Press, 2019).
12. Stephen D. Moore, *Untold Tales from the Book of Revelation: Sex and Gender, Empire and Ecology* (Atlanta: SBL Press, 2014). See chap 6, "Raping Rome."
13. Moltmann, *The Crucified God*, 222.
14. Thomas Jay Oord, *The Death of Omnipotence and Birth of Amipotence* (Grassmere, ID: SacraSage Press, 2023), 120.
15. Oord, *The Death of Omnipotence*, 140. Also: "No creature is equal to or greater than an amipotent God. But the efficacy of amipotence requires creaturely collaboration. Love involves God and creation" (141).
16. Oord, *The Death of Omnipotence*, 148.
17. Oord, *God Can't*.
18. Charles Hartshorne, "Omnipotence," in *An Encyclopedia of Religion*, ed. Vergilius Ferm (Philosophical Library, Inc., 1945), 545, as cited in David Ray Griffin, *God, Power, and Evil: A Process Theodicy* (Louisville: Westminster John Knox Press, 1976), 268.
19. Griffin, *God, Power, and Evil*, 268–269.
20. See my *Face of the Deep: A Theology of Becoming* (New York: Routledge, 2003) for *creatio ex profundis* as more scripturally faithful and existentially compelling than the *ex nihilo*.
21. Griffin, *God, Power, Evil*, 310.

7. Weakness, Folly, Insistence, Glory: The Phenomenal God of John D. Caputo

1. This paper was originally delivered at an event in honor of Caputo's work, at the Simon Silverman Phenomenology Center of Duquesne University on April 14, 2023. For a video recording of the original proceedings, see https://dsc.duq.edu/phenomenology-symposium/33/.
2. John D. Caputo, *Specters of God: An Anatomy of the Apophatic Imagination* (Bloomington: Indiana University Press, 2022).
3. John D. Caputo, *The Insistence of God: A Theology of Perhaps* (Bloomington: Indiana University Press, 2013), 41ff.
4. Caputo, *The Insistence of God*, 181.
5. Caputo, *The Insistence of God*, 176.
6. See Caputo, *The Insistence of God*, 5–7 and chap. 2.
7. Caputo, *The Insistence of God*, 103.
8. Paul Tillich, *Systematic Theology*, vol. 1 (Chicago: University of Chicago Press, 1951), 205.
9. Caputo, *The Insistence of God*, 13.
10. Mary Daly, *Beyond God the Father: Toward a Philosophy of Women's Liberation* (Boston: Beacon Press, 1985), 23–24. According to Wesley Wildman, Mary Daly writes in her autobiography, *Outercourse*, of her experience auditing Tillich's lectures at Harvard during her teaching stint at Cardinal Cushing College. . . . In this discussion, she uses Tillich's concepts of the state of existence as a means to relate to the condition of women's oppression in the world. She construes former conceptions of God as male

and transcendent as having served as forms of nonbeing in the world. A woman's confrontation with nonbeing, manifest in oppression and subjugation, creates anxiety, which limits her full participation in being. Obviously deeply moved by *The Courage to Be*, Daly states that the revelatory confrontation with nonbeing is sparked and fueled by existential courage. And that "courage to be is the key to the revelatory power of the feminist revolution."

Wesley Wildman, "Tillich's Theological Influence on Mary Daly (1928–2010)," Paul Tillich Resources, accessed January 5, 2024, https://people.bu.edu/wwildman/tillich/resources/influence_daly.htm.

11. Paul Tillich, *Dynamics of Faith* (New York: Harper Collins, 1957).

12. Caputo, *Specters*, 196.

13. See my *Face of the Deep: A Theology of Becoming* (New York: Routledge, 2002).

14. John D. Caputo, *The Folly of God: A Theology of the Unconditional* (Salem, OR: Polebridge Press, 2015), 119.

15. Caputo, *Specters*, 151.

16. Alfred North Whitehead, *Process and Reality: An Essay in Cosmology*, corrected edition, ed. David Ray Griffin and Donald W. Sherburne (1929; New York: Free Press, 1978), 351.

17. Caputo's 2006 *Weakness of God* does not engage process theology as such, nor am I claiming it should have. That would not have helped its project: its deployment of a Continental and deconstructive vocabulary in the construction of an actual theology. And doing this as an *anglophone philosopher*—this already verges on the impossible. John D. Caputo, *The Weakness of God: A Theology of the Event* (Bloomington: Indiana University Press, 2006).

18. Caputo, *Specters*, 184.

19. See my *Cloud of the Impossible: Negative Theology and Planetary Entanglement* (New York: Columbia University Press, 2015).

20. Whitehead, *Process and Reality*, 21.

21. David Nikkel, *Panentheism in Tillich and Hartshorne: A Creative Synthesis* (New York: Peter Lang, 1996).

22. See Benedikt Paul Göcke, *The Panentheism of Karl Christian Friedrich Krause (1781–1832): From Transcendental Philosophy to Metaphysics* (New York: Peter Lang, 2018).

23. Caputo, *Specters*, 49.

24. Caputo, *Specters*, 49.

25. Caputo, *Specters*, 244.

26. Caputo, *Specters*, 244.

27. See my exploration of Nicholas Cusa in "Enfolding and Unfolding God: Cusanic *Complicatio*," in *Cloud of the Impossible: Negative Theology and Planetary Entanglement* (New York: Columbia University Press, 2015).

28. Caputo, *Specters*, 308.

29. See Karen Barad, *Meeting the Universe Halfway: Quantum Physics and the Entanglement of Matter and Meaning* (Durham, NC: Duke University Press, 2007).

30. Barad, *Meeting the Universe Halfway*, 283. See also my chapter, "Spooky Entanglements: The Physics of Nonseparability," in *Cloud*, 127–167, esp. 138. Yet on the side of that insistent theological struggle, another question arises. I can't now help wondering why and how the death threat to the human habitat goes hand in hand with the death of God. A kind of twenty-first-century human co-morbidity? Not that

either death is a terminal necessity; possibilities for transformation haunt us, insistently, as well.

31. Paul Davies, *God and the New Physics* (New York: Simon and Schuster, 1983), 103. Also: "The fuzzy and nebulous world of the atom only sharpens into concrete reality when an observation is made" (103).

32. Barad, *Meeting the Universe Halfway*, 396.

33. Bruno Latour, *Facing Gaia: Eight Lectures on the New Climate Regime*, trans. Catherine Porter (Medford, MA: Polity, 2017).

34. "Hottest July Ever Signals 'Era of Global Boiling has Arrived,' Says UN Chief," *UN News*, United Nations, July 27, 2023, https://news.un.org/en/story/2023/07/1139162.

35. Lynn White Jr., "The Historical Roots of Our Ecological Crisis," *Science* 155 (1967): 1203–1207.

36. See Mary-Jane Rubenstein, *Astrotopia: The Dangerous Religion of the Corporate Space Race* (Chicago: University of Chicago Press, 2022).

37. See my *Apocalypse Now and Then: A Feminist Guide to the End of the World* (Boston: Beacon Press, 1996) and *Facing Apocalypse: Climate, Democracy, and Other Last Chances* (Maryknoll, NY: Orbis Books, 2021). See also the two essays in this book, "Creeps of the Apocalypse" and "Apocalypse After All?"

38. Caputo, *Specters*, 340.

39. Caputo, *Specters*, 340–341.

8. Poiesis of the Earth: "A Black and Living Thing"

1. Lucille Clifton, "the earth is a living thing," in *how to carry water: Selected Poems of Lucille Clifton*, ed. with a foreword by Aracelis Girmay (Rochester, NY: BOA, 2020), 143.

2. This essay was originally delivered as a talk at "Hosting Earth," a conference at Boston College organized by Richard Kearney, April 2023. In that earlier form, the essay is forthcoming in *Hosting Earth: Facing the Climate Emergency*, ed. Richard Kearney, Urwa Hameed, and Peter Klapes (London: Routledge, 2024).

3. In the interval since her poem, there has developed a broadly respected , or at least non-dismissible, discourse of Earth as a certain kind of organism, or indeed "superorganism." See James Lovelock: "When I talk of Gaia as a superorganism, I do not for a moment have in mind a goddess or some sentient being. I am expressing my intuition that the Earth behaves as a self-regulating system." James Lovelock, *Gaia: The Practical Science of Planetary Medicine* (New York: Oxford University Press, 1991, 2000), 57. Cf. Bruno Latour, *Facing Gaia: Eight Lectures on the New Climatic Regime*, trans. Catherine Porter (Medford, MA: Polity, 2017), 94ff.

4. "Deterritorialization" works dissidently in relation to territorialization in Deleuze and Guattari.

5. Abdel Mohsen Ibrahim Hashim, "Grief for What Is Human, Grief for What Is Not: An Ecofeminist Insight into the Poetry of Lucille Clifton," *International Journal of English and Literature* 5, no. 8 (October 2014): 182–193.

6. Lucille Clifton, "being property once myself," in *carry water*, 19.

7. James Cone, "Whose Earth Is It Anyway?" *Cross Currents* 50, no. 1–2 (2000): 36.

8. Lucille Clifton, *Mercy* (Rochester, NY: BOA, 2004), 72.

9. Clifton, *Mercy*, 73.

10. Clifton, "the earth," 143.

11. Clifton, "the earth," 143.

12. Clifton, "the earth," 143.

13. Lucille Clifton, *Good News About the Earth* (New York: Random House, 1972), no. 11.

14. In this piece I follow Clifton and use lowercase for "black" where she does. In other essays I generally use the convention of capitalizing it.

15. Clifton, *Mercy*, 192.

9. Amorous Entanglements: The Matter of Intercarnation

1. This essay was published in *Earthly Things: Immanence, New Materialisms, and Planetary Thinking*, ed. Karen Bray, Heather Eaton, and Whitney Bauman (New York: Fordham University Press, 2023).

2. See Diana Coole and Samantha Frost, eds., *New Materialisms: Ontology, Agency, and Politics* (Durham, NC: Duke University Press, 2010); Catherine Keller and Mary-Jane Rubenstein, eds., *Entangled Worlds: Religion, Science, and New Materialisms* (New York: Fordham University Press, 2017); Jane Bennett, *influx & efflux: writing up with Walt Whitman* (Durham, NC: Duke University Press, 2020); Whitney A. Bauman, ed., *Meaningful Flesh: Reflections on Religion and Nature for a Queer Planet* (Santa Barbara, CA: Punctum, 2018); Donna J. Haraway, *Staying with the Trouble: Making Kin in the Chthulucene* (Durham, NC: Duke University Press, 2016); Clayton Crockett, *Energy and Change: A New Materialist Cosmotheology* (New York: Columbia University Press, 2022).

3. See Catherine Keller, *Political Theology of the Earth: Our Planetary Emergency and the Struggle for a New Public* (New York: Columbia University Press, 2018).

4. Espousing the tensive opening of the "to come," Derrida famously offers the messianic, or also messianicity, "without a messiah." See Jacques Derrida, *Acts of Religion*, ed. and int. Gil Anidjar (New York: Routledge, 2002), 362ff.

5. Walter Benjamin, "Theses on the Philosophy of History" (1940), in *Illuminations: Essays and Reflections*, trans. Harry Zohn, ed. and int. Hannah Arendt (Boston: Mariner Books, 2019). For a further discussion of "matter's messianic moment," see my *Political Theology of the Earth*, 100–104.

6. Karen Barad, "Quantum Entanglements and Hauntological Relations of Inheritance: Dis/continuities, SpaceTime Enfoldings, and Justice-to-Come," *Derrida Today* 3, no. 2 (2010): 265. Cf. also Barad, "What Flashes," 48–49.

7. Barad, "Quantum Entanglements," 265.

8. Allen O. Miller was a professor of systematic theology and philosophy at Eden Seminary, where I did the M.Div. He was an important contributor to the World Council of Churches and highly influential on my intellectual development.

9. Panentheism is associated above all with the process thought derived from the philosophy of Alfred North Whitehead. Chapters 3 and 6 offer brief introductions to process theology, which occurs throughout this work.

10. See Mary-Jane Rubenstein, "The Matter with Pantheism: On Shepherds and Hybrids and Goat-Gods and Monsters," in *Entangled Worlds*. See also her full-length study, *Pantheologies: Gods, Worlds, Monsters* (New York: Columbia University Press, 2018), 5.

11. "We must conceive the Divine Eros as the active entertainment of all ideals, with the urge to their final realization, each in its due season. Thus a process must be inherent in God's nature, whereby [god's] infinity is acquiring realization." Alfred North Whitehead, *Adventures of Ideas* (New York: Free Press, 1933/1961), 277, 296.

12. Alfred North Whitehead, *Science and the Modern World* (1925; New York: Free Press, 1967), 175–176.

13. See Catherine Keller, "Tingles of Matter, Tangles of Theology: Bodies of the New(ish) Materialism," in *Intercarnations: Exercises in Theological Possibility* (New York: Fordham University Press, 2017), 60–82. (Also published in *Entangled Worlds*.) I also engage Barad in relation to the whole history of quantum entanglement in chapter 4 of *Cloud of the Impossible: Negative Theology and Planetary Entanglement* (New York: Columbia University Press, 2015), 127–167.

14. Karen Barad, *Meeting the Universe Halfway: Quantum Physics and the Entanglement of Matter and Meaning* (Durham, NC: Duke University Press, 2007), 393.

15. Alfred North Whitehead, *Process and Reality: An Essay in Cosmology*, corrected edition, ed. David Ray Griffin and Donald W. Sherburne (1929; New York: Free Press, 1985), 348.

16. See especially the works of political philosopher William Connolly that explicitly engage Whiteheadian thought: *A World of Becoming* (Durham, NC: Duke University Press, 2011); *Climate Machines, Fascist Drives, and Truth* (Durham, NC: Duke University Press, 2019); *The Fragility of Things: Self-Organizing Processes, Neoliberal Fantasies, and Democratic Activism* (Durham, NC: Duke University Press, 2013).

17. John D. Caputo, *The Insistence of God: A Theology of Perhaps* (Bloomington: Indiana University Press, 2013), 49. See also Chapter 7 of this book.

18. The role of possibilities in Caputo thus inadvertently echoes the work of the divinely proffered possibilities, "initial aim" or "divine lure," of Whiteheadian theology—possibilities that depend upon the creature for their actualization.

19. Caputo, *Insistence of God*, 49.

20. Caputo, *Insistence of God*, 49.

21. Caputo, *Insistence of God*, 14.

22. Whitehead, *Process and Reality*, 7.

23. Gilles Deleuze and Félix Guattari, *What Is Philosophy?* trans. Hugh Tomlinson and Graham Burchell (New York: Columbia University Press, 1994), 36.

24. "Of Learned Ignorance," in *Nicholas of Cusa: Selected Spiritual Writings*, trans. and intro. by H. Lawrence Bond (New York: Paulist Press, 1997), 140.

25. See my *Cloud*, chap. 4, "Enfolding and Unfolding God: Cusan *Complicatio*," 87–123.

26. Deleuze and Guattari, *Philosophy?* 37.

27. Deleuze and Guattari, *Philosophy?* 42.

28. Deleuze and Guattari, *Philosophy?* 43.

29. See Chapter 5 for more on Connolly vis a vis antagonism/agonism.

30. For example, John Grim and Mary Evelyn Tucker, *Ecology and Religion* (Washington, DC: Island Press, 2014). See also Mary Evelyn Tucker and John Grim, eds., *Living Cosmology: Christian Responses to Journey of the Universe* (Maryknoll, NY: Orbis Books, 2016). See also Connolly's frequent (nontheistic) positive engagements of pluralist forms of theism (above).

31. Mel Y. Chen, *Animacies: Biopolitics, Racial Mattering, and Queer Affect* (Durham, NC: Duke University Press, 2012), 237.

32. Sharon V. Betcher, *Spirit and the Obligation of Social Flesh: A Secular Theology for the Global City* (New York: Fordham University Press, 2014), 108.

33. Sharon V. Betcher, "Of Disability and the Garden State," Religious Studies News (March 2013), https://rsn.aarweb.org/spotlight-on/theo-ed/environemental-justice/disability-and-garden-state.

34. For a radically transformed construct of transcendence as embodied and decolonized, see Mayra Rivera, *The Touch of Transcendence: A Postcolonial Theology of God* (Louisville, KY: Westminster John Knox, 2007). Also see the multidimensional work of "enfleshed," a nonprofit that offers spiritual nourishment for collective liberation, co-founded in 2017 by Rev. Anna Blaedel and Rev. M. Jade Kaiser. Robert Monson joined the team of co-directors in 2022. https://enfleshed.com/. Anna Blaedel is currently writing a dissertation with the working title "Sacred Enfleshments: A Queer Theopoetics of Collective Liberation."

35. Karen Barad, *Meeting the Universe Halfway: Quantum Physics and the Entanglement of Matter and Meaning* (Durham, NC: Duke University Press, 2007), 393.

36. Haraway, *Staying with the Trouble*, 11.

37. See Diana Coole and Samantha Frost, eds., *New Materialisms: Ontology, Agency, and Politics* (Durham, NC: Duke University Press, 2010); Catherine Keller and Mary-Jane Rubenstein, eds., *Entangled Worlds: Religion, Science, and New Materialisms* (New York: Fordham University Press, 2017); Jane Bennett, *influx & efflux: writing up with Walt Whitman* (Durham, NC: Duke University Press, 2020); Whitney A. Bauman, ed., *Meaningful Flesh: Reflections on Religion and Nature for a Queer Planet* (Earth: Milky Way; Santa Barbara, CA: Punctum, 2018); Donna J. Haraway, *Staying with the Trouble: Making Kin in the Chthulucene* (Durham, NC: Duke University Press, 2016); Clayton Crockett, *Energy and Change: A New Materialist Cosmotheology* (New York: Columbia University Press, 2022).

10. "Birds with Wings Outspread": Islam, Christianity, and the Earth

1. An earlier version of this exploration was published as "Ecologies of Diversity: Beyond Religious and Human Exceptionalism," in *Nature and the Environment in Contemporary Religious Context*, ed. Muhammad Shafiq and Thomas Donlin-Smith (Newcastle upon Tyne: Cambridge Scholars Publishing, 2018). An even earlier version was presented at the conference "Sacred Texts and Human Contexts: Nature and Environment in World Religions," March 23–25, 2016, at the Hickey Center for Interfaith Studies and Dialogue, which under the leadership of Professor Muhammad Shafiq, continues its comparative work through conferences and publications. A subsequent version is forthcoming in *Open and Relational Theology and its Social and Political Implications: Muslim and Christian Perspectives*, ed. Jonathan J. Foster, Mouhamad Khorchide, Thomas Jay Oord, and Manuel Schmid (Grasmere, ID: SacraSage Press, 2024).

2. Jürgen Moltmann, "Eine gemeinsame Religion der Erde [A Common Religion of the Earth]: Weltreligionen in ükologischer Perspektive [World Religions in Ecological Perspective]," in *Verlag Otto Lembeck* 10/1605, "Okumenische Rundschau" (2011), 26 (my translation). As discussed in my *Cloud of the Impossible: Negative Theology and Planetary Entanglement* (New York: Columbia University Press, 2014), 279–280.

3. See William E. Connolly, *Aspirational Fascism: The Struggle for Multifaceted Democracy under Trumpism* (Minneapolis: University of Minnesota Press, 2017).

4. Several essays in this collection have reflected on the power of the exception (especially 1, 4, 5, and 9). For a wider background see particularly Chapter 1, "Political: Sovereign Exception or Collective Inception," in my *Political Theology of the Earth: Climate, Democracy, and Other Last Chances* (New York: Columbia University Press, 2018).

5. Oliver Milman, "Climate Denial Is Waning on the Right. What's Replacing It Might Be Just as Scary," *The Guardian*, November 21, 2021.

6. Carl Schmitt, *Political Theology: Four Chapters on the Concept of Sovereignty*, trans. George Schwab (1922; Chicago: University of Chicago Press, 2005), 5. See the discussions in Chapters 3 and 5 of the present volume.

7. For an incisive analysis of the history of white supremacy and American exceptionalism in the context of contemporary instances of violence against people of color in the United States, see Kelly Brown Douglas's *Stand Your Ground: Black Bodies and the Justice of God* (Maryknoll, NY: Orbis Books, 2015). See also William Connolly's *The Fragility of Things: Self-Organizing Processes, Neoliberal Fantasies, and Democratic Activism* (Durham, NC: Duke University Press, 2013); and Joshua Barkan's *Corporate Sovereignty: Law and Government under Capitalism* (Minneapolis: University of Minnesota Press, 2013).

8. Cited in *Medieval Worlds: A Sourcebook*, ed. Roberta Anderson and Dominic Aidan Bellenger (New York: Routledge, 2003), 90.

9. For a discussion of this legacy of exceptionalism in the case of political crusades in the distant and not-so-distant past, see my "Crusade, Capital, and Cosmopolis: Ambiguous Entanglements," chapter 8 in *Cloud of the Impossible: Negative Theology and Planetary Entanglement* (New York: Columbia University Press, 2015). For one example of Bush I's "new crusade" language, see the concluding lines of his "Remarks Accepting the Presidential Nomination at the Republican National Convention," Houston, TX, 1992. https://www.presidency.ucsb.edu/documents/remarks-accepting-the-presidential-nomination-the-republican-national-convention-houston. For Bush II's echoes see for example https://www.csmonitor.com/2001/0919/p12s2-woeu.html.

10. Giorgio Agamben, *Homo Sacer: Sovereign Power and Bare Life*, trans. Daniel Heller-Roazen (Stanford, CA: Stanford University Press, 1998).

11. See Mary-Jane Rubenstein, *Astrotopia: The Dangerous Religion of the Corporate Space Race* (Chicago: University of Chicago Press, 2022); and her *Worlds without End: The Many Lives of the Multiverse* (New York: Columbia University Press, 2014).

12. Lynn White Jr., "The Historical Roots of Our Ecological Crisis," *Science* 155, no. 3767 (March 10, 1967): 1203–1207.

13. Pope Francis, *Laudato Si': On Care for Our Common Home*, Papal Encyclical Letter (Huntington, IN: Our Sunday Visitor, 2015).

14. John J. Thatamanil, *Circling the Elephant: A Comparative Theology of Religious Diversity* (New York: Fordham University Press, 2020), 93–94.

15. "Islamic Declaration on Global Climate Change," International Islamic Climate Change Symposium (Istanbul: August 2015).

16. Abdul Aziz Said and Nathan C. Funk, "Peace in Islam: An Ecology of the Spirit," in *Islam and Ecology: A Bestowed Trust*, ed. Richard C. Foltz, Frederick M. Denny, and Azizan Baharuddin (Cambridge, MA: Harvard University Press, 2003), 155–184.

17. Ibrahim Özdemir, "Toward an Understanding of Environmental Ethics from a Qur'anic Perspective," in *Islam and Ecology*, 17.

18. Karen Barad, "Posthumanist Performativity: Toward an Understanding of How Matter Comes to Matter," *Signs: Journal of Women in Culture and Society* 28, no. 3 (Spring 2003): 801–831. For an extended discussion of Barad's work and more generally of the entanglement of quantum physics and negative theology please see "Spooky Entanglements: The Physics of Nonseparability," chapter 4 in my *Cloud of the Impossible*. See also Chapters 7 and 9 in the present volume.

19. Nicholas of Cusa, *De Pace Fidei (1453)*. See *Cloud of the Impossible*, 241ff., and also chap. 3, "Enfolding and Unfolding God: Cusanic *Complicatio*," 87ff.

20. Isabelle Stengers, *In Catastrophic Times: Resisting the Coming Barbarism*, trans. Andrew Goffrey (London: Open Humanities Press, 2015).

21. Catherine Keller, *Political Theology of the Earth: Our Planetary Emergency and the Struggle for a New Public* (New York: Columbia University Press, 2018).

22. Ernst Bloch, *The Principle of Hope*, vol. 1, trans. Neville Plaice and Stephen Plaice (Cambridge, MA: MIT Press, 1995). See also discussion of Bloch in Catherine Keller, *Apocalypse Now and Then: A Feminist Guide to the End of the World*, (Boston: Beacon Press, 1996).

23. Jürgen Moltmann, *The Living God and the Fullness of Life* (Louisville, KY: Westminster John Knox Press, 2015), 171.

24. The image of the whore of Babylon, indeed much of the text, trends misogynist. See Chapters 1 and 4 in this volume along with my *Facing Apocalypse: Climate, Democracy, and Other Last Chances* (Maryknoll, NY: Orbis Books, 2021).

25. Struggle continues since 2016. Laurel Sutherland, "Standing Rock Withdraws from Ongoing Environmental Assessment of Dakota Access Pipeline," *Mongabay*, February 2, 2022.

26. Naomi Klein, *This Changes Everything: Capitalism vs. the Climate* (New York: Simon and Schuster, 2014), 6.

27. "Islamic Declaration."

28. Imam Saffet Catovic quoted in Chris Bentley, "Muslim Environmentalists Give Their Religion—and their Mosques—a Fresh Coat of Green," *The World*, from PRX, January 4, 2017. I am proud that Imam Catovic was a student in Drew University's Graduate Division of Religion as I wrote the first version of this essay; and that since he has been a key member of the Parliament of the World's Religions Climate Action Task Force.

11. Animality, Animacy, *Anima Mundi*: Toward an Age of Enlivenment

1. This essay was presented as a talk in Dresden at *Animate Life: Konferenz zum Futur 2 der Mensch-Tier-Beziehungen*, organized by Prof. Julia Enxing, July 6–8, 2022.

2. Isabelle Stengers, "Reclaiming Animism," *e-flux Journal* 36 (July 2012).

3. Isabelle Stengers, "Reclaiming Animism," *e-flux Journal* 36 (July 2012).

4. Jane Bennett, *Vibrant Matter: A Political Ecology of Things* (Durham, NC: Duke University Press, 2010).

5. The seminar was co-taught with my long-time colleague and collaborator Laurel Kearns, far more expert in animal studies.

6. Caspar A. Hallmann et al., "More Than 75 Percent Decline over 27 Years in Total Flying Insect Biomass in Protected Areas," *PLoS ONE* 12, no. 10 (2017): e0185809. Cf. Paula Kover, "Insect 'Armageddon': Five Crucial Questions Answered," *The Conversation*, October 25, 2017.

7. David L. Clough, *On Animals*, 2 vols. (New York: T&T Clark, 2012 and 2018).

8. Clough, *On Animals*, 1:xiv.

9. Clough, *On Animals*, 1:135.

10. Clough, *On Animals*, 1:18.

11. Mel Y. Chen, *Animacies: Biopolitics, Racial Mattering, and Queer Affect* (Durham, NC: Duke University Press, 2012), 13ff.

12. Carol Adams, *The Sexual Politics of Meat: A Feminist-Vegetarian Critical Theory* (1990; New York: Bloomsbury, 2015).

13. Rosemary Radford Ruether, *God and Gaia: An Ecofeminist Theology of Earth Healing* (New York: HarperCollins: 1994); Elizabeth Johnson, *Ask the Beasts: Darwin and the God of Love* (New York: Bloomsbury, 2014).

14. Zakiyyah Iman Jackson, *Becoming Human: Matter and Meaning in an Anti-Black World* (New York: NYU Press, 2020), 17.

15. Alexis Pauline Gumbs, *Undrowned: Black Feminist Lessons from Marine Mammals* (Chico, CA: AK Press, 2020), 15. For her self-description see her website https://www.alexispauline.com/about.

16. Carol Wayne White, "Polyamorous Bastards: James Baldwin's Opening to a Queer African-American Religious Naturalism," in *Meaningful Flesh: Reflections on Religion and Nature for a Queer Planet*, ed. Whitney A. Bauman (Santa Barbara, CA: Punctum Press, 2018).

17. On another racial front, it must be noted that Ernst Haeckel's books were banned by the Nazis for their naturalism and his approving citation of multiple Jewish authors. Whitney Bauman has done considerable work on the ambiguity of Haeckel's legacy. See *A Critical Planetary Romanticism: Literary and Scientific Origins of New Materialism* (New York: Columbia University Press, forthcoming, 2025).

18. See Stephen D. Moore, ed., *Divinanimality: Animal Theory, Creaturely Theology* (New York: Fordham University Press, 2014).

19. See Elizabeth Kolbert, *The Sixth Extinction: An Unnatural History* (New York: Picador, 2014).

20. Merlin Sheldrake, *Entangled Life: How Fungi Make Our Worlds, Change Our Minds & Shape Our Futures* (New York: Random House, 2020), 12. See also Ann Lowenhaupt Tsing, *The Mushroom at the End of the World: On the Possibility of Life in Capitalist Ruins* (Princeton, NJ: Princeton University Press, 2015).

21. Sheldrake, *Entangled Life*, 16.

22. Sheldrake, *Entangled Life*, 17.

23. Sheldrake, *Entangled Life*, 17.

24. Clayton Crockett, *Energy and Change: A New Materialist Cosmotheology* (New York: Columbia University Press, 2022), 183. Cf. Bruno Latour, *Facing Gaia: Eight Lectures on the New Climate Regime*, trans. Catherine Porter (Medford: Polity Press, 2017), 87.

25. Latour, *Facing Gaia*, 87. Italics his. Cf. Isabelle Stengers, *Cosmopolitics I*, trans. Robert Bononno (University of Minnesota Press, 2010); and, Isabelle Stengers, *Cosmopolitics II*, trans. Robert Bononno (University of Minnesota Press, 2011).

26. Latour, *Facing Gaia*, 87.

27. Isabelle Stengers, *In Catastrophic Times: Resisting the Coming Barbarism*, trans. Andrew Goffey (London: Open Humanities Press, 2015).

28. Johann Gottfried von Herder, "God: Some Conversations" (1787), qtd. in Bennett, *Vibrant Matter*, 92.

29. Bennett, *Vibrant Matter*, 23ff. "Assemblage," of course, echoes Deleuze and Guattari.

30. Bennett, *Vibrant Matter*, 38.

31. Bruno Latour, *We Have Never Been Modern*, trans. Catherine Porter (Cambridge, MA: Harvard University Press, 1993), 144.

32. Bennett, *Vibrant Matter*, 122. Quotation marks in original, though words are Bennett's with exceptions noted by notes in original.

33. References to him recur throughout the so-called new materialism. See, for example, Diana Coole, "The Inertia of Matter," in *New Materialisms: Ontology, Agency and Politics*, ed. Diana Coole and Samantha Frost (Durham, NC: Duke University Press, 2010); Bennett, *Vibrant Matter*, 117; Latour, *Facing Gaia*, 2, 85. See also most books of William Connolly in this millennium.

34. Latour, *Facing Gaia*, 85

35. Alfred North Whitehead, *Process and Reality: An Essay in Cosmology*, corrected edition, ed. David Ray Griffin and Donald W. Sherburne (1929; New York: Free Press, 1985), 105.

36. Alfred North Whitehead, *Modes of Thought* (New York: Free Press, 1938).

37. Process theology, a movement of over half a century, generated by many but especially by John B. Cobb Jr., who, as I write, at age ninety-nine keeps writing books while initiating activist networks devoted to fighting climate change. See the Living Earth Movement (livingearthmovement.eco) and the Cobb Institute (cobb.institute) for just two examples.

38. Whitehead, *Process*, 105.

39. See Catherine Keller, *Face of the Deep: A Theology of Becoming* (New York: Routledge Press, 2003).

40. Julia Enxing, *Und Gott sah, dass es schlecht war: Warum der christliche Theologie uns verplfichtet, die Schoepfung zu bewahren* (Munich: Koeselverlag, 2022).

41. See "Weakness, Folly, Insistence, Glory: The Phenomenal God of John D. Caputo," Chapter 7 in this volume.

42. Matt David Segall, *The Physics of the World-Soul: Whitehead's Adventure in Cosmology* (Gramsmere, ID: SacraSage, 2021), 47. Cf. Whitehead, *Process*, 214–215.

43. Plato writes, "Thus, then, in accordance with the likely account, we must declare that this Cosmos has verily come into existence as a Living Creature endowed with soul and reason . . . a Living Creature, one and visible, containing within itself all the living creatures which are by nature akin to itself." Plato, "Timaeus," in *Plato in Twelve Volumes*, vol. 9, trans. W. R. M. Lamb (Cambridge, MA: Harvard University Press, 1925), 30b–d.

44. See my *Cloud of the Impossible: Negative Theology and Planetary Entanglement* (New York: Columbia University Press, 2015), 107. I have in *Cloud* drawn out that deep affinity between the Cusanic and the process panentheism.

45. See the multidimensional work of "enfleshed," a non-profit that offers spiritual nourishment for collective liberation, co-founded in 2017 by Rev. Anna Blaedel and Rev. M. Jade Kaiser. Robert Monson joined the team of co-directors in 2022. https://enfleshed.com/. Anna Blaedel is currently writing a dissertation with the working title "Sacred Enfleshments: A Queer Theopoetics of Collective Liberation."

12. Dear Young Theologian

1. An earlier version of this essay was originally published in *Letters to a Young Theologian*, ed. Henco van der Westhuizen (Minneapolis: Fortress Press, 2022), 224–239.

2. Odd timeliness—there remains an uncertainty as to this pandemic's closure. (As I move months later through a penultimate revision, I am propped up with pillows, and awaiting word on today's COVID19 test.—December 2023.)

3. Transdisciplinary conferences aimed at multilateral transformation have taken place almost annually at Drew's Theological School since the start of the millennium. Fordham University Press has published the resultant essays in the multiple-volume

series, the Transdisciplinary Theological Colloquia. Dr. John Garza, acquisitions editor for Fordham Press, has been an indispensable partner at the level both of content and of process in this long-term and ongoing collaboration.

4. See Catherine Keller, *Face of the Deep: A Theology of Becoming* (London: Routledge, 2003); Catherine Keller and Laurel C. Schneider, eds., *Polydoxy: Theology of Multiplicity and Relation* (New York: Routledge, 2011).

5. Hence my area at Drew is called Theological and Philosophical Studies in Religion.

6. I am referring, of course, to traditions coming into their own in the late '60s, such as liberation theology in Latin America and as Black theology in the US, of feminist and then womanist and mujerista theologies, theologies of disability and class, and the whole time, the development of ecological theologies.

7. "God is dead! God remains dead! And we have killed him!" Friedrich Nietzsche, *The Gay Science,* ed. Bernard Williams, trans. Josefine Nauckhoff (New York: Cambridge University Press, 2001), 120 (book III, para. 125).

8. See, for example, the significant array of essays, with afterword by Thomas J. J. Altizer, in *Resurrecting the Death of God: The Origins, Influence, and Return of Radical Theology*, ed. Daniel J. Peterson and G. Michael Zbaraschuk (Albany: SUNY Press, 2014).

9. Thomas J. J. Altizer and William Hamilton, *Radical Theology and the Death of God* (Indianapolis: Bobbs-Merrill, 1966). I did in fact meet Altizer at the church I chose to attend and tugged my parents to come hear a lecture he offered there.

10. Rabbi Michael Lerner, *Revolutionary Love: A Political Manifesto to Heal and Transform the World* (Oakland: University of California Press, 2019).

11. See Chapter 9 in this volume.

12. Mary-Jane Rubenstein, *Pantheologies: Gods, Worlds, Monsters* (New York: Columbia University Press, 2018); Richard Kearney, *Anatheism: Returning to God after God* (New York: Columbia University Press, 2010). In this volume, for my version of panentheism see Chapter 9; for Caputo's engagement of panentheism see Chapter 7.

13. For my own work on and in the open-endedness—abysmal and hopeful—of creation, see especially *Face of the Deep: A Theology of Becoming* (New York: Routledge, 2003) and *Facing Apocalypse: Climate, Democracy and Other Last Chances* (Maryknoll, NY: Orbis Books, 2021).

Index

Abrahamic modes. *See* Earth religions
abysmal insistence, 88–92
Adams, Carol, 135
African Americans, 55, 61, 68–69, 102, 104, 136
Agamben, Giorgio, 125
Age of Enlivenment, moving toward, 148; *anima mundi,* 141–43; animalization, 134–37; animate materiality, 137–39; last dance, 143–44; opening in new materialism, 140–41; overview, 133–34; purpose of God in creative advance, 140–41
agonistic pluralism, 72
agony, intimacy of, 81–82
alternative, agonism of: agonism and hope, 71–76; Christosecularizations, 70–71; facing aspirational fascism, 65–68; and malleable religious identity, 68–70
alternative future, possibility of, 26–27
Altizer, Thomas, 148
American Family Association, 69
amipotence, power of, 82–84
amorous agonism, 75
And God Saw That It Was Bad (Enxing), 141
anima mundi, 141–43
animacy hierarchy, 135
animal-vegetable-mineral-sonority cluster, 139
animalization, 134–37
Anthropocene, 15

anxious apophatics, 87
apocalypse: best kind of, 98–99; Christian misreading of, 151; climate apocalypse, 80, 110; creeps of, 11–24; dreamreading, 55–57; Greek word for, 51; Insect Apocalypse, 15, 51; of John of Patmos, 53–54; language, 52; metaforce of, 57–58; nuclear version of, 54; and planetary *kairos,* 23–24; porn queen of, 17–19; and responsible realism, 50–62; rhetoric of, 11–12; salvaging, 21–22; specter of, 61; theodicy and, 78–79; tweeting through, 50–51; weaponizing as the End, 78–79
Apocalypse Now and Then: A Feminist Guide to the End of the World (Keller), 17, 51, 53–54
apocalypsis, term, 16, 51, 78–79
apocalyptic mindfulness, 52, 57–61. *See also* responsible realism
apokalypsis, 5, 9–10, 12, 15, 20–23, 51, 97. *See also* apocalypse
Aquinas, Thomas, 135
arbitrary *(proizvol),* concept, 43
Arctic, 13
Arendt, Hannah, 66–67
Armor of Light, The (film), 70
aspirational fascism, 11, 65–68, 71, 74
Assad, Bashar al-, 124
assemblage, machinic character of, 71
atmosphere, 121–23
Augustine, 59–60, 135

180 / INDEX

Ausnahmezustand. See state of exception
Autopoetic Turn/Overturn, 27, 31

Barad, Karen, 4, 95, 113–16, 119, 128
Barron, Jesse, 15
Barth, Karl, 89, 134–35
basileia tou theou, 48–49
bear, animation of, 101. *See also* "earth is a living thing, a" (Clifton)
becomingness, 115–17
Benjamin, Walter, 112, 113
Bennett, Jane, 7, 117, 134, 138–39
Betcher, Sharon, 120
Bible, faithfulness to, 52
Billion Black Anthropocenes or None, A (Yusoff), 56
bios/mythoi, commitment to, 31
"Black and Living Thing, A," 64
"Black Malpractice" (Carter), 16
black rupture, 20
blackness as earth, 103–4
Blackness, poiesis of, 33–34
Bloch, Ernst, 16, 74
Blombos Cave, cosmogony and, 26
Boff, Leonardo, 14
Book of Revelation, 17–19, 55
Brock, Rita Nakashima, 55
Bush, George W., 125

C-omnipotence, 83–85
capitalism: depredations of, 22; neoliberal, 4, 33, 46, 54, 64, 67, 111; new spirit of, 12, 16; optimism of, 23; spirituality of material transformation serving, 20
capitalism, conflation of conservative Christianity with, 69
capitalocene, 14
Caputo, John D.: and abysmal insistence, 88–91; and cosmopoetic connections, 94–96; and intercarnation, 117–18; and panentheistic perhaps, 92–94; phenomenal God of, 87–88; planetary specters of, 96–99
Carter, J. Kameron, 16, 19–20, 34
Castro, Eduardo Viveiros de, 55
catastrophe: climate catastrophe, 72, 105, 125, 130; ecosocial catastrophe, 21, 124, 131; planetary catastrophe, 15, 79, 124; and salvaging apocalypse, 21–22; turning into catalyst, 124; "we" of, 25–34
Catovic, Saffet, 132
"Ceremony Found, The" (Wynter), 25–26
Césaire, Aimé, 28–29

Chen, Mel, 120, 135
Christ, Jesus: divinity of, 79–82; reading as embodiment of love, 129–30
Christian exceptionalism, 123–26
Christian institutions, 2
Christian nationalism, 6, 65, 68–69
Christianity, 127, 145; critique of, 96; history of, 110; pluralist potentiality in, 129; right wing of, 30, 67; supersession of, 71
Christianity and the New Spirit of Capitalism (Tanner), 14
Christianity, Russian, 41
Christosecularizations, 70–71
Clifton, Lucille, 64; meditation on poetry of, 100–5. *See also* "earth is a living thing, a" (Clifton)
Climate Change Is Racist (Williams), 56
climate crisis, 11, 21, 156n17
climate emergency, 123
Cloud of the Impossible (Keller), 95, 114, 129
Clough, David L., 134–37
Cobb, John B., Jr., 14, 32, 70, 126–27
Coleman, Monica, 32
complicatio, 94, 129
Cone, James, 102
Connolly, William, 18–19, 67, 71, 73, 119
consciousness, coming to, 27
constructive theology, 149–50
cosmogonic "we," 31–33
cosmogony, throb of. *See* "we" of catastrophe
cosmopoetic reduction, 94–96
cosmopoetics, 88, 93
creatio ex nihilo, 30, 32, 57, 91
creatio ex profundis, 30, 91
creative transformation, logos of, 127
creeps, apocalypse: climate crisis, 11; economic endgame, 13–16; economics, 12; fragility of democracy, 11–12; planetary *kairos,* 23–24; porn queen of apocalypse, 17–19; releasing uncertainty, 12–13; salvaging apocalypse, 21–22; spiral of ecosocial demise, 19–21; triple time, 12
Crenshaw, Kimberlé, 27
Crimea, annexation of, 161n7
crisis: and agonism of alternative to, 65–76; climate crisis, 11, 21, 156n17; collective crisis, 1, 145; creeps of apocalypse, 9–24; Earth religions, 122–32; ecological crisis, 32–33, 132; faith in possible, 50–62; intercarnation and, 109–21; and moving toward Age of Enlivenment, 133–44; naming, 3; new globality of, 96; phe-

nomenal God of John D. Caputo, 87–99; planetary crisis, 123; poiesis of Earth, 100–5; political theologies at war, 35–49; power, theodicy, and amipotent God, 77–86; and spirit of planetary crisis, 1–8; times of, 19, 145; "we" of catastrophe, 25–34
critical pluralist assemblage, 72
Crockett, Clayton, 138
cruel optimisms, 75–76
current crisis, witnessing, 2–3

Daly, Herman, 33
Daly, Mary, 89
Danowsky, Déborah, 55
Davies, Paul, 95
Death of God, theology, 145–51
Death of Omnipotence and Birth of Amipotence (Oord), 82
DeLay, Tom, 66–67
Deleuze, Gilles, 119–21
dem dunklen Grund, articulating, 88–89
democracy, dis/closures of, 9–10; creeps of apocalypse, 11–24; exploring breathing room for realism, 50–62; political theologies at war, 35–49; "we" of catastrophe, 25–34
democracy, principle of, 39
denialism, 53–55
Derrida, Jacques, 101
determinism, apocalyptic, 54
Deuteronomy 10, 70
Dickinson, Emily, 51
disability, practice of, 119–20
divinanimality, 136–37
divine power, 6, 47, 60; and abysmal insistence, 90; and grieving and rising, 84; incoherence, 64; rethinking, 64; unquestionable nature of, 37
divine power, views of, 35–36
Doing Theology in the Age of Trump, 65
dreamreading, 55–57
Du Bois, W. E. B., 16

earth, dis/closures of, 9–10; creeps of apocalypse, 11–24; exploring breathing room for realism, 50–62; political theologies at war, 35–49; "we" of catastrophe, 25–34
earth-hawk, ecology of. *See* sky burials, invoking
"earth is a living thing, a" (Clifton), 100; bear imagery, 101; blackness as earth in, 103–4; capturing ecofeminism in, 101–2; exposing double commodification of earth and race, 102; invoking sky burials, 102–3; last word of, 105; preciousness of earth in, 103–5
Earth, poiesis of. *See* "earth is a living thing, the" (Clifton)
Earth religions: alternative to sovereign power of exception, 126–30; ecology of religions, 126–30; overview of, 122–24; shifting climate catastrophe into catalyst, 130–32; treating emergency as emergence, 124–26
Earth, as space for living, 138. *See also* earth, dis/closures of
Eckhart, Meister, 89
ecofeminism, 95, 126; capturing in poetry, 101–2
ecology, 23–24, 27, 72; Abrahamic ecology, 130–32; and cosmopoetic connections, 94–95; crisis overlapping with immigration crisis, 125; of hospitable earth, 14; integral ecology, 56; issues of issues, 98; and planetary crucifixion, 80; in poetry, 100–5; political ecology, 139; of religions, 126–30; of spirit, 128; term, 136
Ecology and Islam, 128
economic endgame, creeps of the apocalypse, 13–16
ecosocial demise, intensifying spiral of, 19–21
ecosocial justice, 9, 15, 28, 34
Ecowomanism (Harris), 56
emergence, treating emergency as, 124–26
End of the World, The (exhibit), 55
enemy, defining, 66
Energy and Change (Crockett), 138
enlivenment. *See* Age of Enlivement, moving toward
entangled difference, 123–24
Entangled Life (Sheldrake), 137–38
entanglements, 12, 16, 24, 48, 91, 94–95, 108. *See also* intercarnation
Enxing, Julia, 141
eschatos (edge), 19–20
Escobar, Arturo, 48
evangel, freedom from, 71
evangelical, label, 68–69
ex profundis. *See creatio ex profundis*
exception: and alternative to current political theology, 123–24; Christ as transcendent exception, 109; climate emergency being treated as, 123; creatures and, 59; and ecology of religions, 126–30; and

exception *(continued)*
  intercarnation, 110–11; miracle as, 66; or emergence, 124–26; political theology of, 42; and process theology, 45; reading sovereignty as, 36–37; treating emergency as, 124–26
explicatio, 94, 129

Facing Apocalypse (Keller), 17, 51, 53, 55
fallen God, concept, 38–39
female figure, vilification of, 17–19
feminism, 135
First Event, 26
Falwell, Jerry, Jr., 68
flesh, code made as, 27–31
Fletcher, Karen Baker, 32
Fold, The (Deleuze), 119
Folly of God, The (Caputo), 90
Foltz, Richard, 40
For the Common Good (Cobb), 33
forsakenness, question of, 79–80
Four Horseman (apocalypse), 53–55
Fox Evangelicals, 65–66
Fox News, religious identity and, 68–70
Foxangelicals, 71–76; and Christosecularizations, 70–71; facing aspirational fascism, 65–68; and malleable religious identity, 68–70
Francis, pope, 126, 131
fungi, plants socially networked by, 137–38
Funk, Nathan, 128

Gaia, 2; facing, 96–99; reading as full of agents, 138
Gaiacentrism, 4–5
Gebara, Ivone, 14, 115
Genesis 1:2, 3
Genesis 1.26–28, sacrality of, 126
Gill, Jon Ivan, 33
global capitalism, 18
glory, alternative to: abysmal insistence, 88–92; cosmopoetic connections, 94–96; overview, 87–88; panentheism, 92–94
God: and *anima mundi*, 141–43; and apocalyptic mindfulness, 59–61; appearing as all-in *(pan-en)*, 111; blame for tragedies, 44–45; of John D. Caputo, 87–99; depending on Russia for redemption, 42–43; in each creature as "lure to becoming," 43–44; emergence of, 118; fallen God, 38–39; and forsakenness, 79–80; insistence of, 93; interdependency of, 44; and intimate agony of, 81–82; loving, responsive face of, 37; mutual immanence of, 115; and power of amipotence, 82–84; primordial nature of, 90; prophecy of mytho-philosophical death of, 145–51; ruin of, 120; theodicy and apocalypse, 78–79; and theology of perhaps, 117–18; Tillichian God, 89
God Can't, 44
god-making *(theopoiesis)*, 88, 99
God, Power, and Evil: A Process Theodicy (Griffin), 78, 85
Godforsakenness, 77–82, 84–86
Goldberg Variations (Bach), 1
Good Friday, 85
Good News about the Earth (Clifton), 102
Grau, Marion, 14
Great Whore, decoding, 17
green-cloaked nativism, 124
grieving, 84–86
Griffin, David Ray, 78, 83, 85
Gumbs, Alexis Pauline, 136

Haeckel, Ernst, 136
Haraway, Donna, 114
Harney, Stefano, 73
Harris, Melanie, 56
Hartshorne, Charles, 92, 115, 141
Hayhoe, Katharine, 58
Herder, Johann Gottfried von, 139
Hiroshima, Japan, 54
Hitler, Adolf, 37
home *(oikos)*, 4, 14, 21–24, 28, 97
Homo narrans, 16, 28
Homo sapiens, 4–5
homodictatorship, 40
hope, agonism and: alternative friendship, 75–76; amorous agonism, 75; current political conditions, 71–72; dissipating political responsibility on Left, 72; hope as enlivening alternative, 73; instability infusing Foxangelicalism, 73–74; omnipotentiality, 74; overdetermined indeterminacy, 74; respectful agonism, 72; undercommons, 72–73
hope in the dark, 61–62
hope, principle of, 16
hostipitality, neologism, 101
How Will Capitalism End? (Streeck), 18
humanimality, 136–39

Ibrahim, Abdel Mohsen, 101–2
Ilyin, Ivan: imagining Russian Christian fascism, 38–39; influence on Putin,

39–40; insight in theology of, 43; and mockery of love, 45; and political challenge of Christian love, 41; Russian unification redeeming creator, 42–43
image of God *(imago dei)*, 96, 126, 128, 134
Incarnation, transmuting. *See* intercarnation
Inflation Reduction Act, 58
Insect Armageddon, 15, 51, 134
insistence, planetary, 96–99
integral ecology, 56
intercarnation: becomingness and, 115–17; caricature of betrayal of messianic moment, 109; creation-honoring justice, 111; Deleuzian influence, 119–21; exception *(excipere)*, 111; inability to refuse responsibility, 110; and messianic coming, 113–14; messianicity, 112; monstrous abbreviation, 112; mounting improbability of stopping planetary overheat, 111–12; and panentheism, 114–19; panentheist deity lacking transcendence, 116–18; perspective of "to come," 112–14, 117, 121; practice of disability, 119–20; proposing Terrapolis, 121; ruins, 120–21; singling up-close juxtaposition, 110–11; and sustainability of *horror pantheismus*, 115; and theology of perhaps, 117–18
intercorporeal generosity, call for, 120
Intergovernmental Panel on Climate Change (IPCC), 157n16
intersectionalism, 6, 45, 56
intersectionality, concept, 27
intimate agony, 81–82
intra-active becomings. *See* becomingness
intra-activity, 4, 128
Is It Too Late? (Cobb), 32–33
Islamic Declaration on Global Climate Change, 127, 132

Jackson, Zakiyyah Iman, 136
John of Patmos, 53–54, 77
juxtaposition, signaling, 110

kairos, planetary, 23–24
Kant, Immanuel, 139
katechon. See restrainer *(katechon)*, role of
Khersonska, Lyudmyla, 49
Khudrī, Abu Sa'īd Al-, 132
Kirill, Patriarch, 38, 40
Klein, Naomi, 131
Krause, Karl, 92
krinein, 3. *See also* crisis

Late Great Planet Earth (Lindsey), 54
Latour, Bruno, 2, 14–15, 96, 138–39
Lewis, David, 39, 46–47
LGBTQIA people, "homodictatorship" and, 40
Lindsey, Hal, 54
Lofton, Kathryn, 20
Logos, 29
Los Angeles Times, 51–52
love, 120; ancient fountain of love, 61; and coercion, 46–47; as correlate power, 47; fragile question of, 40–41; "God is love," 37; honesty and, 75; intimacies of, 108; and mobilizing resistance, 98; mockery of, 45; notion of, 48; power of, 60, 82; Russian world and, 40–41; and self-limiting nature of God, 80
love-tangles, 107–8; Earth religions, 122–32; letter to theologian, 145–51; matter of intercarnation, 109–21; toward Age of Enlivenment, 133–44
Luther, Martin, 135

Man(1), 30
Martin, Jonathan, 68
Massumi, Brian, 119
mater, 2
materiality, animateness of, 137–39
McFague, Sallie, 59, 115
Meeting the Universe Halfway (Barad), 116
messianic coming, 113–14
Miéville, China, 22
Miller, A. O., 114
mindfulness, apocalyptic, 57–61
miracle, as exception, 66
modernity, 16, 20, 30–32, 36, 42, 63, 135, 138–39, 151
Modes of Thought (Whitehead), 140
Moltmann, Jürgen, 4, 14, 79–80, 122
monstrous abbreviation *(ungeheueren Abbreviatur)*, 112
Morton, Timothy, 119
Moskovskiye Novosti, 39
Moten, Fred, 73
Mouffe, Chantal, 72

Nazism, 66
New Creation, 4
New Jerusalem, 21–22, 48, 57–61, 74, 131
new materialism, 2, 113, 117, 120–21, 140
New York Times Magazine, 33
Nicholas of Cusa, 94, 119, 129, 142
Nietzsche, Friedrich, 147–48

nihilism: capturing culture of, 50–52; denialism or, 53–55; dreamreading apocalypse, 55–57
no matter what, phrase, 1
nonhuman animal, theology of, 134–37
nonwhite races, civilizational association of, 135–36
Notstand. See state of emergency
novel becomings. See becomingness
novo creatio ex nihilo, 57–58
nuclear destruction, danger of, 53–54

O'Reilly, Bill, 69
Of Divine Economy: Refinancing Redemption (Grau), 14
oikonomia, 14
oikos. See home
omnipotence: amipotence replacing, 82–84; C-omnipotence, 83–85; deconstruction of, 91
omnipotentiality, 74, 88, 90, 94
On the Peace of the Faith (Nicholas of Cusa), 129
Oord, Thomas Jay, 6, 81, 82–84
Orthodoxy, Russian, 5, 38, 41
othering, entanglements and, 114
Ozdemir, Ibrahim, 128

Pally, Marcia, 23, 67
panentheism, 88; and amorous entanglements, 109–10; and existence of omnianimate deity, 142; and intercarnation, 114–19; panentheistic perhaps, 92–94; process theology and, 141, 149; process thought and, 170n9
Pantheologies (Rubenstein), 115
Patriarchate, 40
Patterson, Jacqueline, 55–56
Physics of the World-Soul (Segall), 141
planetary crisis, 123; spirit of, 1–8
planetary *kairos*, 23–24
planetary possibility, spirit of, 3–4
planetary specters, 96–99
plantationocene, 16
pluriversal politics, 48–49
poetry, meditation on. See "earth is a living thing, a" (Clifton)
political struggle, 42
Political Theology of the Earth, 74
political theology, war of: and applied Russian metaphysics of totality, 42; creaturely intersectionalism, 45–46; famous sentence, 157n18; God in each creature as "lure to becoming," 43–45; good Russia against evil West, 46–47; identifying sovereignty, 36–37; imagining Russian Christian fascism, 38–39; loving, responsive face of God, 37; pluriversal politics, 48–49; Putin political theology of sovereign might, 37–38; role of restrainer *(katechon)*, 46–47; Russian unification redeeming creator, 42–43; views of divine power, 35–36
Pompeo, Mike, 13
porn-apocalyptic image, 17–19
possibility, concept of, 3–4
possibility, faith in: apocalyptic mindfulness, 57–61; cultural nihilism, 50–52; dreamreading apocalypse, 55–57; hope in the dark, 61–62
potentiality, galvanizing, 82–83
power, alternatives to, 63–64; agonism of alternative, 65–76; meditation on poetry, 100–105; theodicy and amipotent God, 77–86
primordial nature, 90
Principle of Earth, The (Bloch), 74
Principle of Hope, The (Bloch), 16
principle of the ultimate, defining, 91–92
Process and Reality: An Essay in Cosmology (Whitehead), 31–32, 43, 90, 118
process theology, 43, 90, 126–27; accessible work of, 44; amipotence and, 82–83; creaturely intersectionalism and, 45; divine lure and, 60–61; emergence of, 32–33; grieving and, 84–86; half-century pathway of, 149; and intimate agony, 81–82; language of weakness, 91; lending to political theology of democracy, 45–46; and panentheistic perhaps, 92; persistence in God-inflected cosmology, 140–41; question of theodicy found in, 78–79; rising and, 84–86; systematic alternative offered by, 64. See also panentheism
process thought, 32–33, 85, 90, 170n9
propertied present, 13
prophecy. See dreamreading
prosthesis, 120
Protestant dispensationalism, 54
Putin, Vladimir, 36; and annexation of Crimea, 161n7; good Russia against evil West, 46–47; Ilyin influence on, 39–40; and love in relation to homogenizing theopolitics of Russian world, 40–42; and mockery of love, 45; political

theology of, 37–38; role of restrainer *(katechon)*, 46–47; warning of "homodictatorship," 40

Qur'an, 127–28

Radical Theology and the Death of God (Altizer), 148
Ragnarök, 147–48
reasonable realism: apocalyptic mindfulness, 57–61; dreamreading apocalypse, 55–57; hope in the dark, 61–62
religions, ecology of, 126–30
religious identity, malleability of, 68–70
repair of the world *(tikkun olam)*, 142–43
respectful agonism, 72
responsible realism, cultural nihilism and, 50–52
restrainer *(katechon)*, role of, 46–47
Revelation Six, 58–59
Rieger, Joerg, 14
rising, 84–86
Rubenstein, Mary-Jane, 115
Ruether, Rosemary Radford, 135
rupture, 20–23
Russell, Bertrand, 32–33
Russia: acting as *katechon*, 47; alternative to autocratic oneness in, 48; concept of "arbitrary" in, 43; consolidation under manly force, 40–41; good Russia against evil West, 46–47; and homodictatorship, 40; imagining Russian Christian fascism, 38–39; invasion of Ukraine, 53; love in relation to homogenizing theopolitics of Russian world, 40–42; role of restrainer *(katechon)*, 46–47; Russian Orthodoxy, 5, 38, 41; Russian-Ukrainian relations, 39; spiritual organism of, 38–39, 42; unification redeeming creator, 42–43. See also Russian world *(russkii mir)*
Russia's New Authoritarianism (Lewis), 46
Russian Revolution, 38
Russian world *(russkii mir)*, 38, 40; and applied Russian metaphysics of totality, 42; drawing upon history of Russian Orthodoxy, 38; good Russia against evil West, 46–47; love in relation to homogenizing theopolitics of, 40–42
russkii mir. See Russian world

Said, Abdul Aziz, 128
salvage, apocalypse and, 21–22

salvage communism, 22
Schelling, Friedrich, 88–89
Schmitt, Carl, 36, 39, 70–71, 125; and aspirational fascism, 65–68
Scientific American, 79
Second Chechen War, 46
Second Event, 26
Second World War, 53–54, 125
secularization, exposing, 70–71
Segall, Matt, 141
self-identified evangelicals, 68–69
Sexual Politics of Meat: A Feminist-Vegetarian Critical Theory, The (Adams), 135
Sheldrake, Merlin, 137–38
sky burials, invoking, 102–3
soap, marketing, 20
Social Flesh, 120
Society of Friends, 75
solidarity, 80, 121, 130, 132, 151; with animality, 135; attracting, 73; earthbound solidarity, 7, 98; ecosocial solidarity, 6, 76; enabling communication, 74; friendships possible in politics of, 75; grounding, 25–27; intersectional web of, 72; outgrowing "cruel optimisms," 75–76; and planetary *kairos*, 23–24; sciences working in, 31; species-oriented, 27
Solnit, Rebeca, 73
South Africa, 25–26, 29
sovereign exceptionalism, 36–37
sovereignty of the exception, 155n6
Specters of God: Anatomy of the Apophatic Imagination (Caputo): abysmal insistence, 88–92; cosmopoetic connections, 94–96; overview, 87–88; panentheism, 92–94; planetary specters, 96–99
speed-creeping, 11–12, 14–16, 19, 24
Spirit of Life, The (Moltmann), 4
state of emergency *(Notstand)*, 36; legal notion of, 123
state of exception *(Ausnahmezustand)*, 36
Stengers, Isabelle, 2, 138
Streeck, Wolfgang, 18, 158n26
Sullivan, Amy, 65, 68–70
Super, Natural Christians (McFague), 59

Tanner, Kathryn, 12–13, 14, 16; *eschatos* of theological vision of, 19–20
tawhid, forging sense of, 128–30
tehom, 29–30, 91, 94
Terrapolis, proposing, 121

theodicy: and apocalypse, 78–79; and forsakenness, 79–80; and grieving, 84–86; intimate agony, 81–82; overview, 77–78; and panentheism, 117–18; and political theology of sovereign One, 47; power of amipotence, 82–84; questions of, 6, 35–36, 44; and rising, 84–86; standard theodicy, 42
theologian, letter to, 145–51
theology: Christian theology, 7, 109, 123, 129, 139; ecological theology, 2; exposing secular infinite, 13–14; secularization of, 70–71. *See also* political theology, war of; process theology
Theology of Hope, The, 130
theopoiesis. *See* god-making
theos, 2
Third Event, 26
This Changes Everything: Capitalism vs. the Climate (Klein), 131–32
tikkun olam. See repair of the world
Tillich, Paul, 1, 88–89, 92, 134
Timaeus, 141
"to come," perspective of, 112–14, 117, 121
tohu va bohu, phrase, 29–30
triple temporality, 21
Trump, Donald, 18, 71–72
Trumpism, age of, 67
Trumpocalypse, 55
Trumpocalypse, 18

Ukrainian students, virtual talk with: and applied Russian metaphysics of totality, 42; creaturely intersectionalism, 45–46; God in each creature as "lure to becoming," 43–45; good Russia against evil West, 46–47; identifying sovereignty, 36–37; imagining Russian Christian fascism, 38–39; loving, responsive face of God, 37; pluriversal politics, 48–49; Putin political theology of sovereign might, 37–38; role of restrainer *(katechon)*, 46–47; Russian unification redeeming creator, 42–43; views of divine power, 35–36
ultimate concern, 1
undercommons, 72–73
Underground Rap as Religion (Gill), 33

ungeheueren Abbreviatur. See monstrous abbreviation
Ungrund, 93–94, 96–97
United States: Inflation Reduction Act in, 58; nationalist/globalist partnership in, 18–19; power of "us" in, 66–68; Protestant dispensationalism in, 54
"Unparalleled Catastrophe for Our Species?" (Wynter), 25–26
unprecedented Second Emergence, 27
unveiling, apocalyptic, 20–21
Urban II, pope, 125

Vibrant Matter (Bennett), 138–39

Wagner, Richard, 147
War on Christmas, 68–70
"we" of catastrophe: code made flesh, 27–31; cosmogonic "we," 31–33; overview, 25–27; poiesis of blackness, 33–34
Weber, Max, 14
West, evilness of, 46–47
What Does the White Evangelical Want (DeLay), 66–67
White Evangelicals and Right-Wing Populism: How Did We get Here? (Pally), 67
white supremacism, affective field of, 69
white supremacism, warning of role of, 66–67
White, Carol Wayne, 32, 136
White, Lynn, 96
Whitehead, Alfred North, 31–32, 43, 64, 73, 83, 88, 90, 118; and animate futures, 140–41
Whore of Babylon, 56–57, 77
"Whose Earth Is It Anyway?" (Cone), 102
Williams, Jeremy, 56
womanist thinkers, 32
Word as code, 28–29
world religions, transforming. *See* Earth religions
World War II, 53–54, 125
world, propertization of, 16
WWJ(N)D, question, 65, 75
Wynter, Sylvia, 25, 34

Yusoff, Kathryn, 56

Catherine Keller is George T. Cobb Professor of Constructive Theology in The Graduate Division of Religion, Drew University. She works amid the tangles of ecosocial, pluralist, feminist philosophy of religion and theology. Her books include *Face of the Deep: A Theology of Becoming*; *On the Mystery*; *Cloud of the Impossible: Negative Theology and Planetary Entanglement*; *Political Theology of the Earth: Our Planetary Emergency and the Struggle for a New Public*. She has co-edited several volumes of the Drew Transdisciplinary Theological Colloquium, most recently *Political Theology on Edge: Ruptures of Justice and Belief in the Anthropocene*. Her latest monograph is *Facing Apocalypse: Climate, Democracy, and Other Last Chances*.

www.ingramcontent.com/pod-product-compliance
Lightning Source LLC
Chambersburg PA
CBHW020412080526
44584CB00014B/1284